Letters from Kimberley

Letters from Kimberley

Eyewitness Accounts from the South African War

Edward M. Spiers

FRONTLINE BOOKS, LONDON

Letters from Kimberley:
Eyewitness Accounts from the South African War

This edition published in 2013 by Frontline Books,
an imprint of Pen & Sword Books Ltd,
47 Church Street, Barnsley, S. Yorkshire, S70 2AS
www.frontline-books.com

Copyright © Edward Spiers, 2013

The right of Edward Spiers to be identified as the
author of this work has been asserted by him in accordance
with the Copyright, Designs and Patents Act 1988.

ISBN: 978-1-84832-657-6

All rights reserved. No part of this publication may be reproduced,
stored in or introduced into a retrieval system, or transmitted, in any form,
or by any means (electronic, mechanical, photocopying, recording
or otherwise) without the prior written permission of the publisher.
Any person who does any unauthorized act in relation to this publication
may be liable to criminal prosecution and civil claims for damages.

CIP data records for this title are available from the British Library

For more information on our books, please visit
www.frontline-books.com, email info@frontline-books.com
or write to us at the above address.

Printed and bound by CPI Group (UK) Ltd, Croydon, CR0 4YY

Typeset in ITC Galliard 10½/13pt

Contents

	List of Illustrations	vii
	List of Maps	viii
	Acknowledgements	ix
Introduction	Kimberley: The Siege and its Significance	1
Chapter 1	Defending 'Diamond City'	11
Chapter 2	Relief Force: Advancing to the Modder River	37
Chapter 3	Magersfontein: Highlanders 'Marched to their Graves'	77
Chapter 4	Kimberley: Beleaguered and Bombarded	107
Chapter 5	Kimberley Relieved: Cronjé Surrenders	127
Chapter 6	Assessing the Kimberley Siege	165
	Select Bibliography	185
	Index	191

List of Illustrations

1. The searchlight at Wesselton Mine, with soldiers of the Loyal North Lancashire Regiment. *McGregor Museum, Kimberley photographs*
2. Lt-Col Robert Kekewich. *McGregor Museum, Kimberley photographs*
3. Cecil Rhodes, Mrs Rochfort Maquire, and defenders of Kimberley. *National Army Museum* (NAM 1971-01-36-5-13)
4. 'Relief of Kimberley. Charge of the Brigade of Guards'. *A. S. K. Brown Military Collection, Brown University Library*
5. 'Lord Methuen's advance . . . Crossing the Modder River'. *A. S. K. Brown Military Collection, Brown University Library*
6. Lt-Gen Lord Methuen. *A. S. K. Brown Military Collection, Brown University Library*
7. Kimberley people waiting to draw their rations. *McGregor Museum, Kimberley photographs*
8. Miss Agnes Oliver with artillery shells. *A. S. K. Brown Military Collection, Brown University Library*
9. Women and children waiting to go down a mine in Kimberley. *McGregor Museum, Kimberley photographs*
10. 'Advance on Kimberley . . . Lancers at Klip Drift'. *A. S. K. Brown Military Collection, Brown University Library*
11. 'Entrances to the underground tunnel at Kimberley'. *A. S. K. Brown Military Collection, Brown University Library*
12. 'The 10th Hussars Crossing Klip Drift'. *A. S. K. Brown Military Collection, Brown University Library*
13. 'General French's meeting with Mr. Cecil Rhodes'. *A. S. K. Brown Military Collection, Brown University Library*
14. 'General Cronjé in Captivity'. *A. S. K. Brown Military Collection, Brown University Library*

List of Maps

1. Theatre of Operations   10
2. Kimberley Besieged, 14 October 1899–15 February 1900   13
3. Battle of Belmont, 23 November 1899   43
4. Battle of Graspan, 25 November 1899   53
5. Battle of Modder River, 28 November 1899   62
6. Battle of Magersfontein, 11 December 1899   82

Acknowledgements

I should like to acknowledge the grant from the Scouloudi Foundation in association with the Institute of Historical Research, which enabled me to complete the research for this work.

I should like to acknowledge, too, the kind permission of the Trustees of the National Library of Scotland to quote from the papers of the first Earl Haig in their possession; Dr A. Massie for permission to quote from several archival collections in the possession of the National Army Museum; to the Rhodes Trust and the Bodleian Library, University of Oxford, for permission to quote from the papers of Cecil Rhodes; the Fusiliers Museum of Northumberland for permission to quote from collections of papers in its possession; the Royal Engineers, Library and Archive for permission to quote from papers in its possession; and to Mr James Methuen-Campbell for permission to quote from the papers of the third Baron Methuen in the Wiltshire and Swindon History Centre. I should also like to recognize the assistance of many other individuals: Ms Lauren Jones and Adam Walsh, Royal Engineers Museum, Library and Archive; Miss Jane Davies, curator, Lancashire Infantry Museum, Fulford Barracks, Preston; Ms Lesley Frater, Fusiliers Museum of Northumberland, Alnwick Castle; Ms Lucinda Jones, Wiltshire & Swindon History Centre; Ms Lucy McCann, Bodleian Library of Commonwealth & African Studies, Rhodes House, Oxford; Mr Thomas B. Smyth, Black Watch Regimental Archive, Balhousie Castle, Perth; and Major L. White of Cornwall's Regimental Museum, Bodmin. I should also like to thank the staffs of the British Library (Newspaper Collection) at Colindale, the Templer Study Centre of the National Army Museum, the National Library of Scotland, and of the Reference and Local Studies Centres in Liverpool Central Library, Sheffield Central Library, Wakefield Local Studies Library and Leeds Central Library.

I should also like to express my thanks to various colleagues who have assisted me in this project, namely Professors John Gooch, Andrew Thompson and Richard Whiting (University of Leeds), Professor Ian F. W. Beckett (University of Kent), Professor Fransjohan Pretorius (University of Pretoria), and Dr Jeremy A. Crang (University of Edinburgh).

I am particularly grateful to David Appleyard for the services of the Graphic Support Unit (University of Leeds) in the preparation of the maps; to Peter Harrington, Anne S. K. Brown Military History Collection, Brown University, Rhode Island, for his assistance in finding images for the volume; to the McGregor Museum, Kimberley, South Africa, for permission to use photographic images from its collections; to Richard Dabb for permission to use an image of Cecil Rhodes from the collection of the National Army Museum; and to the editorial support and encouragement of Michael Leventhal, Stephen Chumbley and Kate Baker. As ever, I remain profoundly appreciative of the support and tolerance of Fiona, my wife, and Robert and Amanda, our children, for enduring the preparation of another book.

Edward M. Spiers

Introduction

Kimberley: The Siege and its Significance

Only three days after the expiry of the Boer ultimatum on 11 October 1899, which precipitated the South African War (1899–1902), the siege of Kimberley began. It would last 124 days from 14 October 1899 to 15 February 1900. This siege, alongside the investments of Mafeking (Mafikeng) and Ladysmith, was soon regarded as an iconic episode in the first part of the war, and these towns became early objectives for the relief forces sent from the United Kingdom and the colonies. If Kimberley possessed neither the strategic significance of Ladysmith nor a charismatic leader like Colonel R. S. S. Baden-Powell in Mafeking, it was by far the largest and wealthiest town invested. With its population swollen to nearly 50,000 by incoming refugees, it had 13,000 whites, 7,000 coloureds and Indians, and 30,000 black people, according to the categorization of the time. Known as 'Diamond City', Kimberley was an obvious target on account of its mineral wealth but it was also a great industrial centre, making it 'a plum deposit of capital, coal, foodstuffs and other stores, railway equipment, engineering workshops, scrap iron (potential shrapnel), and dynamite'.[1] Moreover Kimberley, located in northern Cape Colony, was highly vulnerable being only a few miles from the Orange Free State but 600 miles (966 km) from the coast. Nor did the paucity of British forces in Natal and Cape Colony – 10,289 men and 24 artillery pieces in June 1899 – pose much of a deterrent or offer the prospect of significant relief.[2] Compounding this vulnerability was a

---

1 B. Nasson, *The South African War 1899–1902* (London: Arnold, 1999), p. 99; see also F. Pretorius, *The A to Z of the Anglo-Boer War* (Lanham, Maryland, and Plymouth, UK: Scarecrow Press, 2009), p. 213.
2 Only belatedly did the British government approve the dispatch of 10,000 re-inforcements, mainly from India, but these were destined for Natal in October 1899.

political incentive for seizing Kimberley, namely the return of Cecil John Rhodes to Kimberley on 10 October just before the outbreak of war. He was, in the eyes of many Boers, 'the arch-enemy of Afrikanderdom'.[3]

Boer enmity towards Rhodes, and their grievances over Kimberley, derived from the origins of the town amidst the upsurge of diamond prospecting in the early 1870s. Located on the Vooruitzigt farm near the confluence of the Vaal and Orange Rivers, the town was first known as New Rush after the frenetic stampede of prospectors and speculators, who sought the newly found mineral wealth. A dispute soon erupted over the ownership of the diamond fields, with the claims of the local Griqua leader, Nikolaas Waterboer, challenged by the Transvaal and the Orange Free State. Cape Colony supported Waterboer, and in subsequent mediation between the claims of the Transvaal and Waterboer (the Free State refused to participate), Robert Keate, the lieutenant-governor of Natal, ruled in favour of Waterboer. Under various proclamations, the territory of Waterboer became known as Griqualand West (27 October 1871) with a government similar to that of Cape Colony. On 5 July 1873, New Rush was renamed Kimberley after Lord Kimberley, the secretary of state for the colonies, and three years later the Free State was persuaded to renounce its claims for a financial settlement of £90,000. On 15 October 1880 Griqualand West was formally incorporated within Cape Colony,[4] a development that hardly assuaged the Boers' sense of grievance.

Festering resentment persisted despite the discovery of gold on the Witwatersrand in 1886, and the flocking of diggers from all over the world, including thousands of *Uitlanders* (outsiders), into the Transvaal. Within a decade Johannesburg in the centre of the gold fields eclipsed Kimberley (and Cape Town) to become the largest town in South Africa, and far greater fortunes were to be made out of gold than diamonds. Kimberley and the diamond mining industry were changing anyway. The completion of the railway to Kimberley on 28 November 1885 ushered in a new era, linking the town more directly to the coastal ports, while the amalgamation of local mining companies left De Beers Consolidated Mines with a monopoly over diamond production in Griqualand West. The company dominated the diamond mining, trading, and industrial manufacturing sectors (and effectively Kimberley itself) from 1888

---

3 L. S. Amery (ed.), *The Times History of The War in South Africa 1899–1902*, 7 vols (London: Sampson Low, Marston and Co., 1900–9), vol. 2, p. 135; see also L. Creswicke, *South Africa and the Transvaal War*, 6 vols (Edinburgh: T. C. & E. C. Jack, 1900), vol. 2, pp. 65–6.
4 B. Roberts, *Kimberley: Turbulent City* (Cape Town: David Philip, 1976), pp. 23, 30, 59–61, 115, 155, 184.

onwards. By the late 1890s, Kimberley was the production centre for about 90 per cent of the world's diamonds.[5]

Cecil John Rhodes (1853–1902) had made his fortune in the diamond industry, founding the De Beers Mining Company in 1880, and subsequently De Beers Consolidated Mines. He belatedly became involved in gold mining and formed a company with Charles Rudd in 1887, which became Consolidated Gold Fields of South Africa in 1892, with Rhodes as the managing director. He utilized his vast wealth, political connections (as a member of the Cape parliament since 1881, prime minister of Cape Colony from 1890, and a privy councillor), as well as his British South Africa Company (with its Royal Charter, 1889) to secure mining concessions (and British imperial expansion) in the territory north of the Limpopo River. By eventually seizing this country in 1890, later known as Rhodesia, Rhodes clashed once more with President Paul Kruger[6] of the Transvaal. Rhodes had already thwarted the westerly ambitions of the Transvaal by supporting the military expedition of 1884–5 to assert British sovereignty over Bechuanaland (now Botswana). He now envisaged an unbroken belt of British territory from the Cape to Cairo, and, unable to find a second Witwatersrand in Rhodesia, decided that Kruger had to be overthrown by force and the Transvaal brought into a British federation.

He duly supported the planning of a *coup d'état* by 510 mounted police and volunteers led by his devoted friend, Dr Leander Starr Jameson. Launched from Bechuanaland on 29 December 1895, the raid proved a complete fiasco. Jameson and his column were forced to surrender on 2 January 1896, the *Uitlanders* failed to rise in revolt, and Rhodes had to resign the premiership of the Cape. The raid also convinced the Boers, who made no distinction between the imperialist vision of Rhodes and the aims of British policy, that Britain wanted to seize their country.[7]

---

5   Roberts, *Kimberley*, pp. 239, 263; R. I. Rotberg, *The Founder: Cecil Rhodes and the Pursuit of Power* (New York: Oxford University Press, 1988), p. 624.
6   President Stephanus Johannes Paulus (Paul) Kruger (1825–1904) was the last president of the South African Republic (Transvaal), who spent half a century militarily and politically upholding the state's struggle for independence. After the Jameson Raid, he imported massive amounts of modern armaments into the Transvaal, concluded an alliance with President Marthinus T. Steyn of the Orange Free State (1897), and, in subsequent negotiations with Britain at the Bloemfontein conference (May–June 1899), made only minor concessions before delivering an ultimatum (9 October 1899) to the British government. After the defeat at Bergandal (21–27 August 1900), Kruger fled to Europe, where he failed to raise support for the Boer republics. He died in Switzerland.
7   Rotberg, *The Founder*, pp. 10–11; Roberts, *Kimberley*, p. 250; Pretorius, *A to Z*

Although Rhodes was not involved in the subsequent negotiations and the crisis that preceded the outbreak of war in 1899, his dramatic re-entry into Kimberley on the eve of war ensured his pre-eminence in the ensuing siege. Based in the Sanatorium, a handsome hotel south-east of the town, Rhodes was not only an obvious target for the besieging forces but also a massively influential personality within the invested town. In some accounts, the pivotal controversy of the siege centred upon the fraught relationship between Rhodes and Lieutenant-Colonel Robert G. Kekewich, who commanded all the troops in the Kimberley area. Kekewich had only arrived in Kimberley on 13 September. He had been sent as a 'special adviser' by Sir Alfred Milner, the governor of Cape Colony and high commissioner for Southern Africa, who suspected that neither the Cape government nor Sir William F. Butler, the commander-in-chief in South Africa, had done enough to protect the highly vulnerable Kimberley. When Milner received confirmation of his worst fears from Kekewich, he secured his appointment as commander of all the forces in Griqualand West and the dispatch of some 600 regular reinforcements to Kimberley.[8]

While Kekewich, an unassuming and rather inarticulate Devonian, would prove a tactful, efficient and energetic, if not particularly charismatic, commander of Kimberley, the impulsive, self-opinionated and influential Rhodes also threw his energies, resources (and those of De Beers) into the defensive effort. What irritated and at times enraged Rhodes, who was all too aware of his failing health, was the apparent 'helplessness' of the isolated Kimberley, and periodically he 'railed against the incompetence of the local command and the British forces in South Africa'.[9] The ensuing rift became more pronounced towards the end of the siege, when the Boers began bombarding the town with 94-pound (43-kg) shells from their 'Long Tom' gun (7–14 February 1900),[10] and was known to contemporaries almost as soon as the siege was over. Arthur Conan Doyle, then a war correspondent, wrote of 'the painful but notorious fact' that 'considerable friction' existed 'between the military authorities and a section of the civilians, of whom

---

of the Anglo-Boer War, pp. 194–5, 381–3; E. Longford, Jameson's Raid (London: Weidenfeld & Nicolson, 1982, 2nd edition).
8   Lieutenant-Colonel W. A. J. O'Meara, Kekewich in Kimberley: Being an Account of the Defence of the Diamond Fields October 14th, 1899–February 15th, 1900 (London: Medici Society, 1926), pp. 14–17.
9   Rotberg, The Founder, pp. 627, 632; on Kekewich, see B. Gardner, The Lion's Cage (London: Arthur Barker, 1969), pp. 28–9, 36–7, and O'Meara, Kekewich in Kimberley, pp. 16–17, 52, 58, 140.
10   L. Changuion, Silence of the Guns: The History of the Long Toms of the Anglo-Boer War (Pretoria: Protea Book House, 2001), pp. 66–72, 77, 165; on the repercussions

Mr. Rhodes was chief'. In spite of all the assistance rendered by Rhodes during the siege, 'it is a fact', claimed Doyle, 'that the town would have been more united, and therefore stronger, without his presence. Colonel Kekewich and his chief staff officer, Major O'Meara, were as much plagued by intrigue within as by the Boers without.'[11]

Although some biographers of Rhodes defended his conduct, alluding to his many services on behalf of the besieged town, and claiming that the friction reflected a degree of mutual misunderstanding,[12] many modern scholars have been much more critical of his conduct in the 'siege within a siege'.[13] They have denounced Rhodes for his selfish and overbearing behaviour towards Kekewich; for evading curfew, censorship, and other restrictions that applied to all civilians under martial law; for his breach of confidences, reckless proposals, and readiness to spread alarm; and for his meddling in the defences of the town. They have deplored, too, his vindictiveness towards Kekewich after the siege, namely briefing Major-General John French against him, opposing the award of a sword of honour from grateful citizens in Kimberley, and deprecating the colonel in private conversations.[14]

By focusing upon eyewitness accounts from the siege, involving 50,000 people, this book will not necessarily throw new light on a controversy largely conducted in private meetings,[15] but a comparison of the diaries of Kekewich and his biographer, Colonel O'Meara, confirms that Kekewich was more charitable than his much-quoted staff officer towards Rhodes. He frequently paid tribute to the assistance of Rhodes,

---

of the shells, see Lancashire Infantry Museum (LIM), Lt Colonel Kekewich, diary, 7–10 February 1900, pp. 277, 282–3, 286–8.
11 A. Conan Doyle, *The Great Boer War* (London: Smith, Elder & Co., 1900), pp. 302–3. O'Meara was the main intelligence officer and censor.
12 J. G. Lockhart, and The Hon. C. M. Woodhouse, *Rhodes* (London: Hodder & Stoughton, 1963), pp. 441–2; and H. Hensman, *Cecil Rhodes: A Study of a Career* (Cape Town: C. Struik, 1974), pp. 335–45.
13 T. Pakenham, *The Boer War* (London: Weidenfeld & Nicolson, 1979), ch. 27.
14 Rotberg, *The Founder*, pp. 627–8; Pretorius, *A to Z of the Anglo-Boer War*, pp. 206, 382–3; Gardner, *Lion's Cage*, pp. 57, 70–1, 172–3, 186–7, 190–1; Pakenham, *Boer War*, pp. 183, 185–6, 320–23, 327–8; A. Thomas, *Rhodes: The Race for Africa* (London: Penguin Books, 1997), pp. 360–5; Field Marshal Lord Carver, *The National Army Museum Book of the Boer War* (London: Pan Books, 2000), pp. 90–3; J. Downham, *Red Roses on the Veldt: Lancashire Regiments in the Boer War, 1899–1902* (Lancaster: Carnegie Publishing, 2000), pp. 57–61, 64–5, 68–70.
15 Although Rhodes's secretary delivered communications between the 'two irate men', modifying the language in which they 'couched their messages', he blamed neither man. P. Jourdan, *Cecil Rhodes: His Private Life by His Private Secretary* (London: John Lane The Bodley Head, 1911), p. 110.

supported his controversial policy of trying to expel blacks from the town (even if he doubted it would work), and acknowledged the extent of his influence by making the oft-quoted remark that 'Kimberley is De Beers and De Beers Rhodes.'[16] While the leading citizens of Kimberley commended the professionalism and generosity of Kekewich, they found O'Meara much less impressive. Robert H. Henderson, the mayor of Kimberley in 1899, regarded O'Meara as 'an evil influence'.[17] Sir David Harris, a distinguished soldier and politician in Kimberley, observed that O'Meara had 'an unhappy knack of rubbing civilians up the wrong way. Suspicious and cynical, and deficient in diplomatic tact, he caused much friction, and at times made matters rather difficult for Kekewich.'[18] George A. L. Green, then the young editor of the Kimberley newspaper, the *Diamond Fields Advertiser*, accepted that Kekewich, whom he described as 'always courteous and considerate' was 'personally blameless' in the row. He thought, nonetheless, that Kekewich might have profited from the continued support of his original second-in-command, Lieutenant-Colonel H. Scott Turner, a dashing and very popular Black Watch officer, who had better relations with Rhodes, having served under him as a magistrate in Rhodesia. But Scott Turner was killed in action (28 November 1899), forcing Kekewich to rely on O'Meara, who 'made the mistake of taking all the great man's petulant outbursts seriously' and of regarding Rhodes as just 'an ordinary civilian'.[19] Whatever the truth of such allegations, O'Meara was fiercely partisan, even circulating copies of his diaries in Kimberley after the siege,[20] before they became the basis of his biography of Kekewich, and the source of many criticisms of Rhodes. As Brian Roberts has noted, 'Several ill-informed accounts of the siege of Kimberley have been based on his biased observations.'[21]

---

16 LIM; compare Kekewich, diary, 2, 7–9 November, 12, 16 and 19 December 1899, pp. 44, 47, 49, 125, 134 and 141 with *Diary Written Shortly After the Siege. Written by Major O'Meara, Chief Staff Officer to Colonel Kekewich* (hereafter O'Meara diary), pp. 50–3, 59, 63–5. Mrs Rochfort Maguire, a close friend of Rhodes, had used a similar phrase in her published diary, 'Life in Kimberley during the Siege', *The Times Weekly Edition*, 23 March 1900, p. 183.
17 R. H. Henderson, *An Ulsterman in Africa* (Cape Town: Unie-Volkspers Beperk, 1944), p. 77.
18 Colonel Sir D. Harris, *Pioneer, Soldier and Politician* (London: Sampson, Low, Marston & Co., 1930), p. 173.
19 G. A. L. Green, *An Editor Looks Back: South African and other Memories, 1883–1946* (Cape Town: Juta & Co., 1947), p. 83.
20 Rhodes House, Oxford (RH), Rhodes Mss., Afr. 228/C28, f. 191, W. E. Chapman to C. J. Rhodes, 7 November 1901.
21 Roberts, *Kimberley*, p. 317.

Nevertheless, despite the lack of special correspondents in Kimberley other than G. M. C. Luard of Reuters,[22] Rhodes managed to convey his anxieties both directly to friends in the Cape and Britain via dispatch riders and black runners, and indirectly through the editorials of the *Diamond Fields Advertiser*. While Kekewich sought to reassure the relief column that the situation was 'not critical' in Kimberley, sending messages by dispatch riders and later, as the column approached the Modder River, by using searchlights at night and heliographs by day, Rhodes continued to press for immediate relief, even intercepting dispatch riders to learn of the movements of the column.[23] As early as 18 October, Milner was complaining about Rhodes sending him 'panicky telegrams about immediate relief, which is impossible', although he recognized that 'If Kimberley falls, we cannot hold the whole of the Colony.'[24] Within the month Milner informed Joseph Chamberlain, the colonial secretary, that 'I write this quaking, for one fears every hour for Kimberley.'[25] So Rhodes was not alone in his anxieties, and the *Daily Mail* championed his concerns.[26]

Many metropolitan and provincial newspapers reported upon the siege, with some Lancastrian newspapers following the fortunes of the men of the Loyal North Lancashire Regiment, half of whom were in Kimberley and the other half in the relief column.[27] By publishing uncensored extracts from the letters of soldiers and civilians alike, this work will use eyewitness testimony and reveal its contents, which have not been seen in this form before. The 261 letters were nearly all published in the metropolitan and provincial press (with only a few

---

22   Some London newspapers sought links with George Green and other members of his staff on the *Diamond Fields Advertiser*, J. Beaumont, 'The British Press during the South African War: The Sieges of Mafeking, Kimberley and Ladysmith', in M. Connelly & D. Welch (eds), *War and the Media: Reportage and Propaganda, 1900–2003* (London: I. B. Tauris, 2005), pp. 1–18, at p. 3.
23   O'Meara, *Kekewich in Kimberley*, pp. 57, 59, 61, 73, 78–81; Major-General Sir F. B. Maurice, and M. H. Grant, *History of the War in South Africa 1899–1902*, 4 vols (London: Hurst & Blackett, 1906–10), vol. 2, pp. 71; 'Kimberley Talking Nightly', *Cheshire Observer*, 17 February 1900, p. 7.
24   Sir A. Milner to Lord Selborne, 18 October 1899, C. Headlam (ed), *The Milner Papers,* 2 vols (London: Cassell, 1933), vol. 2, p. 24; see also RH, Rhodes Mss., Afr. S227, Telegrams 24, f. 1301, Rhodes to Milner, 5 November 1899.
25   Sir A. Milner to J. Chamberlain, 9 November 1899 in J. L. Garvin, *Life of Joseph Chamberlain*, 6 vols (London: Macmillan, 1932–69), vol. 3, p. 493.
26   'Kimberley Wants Troops', *Daily Mail*, 24 October 1899, p. 5.
27   'Lancashire Troops at Kimberley' and 'Loyal North Lancashire Regiment', *Preston Herald*, 16 December 1899, p. 5.

culled from regimental and personal archives). They supply insights into contemporary perceptions of the siege and the fierce and bloody attempts to relieve the town over a period of three months.

The extracts are reproduced in their original form to reflect the feelings of residents during and after the siege, and of officers and other ranks as they struggled to cope with the demands of modern warfare. By culling the material from the British press, they indicate how newspaper readers (and their editors) came to understand and respond to events in connection with this siege. In so doing, the letters uncover a broader range of contemporary opinion than the memoirs and diaries of individuals, often written up after the event, whether by civilians in Kimberley[28] or soldiers in the relief force.[29] They also provide first-hand commentary on events in the field, particularly the challenges of crossing fire-zones swept by smokeless-powder, flat-trajectory, magazine rifles. These challenges would prove just as daunting whether faced by raw youngsters in their first battles or by weather-beaten veterans of former wars in Africa and India. They would shatter the complacency in Britain and the widespread under-estimation of a highly mobile enemy that was well armed, adept at field-craft, and sometimes entrenched under the skilful direction of General Koos de la Rey.[30] The letters will further testify to the way in which Britain, as an imperial power, was able to recover from initial defeats, and to exploit the passivity of the Boers, by deploying massive military forces across the seas and projecting them rapidly to the front by rail. They also reveal some of the social effects of the war, particularly the displacement of refugees at the outset, and the destruction of homes and property by both belligerents.

---

28 E. Oliver Ashe, *Besieged by the Boers A Diary of Life and Events in Kimberley during the Siege* (London: Hutchinson, 1900); and C. Meyer, *Days of Honour during The Siege of Kimberley 1899/1900*, trans. by V. Matter (Kimberley: Kimberley Africana Library under the auspices of the Friends of the Library, 1999).

29 L. March Phillipps, *With Rimington* (London: Edward Arnold, 1902); and Captain E. Lloyd, *Boer War: Diary of Captain Eyre Lloyd, 2nd Coldstream Guards* (London: Army and Navy Co-operative Society, 1905).

30 General Jacobus Herculaas 'Koos' de la Rey (1847–1914) was a successful farmer in the Lichtenburg area of the western Transvaal. Having fought black peoples in the western Transvaal, and served in the Anglo-Transvaal War (1880–1), he was later a member of the Volksraad in which he opposed Kruger's drive for war. Once the war began, he served loyally and resourcefully. He mounted the first successful ambush of an armoured train (Kraaipan, 12 October 1899), demonstrated considerable tactical flair in advocating recourse to trench warfare, and later, as a guerrilla leader, refined the art of charging on horseback and firing from the saddle (as at Tweebosch, 7 March 1902). A signatory to the Peace of Vereeniging (31 May 1902), he was later shot dead at a roadblock in 1914.

In examining these events, the approach will be chronological, that is by date of publication in the British press rather than by the date when the letters were written or sent. As some correspondents wrote about several events in a single letter, particularly those soldiers who fought in three battles within six days, their letters will be numbered and where more than one extract comes from the same letter, links to previous passages will be identified by reference to these numbers. Moreover, as newspapers often published several letters under the same headline (twenty-seven in one issue of the *Blackburn Times*),[31] full references with subheadings are given with each letter. Where these letters refer to principal individuals or events, or err in their commentary (and defeated soldiers often exaggerated the numbers of enemy faced and killed), the letters are annotated, and perspectives from a few enemy letters added. More editorial commentary can be found in the introductory sections of each chapter and in the maps and illustrations. The final chapter will assess the significance of this correspondence, particularly its value at the time and subsequently, in understanding how the participants coped with the challenges of enduring a siege and securing its relief.

---

31 'Letters from Local Soldiers at the Front', *Blackburn Times*, 13 January 1900, p. 3.

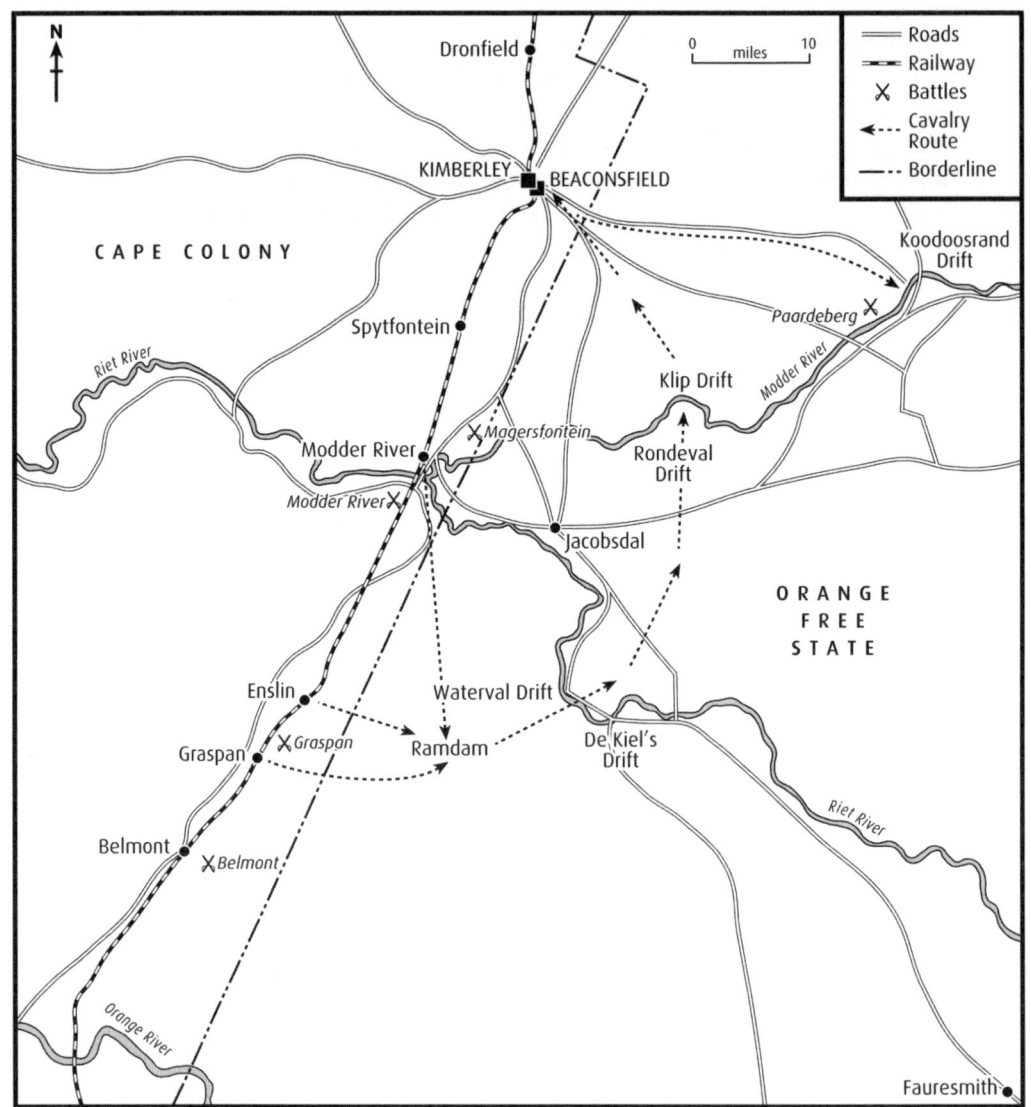

Map 1 Theatre of Operations

Chapter 1

Defending 'Diamond City'

Kimberley and its Defences

Kimberley was hardly an attractive town. When Anthony Trollope visited it at the height of the diamond diggings in October 1877, the intense heat, dust (including great dust storms blown in from the Kalahari Desert), swarms of flies, the lack of trees or greenery, and the profusion of corrugated iron dwellings appalled him: 'the place itself was distasteful to me in the extreme'.[1] After two decades the heat, dust and corrugated iron were still as conspicuous but the population of the town had quadrupled and it had grown more prosperous, with a growing sense of civic pride. Kimberley had secured its own water supply, electric street lighting (the first town to do so in the southern hemisphere), hospital, library, schools and railway station. A building craze had followed the mining amalgamation, including a model village for the workers of De Beers in Kenilworth; the erection of government buildings and a Post Office in Market-square, transforming the town's centre; and the construction of new buildings with brick frontages, verandahs and cast-iron balconies. Large compounds contained the black workers with sleeping quarters for hundreds of men, kitchens, baths, stores, mess rooms, dispensaries, sick wards and guardrooms. The mines, too, had changed: the Dutoitspan and Bultfontein mines had closed and the other great holes were no longer teaming with workers, as Trollope described, since their men were now working out of sight in tunnels.[2] If the great slag heaps round the

---

1 A. Trollope, *South Africa*, reprint of the 1878 edition with an introduction and notes by J. H. Davidson (Cape Town: A. A. Balkema, 1973), pp. 9, 369–70; see also Creswicke, *South Africa and the Transvaal War*, vol. 2, pp. 64–5.
2 Trollope, *South Africa*, pp. 359–62; Roberts, *Kimberley*, 189–91, 195, 244–6, 269–71, 291–2.

town bore witness to the source of the town's prosperity, Kimberley still boasted of some notable constructions in the late 1890s. It established the first South African mining school in 1896; a Theatre Royal with an elegant and spacious interior in 1897; the third Kimberley Club in 1898 (after the first two clubs had been destroyed by fire); and a new Town Hall built in classical style, and completed in September 1899 just before the onset of hostilities.[3]

The secret mission by which Lieutenant-Colonel Kekewich was 'sneaked' into Kimberley enabled a prompt construction of the town's defences. These included several redoubts and entrenched positions on the outskirts, notably at the water-supply reservoir and golf links (south-west of the town); at De Beers Mine (east of the town); at the Kimberley Mine (west of the town); and at several advanced posts, the most important of which was the Premier Mine, some four miles (6.4 km) east from the centre of Kimberley with an abundant supply of water. The heaps of debris from the mines, some 60 to 70 feet (18–21 m) high, skirting the north, south and east, facilitated the choice of sites. A network of barbed wire obstructed all approaches save by the roads, and fields of fire were cleared in front of the line of defence, with some of the cleared material used to construct a line of obstacles filling gaps between the works. While five searchlights, installed by De Beers, could scan the surrounding veld by night, and buried land mines acted as a further deterrent, observation posts were erected, particularly the so called 'conning tower', some 155 feet (47 m) high. The conning tower, with telephonic communications, allowed the garrison commander, equipped with a telescope, to observe any movements across the veld out to 8–10 miles (13–16 km), exercise direct control over his force, and communicate with the various gun positions on the perimeter.

Once it was decided to extend the outer defences to include the south-eastern town of Beaconsfield, extra forts were erected and the circumference stretched over 11½ miles (17.7 km), or in some estimates, nearly 14 miles (22 km). As Kimberley possessed only the Diamond Fields Artillery (97 men), Diamond Fields Horse (178 men), the Kimberley Rifle Volunteers (about 400 strong), and a body of Cape Mounted Police (another 400 men), Kekewich immediately requested regular reinforcements and began to raise a Town Guard from the civilians. On 20 September four companies of his own regiment, the Loyal North Lancashires (over 400 men), a detachment of 21 mounted infantry from the same regiment, about 100 Royal Artillery and 50 Royal Engineers

---

3 Roberts, *Kimberley*, pp. 263, 304–9.

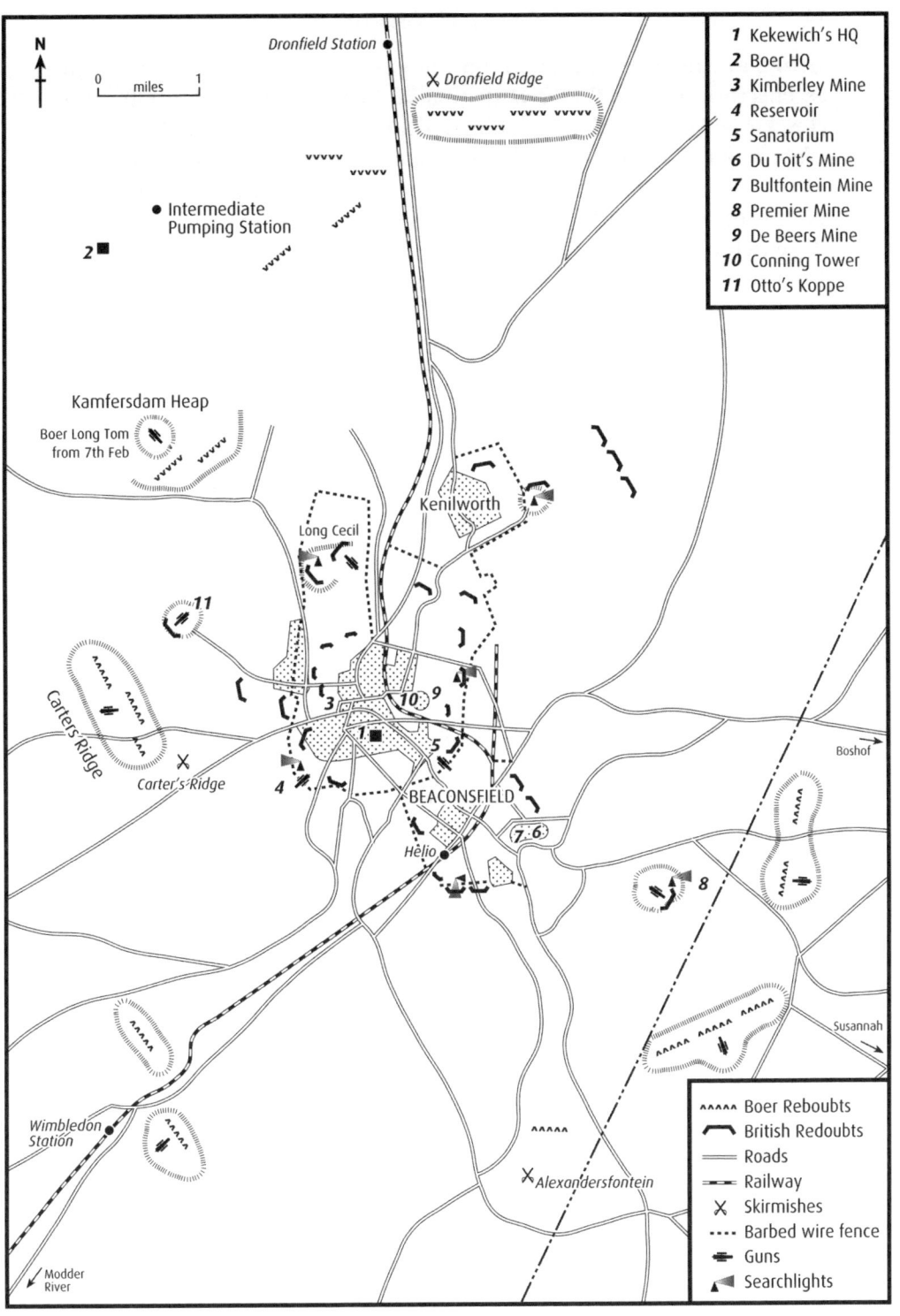

Map 2 Kimberley Besieged, 14 October 1899–15 February 1900

arrived in Kimberley. Kekewich now possessed 14 guns, 12 of which had an effective range of 2,500 yards (2.3 km) and two of only 2,000 yards (1.8 km). After Cecil Rhodes arrived, he raised a body of Kimberley Light Horse, giving Kekewich a combined mounted force of about 864 men by 26 November. Rhodes also assisted in arranging that 300,000 gallons of water should be pumped into the waterworks reservoir, while Kekewich ordered that all available rail and food supplies be brought into Kimberley from Vryburg station to the north and Modder station to the south. Finally, he took possession of six machine guns, 442 rifles and three-quarters of a million rounds of ammunition, which the De Beers Company had stockpiled at the time of the Jameson Raid.[4]

1

A Manx lady recalled that

> For many weeks we had been hearing of the likelihood of war being declared with the Transvaal, but it always seemed in the distance until one morning in September there arrived in Kimberley about 500 of the Loyal North Lancashire Regiment under the command of Colonel Kekewich.[5] The band played as they marched through the principal streets and camped on the veldt just outside the town. There were great crowds of men, women and children following, especially natives. No doubt there were many who had never seen a real live soldier before and looked on them, as they marched with guns on their shoulders, rugs and haversacks slung behind, bandoliers around them, and looking very travel-stained, as a sort of curio. We felt that morning things were beginning to look serious. For about three weeks we were hearing of redoubts getting built, trenches being dug, a town guard formed, also a mounted corps known as the Kimberley

---

[4] Kekewich (Q. 21,853), Minutes of Evidence taken before the Royal Commission on the War in South Africa, vol. 2, Cd. 1791 (1904), XLI (hereafter Evidence before the Elgin Commission), pp. 560–1; O'Meara, *Kekewich in Kimberley*, pp. 15–21; Maurice, *War in South Africa*, vol. 2, pp. 40–53; Pretorius, *A to Z of the Anglo-Boer War*, p. 212.

[5] Lieutenant-Colonel Robert G. Kekewich (1854–1914) served with the Buffs in Perak (1874) and the Sudan (1885 and 1888), before gaining his majority with the Royal Inniskilling Fusiliers (1890) and command of the 1st Battalion, Loyal North Lancashire Regiment, in 1898. Despite his successful defence of Kimberley, the rift with Rhodes occasioned his removal from command in Kimberley and delayed the award of field command in South Africa. Promoted major-general by the end of the war, he had to retire on account of failing health in 1914 and committed suicide.

Light Horse. Our Volunteers were called into camp to be drilled along with the regulars: it seemed almost certain we would be in the midst of war.

'Horrors of the Siege', *Isle of Man Weekly Times and General Advertiser* (henceforth *Isle of Man Weekly Times*), 16 June 1900, p. 5

2

Writing home on 28 October, Private Robert Gregson described how the four companies of the 1st Battalion, Loyal North Lancashires, had travelled for two days and three nights on a train from Cape Town before

we marched into Kimberley the day after, their [*sic*] was a jolly lot of cheering as we marched through. The war had not started then but the Boers had threatened to blow Kimberley up and their [*sic*] was only the Volunteers to stop them until we arrived on the scene.

Lancashire Infantry Museum (LIM), Private R. Gregson to his mother, 28 October 1899

3

The precariousness of Kimberley was evident to residents, such as Hugh Sinclair, formerly of Largs, Ayrshire, and now a resident of De Beers Terrace, Kimberley. As he wrote to William Cook of Kilbirnie, north Ayrshire, in a letter dated 8 October,

things have turned out serious with us here at Kimberley. If you have a map of South Africa, you will see that we are only an hour's ride from the border of the Free State, and as you are aware that State has joined the Transvaal against us. They have a commando lying about three hours from us about 5,000 strong with two batteries of artillery. We are all sworn in again – all the old Volunteers – so I am going to see active service once more.

'The Kimberley Defence Force', *Glasgow Herald*, 7 November 1899, p. 5

4

J. F. 'Fred' Byrne, who played rugby football for Moseley, England and the British Lions, explained in a subsequent interview that he was one of the many refugees who had arrived in Kimberley

upon one of the last trains which left Mafeking. There were hundreds of women and children fleeing towards Cape Colony at that time

... and it was painful to see those poor creatures, all too poorly provided for their dreary and painful ride of 800 miles [1,287 km], thirteen or fourteen being often packed in a carriage ... Happily for Kimberley in its dire straits, Mr More, the railway traffic manager ... accomplished a noteworthy achievement. He was aware that a large consignment of flour was lying on the railway at Modder River, and he sent down a train only a few hours before the ultimatum expired to bring it into the town. He hardly dared hope that it would get through, for war was practically commenced, but success awaited him. Hundreds of sacks of flour were taken into Kimberley that Saturday afternoon, and a few hours afterwards the Boers had blown up the railway culverts and isolated the town ...

All round the town, in a circle the circumference of which measured some thirteen miles [21 km], trenches and redoubts had been thrown up by the besieged, and were manned by the Town Guard, some of whom camped under canvas but many of whom, including Mr Byrne, took their rest on the open veldt with no roof over their heads save the broad canopy of heaven.

'In Beleaguered Kimberley', *Birmingham Daily Post*,
20 March 1900, p. 7

Boer Investment of Kimberley

In the first week of the war Free Staters, initially from the Boshof, Jacobsdal and Kroonstad commandos under General Christiaan J. Wessels, moved on Kimberley and some 4,800 men took up positions to the east of the town down to Alexandersfontein. After a request from President Marthinus T. Steyn,[6] they received support from 2,200 Transvaalers under General Koos de la Rey, who were released from the operations near Mafeking, where de la Rey had captured an armoured train at Kraaipan (12 October). Arriving on 30 October, these reinforcements completed the siege on the western side of Kimberley from the northern Dronfield Ridge round the intermediate pumping station, through Carter's Ridge to Wimbledon Ridge in the south. During the course of the siege, the Boers repeatedly moved their gun emplacements and, in the months of

---

6   Marthinus Theunis Steyn (1857–1916) was the last president of the Orange Free State. After the Jameson Raid he cemented ties with the Transvaal in an offensive and defensive alliance (1897) but tried to broker a deal between Milner and Kruger at the Bloemfontein conference (May–June 1899). Thereafter he supported the hostilities energetically, and avoided capture throughout the war before retiring as president on 29 May 1902 on account of ill health.

November and December, detachments of Transvaalers went south to confront the relief force. After an election on 8 January, the command of all Boer forces in siege of Kimberley passed to General Ignatius Ferreira, who had led the Free State forces at the battle of Magersfontein.[7]

5

A Dundonian, Thomas Bennet was another refugee who had fled from the Orange Free State and promptly enrolled

> in one of the volunteer corps that were hastily organised for the defence of the town. The men were all armed with the Lee-Metford rifle, and had only been partially drilled when the ultimatum expired. With the exception of five hundred men of the Lancashire Regiment, some Royal Artillery and Engineers, the garrison was composed of Colonials. There were the Diamond Fields Artillery, Diamond Fields Horse, the Kimberley Rifles, the Town Guard, and a body of Mounted Police. It became evident that the Boers meant to lay siege to the town when the telegraph wires were cut and the railway destroyed on the south and north. Preparations were immediately made for the defence. Forts were built, rifle pits dug, and shelters constructed all round. It was arranged that as soon as the enemy appeared in sight the sirens at the mines would sound blasts as the alarm . . .
>
> [On Sunday 15 October] Mr Bennet went to the Presbyterian Church in Kimberley. The service had just begun, and the congregation were singing a hymn about war when the sirens sounded the dread alarm. The organist started to his feet, the music ceased, and in three minutes the church was empty. The streets were crowded, and the men were hurrying hither and thither with their rifles and bandoliers over their black Sunday coats. The troops were mustered, and marched to their posts ready to meet the enemy, but the Boers did not that day venture within range of the guns.
>
> 'In a Besieged City', *Courier and Argus* (Dundee), 24 May 1900, p. 3

6

There were personal preparations, too, as H. A. Oliver, the future mayor of Kimberley, recounted in a letter of 23 October:

---

7   Pretorius, *A to Z of the Anglo-Boer War*, pp. 115, 146, 213; Maurice, *War in South Africa*, vol. 2, p. 54.

Last month I bought a large quantity of provisions and hid them under the floors and in the roof, so we shall be fairly well off, unless our house gets burnt down. I also bought some large tanks and had them filled with water, which should last us for a month. Should the siege last longer than that I may have to kill our cows and horses, as we could not spare water for them unless we get rain.

We have fortified the town to the best of our ability. We have a number of Maxims[8] and small field pieces, but should they bring heavy siege guns against us, our only chance would be to go out and attack them, in which case we should lose heavily. We have about 500 Imperial troops, 600 Volunteers, and almost 3,000 citizens formed into a Town Guard. I am one of the latter . . .

We have arranged alarm signals at the outlook stations, which can be heard all over the town. If there is any movement of the enemy the alarm is sounded, and we all rush to our posts . . .

We can see the Boer camps all round us about eight miles [13 km] off; with the aid of glasses we can see their men. They are evidently strengthening their positions. Several times our mounted men have gone out, about 250 strong, when the Boers have been near, but they have always retired on their main body. Evidently they want to draw our men on to their fortified positions, and then cut them off. I hope our commanding officers won't be caught in that way.

'The Siege of Kimberley', *Derby Mercury*,
4 April 1900, p. 2

7

W. O. Lunson found himself undertaking more specialist defensive duties:

On the first day of the siege we came under the direction of the Director of Army Telegraphs. After one night in the trenches, it was thought we should be more useful by taking charge of the telephones in the various redoubts. This was not at all bad at the start, especially one place which was a crow's nest some 80 feet [25 m] high, built above the head gear of the Debeer's [*sic*] Mine, from whence a splendid view of the surrounding country was obtainable. The first climb or two was not altogether to the liking of one's nerves, but after

---

8   Named after their inventor, Hiram Maxim, these machine guns weighed 60 lb (27 kg), had a range of about 1,000 yards (900 m), and could fire at a rate of 500 rounds per minute (but this was a theoretical capacity as they had belts of 250 rounds and had to be fired in bursts to avoid overheating).

one or two trips to the top for a six hour duty, one did not take long to get used to it.

'The Siege of Kimberley', *Wells Journal*, 12 April 1900, p. 5

There were also some reserved occupations. As A. W. Newsham of the Cape Government Railway informed his father, 'When the proclamation was made and martial law established on October 15, we formed a railway corps, and were sworn in. We had to protect railway property, so could not join the town guard, who did duty 12 miles [19 km] round from Market Square.'

'A Sheffield Man in Kimberley', *Sheffield Daily Telegraph*, 21 March 1900, p. 5

8

Not everyone, though, responded so positively. As A. G. Akenhead recalled,

> Nothing of any importance happened until the 13th of October when all communication was cut off from outside, and we found ourselves really besieged. A day or two after the shopkeepers, hoping to reap a golden harvest, started raising their prices, and a few hours saw rises of 25 per cent, 50 per cent, and in some things 100 per cent.[9] But Kekewich was equal to the occasion, and proclaimed martial law, and proclamations came thick and fast regulating the prices of necessaries and down tumbled the prices again. As the time wore on, and there seemed no hope of being relieved, the supplies had to be curtailed, but until about Christmas we could get nearly everything we required, and got fowl for dinner on that day . . . We all give Colonel Kekewich great praise for the manner in which he regulated the food supply.

'The Siege of Kimberley', *Western Mail*, 15 May 1900, p. 6

---

9   See also Carl Meyer, *Days of Honour during The Siege of Kimberley 1899/1900*, trans. by V. Matter (Kimberley: Kimberley Africana Library under the auspices of the Friends of the Library, 1999), p. 19.

Conducting the Siege

Kekewich had resolved to conduct an aggressive defence of Kimberley, thereby stealing the initiative from the enemy. 'I kept on sortieing [*sic*] at them, making reconnaissances in force, and that kind of thing, and they did not know where and when these were coming off.'[10] For this strategy, he needed a mobile force, so employing his mounted units and where appropriate the armoured train.[11]

9

Military service now differed markedly between the various corps. Writing on 20 October, Horace Pattrick informed his mother that he had left the Town Guard, as they were 'only for duty in the town or within eight miles [13 km] of it', to join the newly formed Kimberley Light Horse:

> I expect now I have joined this horse troop I shall see service of a different sort . . . We are to have five shillings [25p] a day from the Government and De Beers are giving us half-pay all the time we are away and free rations as well, so that we are not badly paid for soldiers . . . One of the Directors, too, is giving 2s. [10p] a day to the wife of any man who is away in the volunteers or the Light Horse that I am in, and 9d. [3½p] for every child he may have, all out of his own pocket. Mr. Rhodes has also promised that any married man living in a house belonging to the Company shall live rent free for the time he is engaged in the war. I do not suppose there is another place in the world where a firm of any sort would treat their men as they are treated here . . .
>
> [On 15 December he added] I have been in nine or ten fights during the siege; in fact, I have been in everything except the first little affair our fellows had, and that day I had to stop in the camp, as I happened to be Orderly Corporal that week. I was made corporal when the troop was formed, and since then I have been promoted to Sergeant.

---

10   Kekewich (Q. 21,890), Evidence before the Elgin Commission, vol. 2, p. 562.
11   The train consisted of an engine and tender completely armoured save for the funnel to within 9 inches (23 cm) off the ground, with armoured trucks coupled in the front and rear. The trucks had loopholes and a Maxim gun on a swivel, LIM, Major A. McCallum Webster, 'Reminiscences of the Kimberley Armoured Train', 1899.

Of course our fights have only been small affairs compared to what Lord Methuen[12] is having, but I do not think they will have any hotter than some of ours have been. For one reason we have had to go out to attack every time for the Boers have never once made an attack on us the whole time they have been here, and we have had to attack them lying behind breastworks and every other cover they could make; you fancy it was warm work. Another thing we were never more than five or six hundred strong in the three troops (the Cape Mounted Police, Diamond Fields Horse, and Kimberley Light Horse). The foot soldiers have had no fighting at all except a shot now and then. The Town Guard had absolutely nothing to do the whole time except lay in the forts all day.

The Boers have scarcely ever been nearer than three or four miles [4.8–6.4 km] to the town.

'At the Siege of Kimberley with the Light Horse', *Essex County Standard, West Suffolk Gazette and Eastern Counties Advertiser* (henceforth *Essex County Standard*), 24 March 1900, p. 6

10

'Life in the trenches', argued Bennet, continuing his letter (5), 'was arduous and trying' but

consisted more of watching and waiting than fighting. The men constructed shelters to protect them from the shell fire by scooping out the ground and supporting the roof with bricks and covering it with wood or corrugated iron, over which sandbags were piled, and these again were covered with a thick layer of sand. Everyone had their little brick hut. Patrols and pickets were sent out at nights, and the country all round was swept by searchlights.

'In a Besieged City', *Courier and Argus* (Dundee), 24 May 1900, p. 3

---

12 Lieutenant-General (later Field Marshal) Paul S. Methuen, third Baron Methuen (1845–1932) served under Sir Garnet Wolseley in the Asante expedition (1874) and in Egypt (1882), and with Sir Charles Warren's Bechuanaland expedition (1884–5). His command of the 1st Army Division ended in disaster at Magersfontein but he remained active throughout the war until severely wounded in the defeat at Tweebosch (7 March 1902). He remained friends with Koos de la Rey, the victor of this battle, who treated him well in the aftermath. Methuen served as the General Officer Commanding in South Africa (1908–12).

Another Scot, James Main, agreed that manning the redoubts was fairly tedious:

> When not on duty we had all to be in camp by seven o'clock, and lights out at nine. We had 15 men and 2 non-coms [non-commissioned officers] for guard every night, and the whole camp had to turn out in full war equipment at 3.30 every morning, and wait for daybreak. Then we could retire, say, about four o'clock to five o'clock, after which we had to turn out again for a good hour and a half's drill. It was rather tiresome, but we had to grin and bear.
>
> 'Kimberley Defenders', *Courier and Argus* (Dundee), 3 April 1900, p 5

11

Drummer Ben Nightingale (Loyal North Lancashires) probably expressed the concerns of several regulars about the quality of their colonial comrades:

> The men who garrisoned Kimberley were 450 of the Loyal North Lancashires, 50 of the Royal Engineers, and about 100 garrison artillery. This made about 600 Imperial troops. Then they formed a Town Guard of the civilians. They were not of much use, as they never went out to face the enemy, but they used to man the defences when we went out. Then we had a few volunteers, and some men who formed a company of Light Horse. We had to show them how to go about it. So you see what a fix we were in for a fighting force. We had only 7 lb. guns, the least in the service. You may think what good they were when we could not reach the Boers with them from town. We used to go out to have a bit of a do with them until they got the town properly surrounded; then they showed their bravery by shelling the town.
>
> 'Letters From Local Soldiers at the Front', *Blackburn Times*, 24 March 1900, p. 3

12

One of the MacBean brothers from Inverness came to a more perceptive assessment. Although part of the Town Guard, he accepted that 'The hardest work fell on the Mounted Police, the Mounted Volunteers, and the Light Horse.' These units, he added, were all camped together, and their duties were mostly outside the town – patrolling the veldt, guarding cattle, and, of course, they were the only serviceable force for attacking the Boers, as the regulars had only 25 mounted men. The regulars were camped all the time in the centre of Kimberley . . . ready to go to any part of the town that was threatened. Being nearly all infantry, they were useless to send out for attacking purposes. Their number (650 in all) were so small as to make them very little use in the veldt.

'A Highland Family in Kimberley',
Inverness Courier, 13 April 1900, p. 6

13

Yet co-ordinated sorties were possible initially, so long as coal was available for the armoured train commanded by Major A. MacCallum Webster. At Dronfield (24 October 1899) the train supported action by mounted units under the command of Lieutenant-Colonel H. Scott Turner. Further support could be summoned by heliograph, notably the Volunteer Artillery by road and a troop train with regular reinforcements. H. A. Oliver, adding to his letter (**6**) with one written on 26 October, summarized the skirmish:

On Tuesday about 1,000 mounted Boers came within sight of the town, and seemed to be making for where our cattle were feeding on the outskirts. Our mounted men, about 500 in all, with the Volunteer Artillery, taking two field guns and two Maxims, also 150 of the Lancashire Regiment, went out to meet them.[13] They retired to a hill about six miles [10 km] from the town; a very strong position.[14] They hid among stones and bush; our men attacked them, and after two hours' fighting they bolted, leaving their Commander dead on the field. Although they tried to carry off their dead and wounded, our men secured his pocket-book and papers, which contained some valuable information. We do not know what their total loss was, but they must have suffered to make them run,[15] as we found instructions on the Commandant to take our cattle at any cost, and we saw our

---

13   The primary aim was to examine the Riverton Pumping Station.
14   This was near Dronfield.
15   The Boer losses were 2 killed and 7 wounded while the British suffered 3 men killed, 3 officers and 18 men wounded, Pretorius, *A to Z of the Anglo-Boer War*, p. 213.

shells burst in their midst frequently. We lost four killed and nineteen wounded: the latter are all in hospital doing well.

'The Siege of Kimberley', *Derby Mercury*,
4 April 1900, p. 2

The Early Shelling of Kimberley

On 4 November Commandant C. J. Wessels sent an ultimatum to Kekewich demanding his unconditional surrender or, failing that, allowing the women and children of all nationalities to leave the town. Kekewich rejected the surrender but informed the Boer community, of whom only one family took advantage of the offer. After forty-eight hours the ultimatum expired and the shelling of the outer defences began, with a more concerted bombardment of the town from several different directions on 11 November. A new phase of the siege had begun.

14

James Brander Dunbar of Pitgaveney, Morayshire, a lieutenant in the Town Guard, recorded in his diary for 4 November: 'Ultimatum sent by leader of Boer commando, unless we surrender before 6 a.m. Monday that he will shell the town; to remove women and children to a place of safety if we do not surrender; that he will give protection to anyone in the Boer camp.'

'A Diary of the Siege of Kimberley', *Northern Scot and
Moray & Nairn Express*, 24 March 1900, p. 6

15

One lady observed that 'On November 7th the Boers started shelling Kimberley, but all the shells fell on the veldt, and we didn't mind in the least. On the 15th the enemy shelled very heavily from 5 a.m. until 7 a.m., and then I was really frightened, for the shells were falling all around the house.'

'Siege of Kimberley', *Bristol Mercury and Daily Post*,
14 April 1900, p. 6

Serving on 'an advanced redoubt', George Palmer, a sergeant in the Town Guard, explained that 'The nearest shells came within 400 or 500 yards [366 or 457 m] only, so that the only time I came within range of the Boer shell fire was when I left the redoubt to visit my house and family . . .'

'Through the Siege of Kimberley', *Doncaster Gazette*, 13 April 1900, p. 8

16
The Manx lady, continuing her letter (**1**), described how

> The shells crashed overhead, and burst all around us. It was marvellous how we escaped from being struck[16] – one shell exploded only five yards [4.6 m] from our verandah. I must say I never felt very nervous. Nearly everyone had dug-outs to run into . . . [and a dug-out] is a hole dug in the ground, five or six feet [1.5–1.8 m] deep, reminding one of a grave. There is a roof of rails, sleepers or very thick wood, then sheets of corrugated iron, and on top piles of sandbags, loose sand, and stones, several feet high. We had nearly 300 bags full of sand on ours. At one corner there is a small opening where we can get in and out; and there mothers rushed with their little ones, into the damp earth for protection from these cowardly Boers . . . One family in the next street to ours has suffered very severely from the Boer shells; the mother's leg was so badly crushed it had to be amputated; one child had both leg and arm broken, and another died from its wounds a few hours after – all from one shell.[17]

'Horrors of the Siege', *Isle of Man Weekly Times*, 16 June 1900, p. 5

17
Some were much more shaken and alarmed by the experience. As a young lady from York reflected:

> These shells are terrible things. Thousands have fallen into shops, smashing the whole place to atoms. Men, women, and children have been killed, struck in the street, and in their homes. Just fancy sitting in your room, and suddenly a bugle sounds from a high hill and screaming and praying, waiting for it to come, praying it may not

---

16 Kekewich expressed a similar sentiment in his diary, 14 November 1899, LIM.
17 This family was extremely unlucky. While the Boers fired over 8,000 shells into Kimberley, they killed only nine persons and injured another twenty-two, Maurice, *War in South Africa*, vol. 2, p. 69.

strike you . . . Then is the time to pray; then it is the time you think there is a God . . .

The shells have done a lot of damage. I have got two big pieces and will try and get more.

'The Siege of Kimberley. A York Lady's Experiences',
Yorkshire Evening Press, 26 March 1900, p. 3

Another lady, Miss Jessie R. Guild, who had only settled in Kimberley in the previous August, recalled that 'It was no picnic to be in those splinter-proof holes. It was suffocating, as this time of year it is fearfully hot. The shells fell close to us, and we had narrow escapes, and the noise they made rushing through the air made one's flesh creep.'

'Life in Kimberley Story of the Siege. Wormit Lady's Experiences',
Courier and Argus (Dundee), 24 March 1900, p. 4

18

In fact the damage from the 8,000 shells was relatively light. As early as 13 November, H. A. Oliver, continuing his letter (**6, 13**), observed:

For several days last week they shelled the town; our guns replied; and beat them off after two to three hours' fighting. Their shells did very little damage, only killing one native woman . . . They hit a number of houses, but the damage was not very great in any instance; one went through a bedroom and fell between two beds in which children were sleeping, but it did not explode and no serious harm was done.

'The Siege of Kimberley', *Derby Mercury*,
4 April 1900, p. 2

19

Albert Clucas (Kimberley Light Horse) also noticed how familiarity with the early shelling bred contempt:

The children were very little afraid of the shells; indeed, if one exploded close to our house they would rush out and try and find as many pieces of the shell as possible. Some nights we spent sitting all night on the stoop at the front of the house, listening to the shells flying over and around us in every direction – sometimes exploding so near as to fill the house with smoke from the shell when it burst . . . One passed just over the roof, went in through an open window of a house (the gable of which faces us) and passed through the dining room out through the door, and exploded in the yard, doing no damage. The people had just left the room, and were in the front at the time. Another shell struck the road seven yards [6.4 m] from our front door, and exploded in the yard, doing no damage.

'Experiences of the Kimberley Siege', *Isle of Man Weekly Times*, 31 March 1900, p. 1

20

Although collecting shell fragments became commonplace during the siege (**17**), the bombardments had psychological effects. As Mrs Griffiths, a Welsh lady who lived in the exposed suburb of Kenilworth[18] near the mines, recalled: 'We were very fortunate; but it was trying to one's nerves to hear shells constantly whizzing over one's head.'

'Kimberley during the Siege', *Western Mail*, 28 April 1900, p. 4.

Discretion had to be exercised, as R. Hilliard, a captain in the Town Guard, remembered, when 'They used to shell regularly from Susannah, Dronfield, Kamfersdam, Carter's Ridge, and Wimbledon, and when all these places were going at once one had to be careful. The siege was, however, very monotonous.'

'Another Letter from Kimberley', *Essex County Standard*, 24 March 1900, p. 6

21

However minimal the damage and casualties, many deplored the fact that the Boers had chosen to bombard a town, placing women and children at risk. Bennet, continuing his letter (**5, 10**), maintained that

> Their conduct was disgraceful and barbarous. Wherever the Red Cross was hoisted that building was selected as a target for their artillery practice. The Nazareth Home, an institution maintained by the public for the education of orphan and destitute children, was fired at day by day. The first person killed was a Kaffir woman.

---

18   Located three miles (4.8 km) from Kimberley centre, Kenilworth was a model village built for the employees of De Beers. As prescribed by Rhodes, it had broad avenues, lined with double rows of eucalyptus trees, villas built in luxuriant gardens, an orchard with over 8,000 trees and a wide range of social facilities. Roberts, *Kimberley*, p. 271. Lieutenant W. Gordon Grant served in the Kenilworth Defence Force, 'Besieged in Kimberley', *Northern Scot and Moray & Nairn Express*, 31 March 1900, p. 6.

She was struck on the head just as she was coming from her washing house.

'In a Besieged City', *Courier and Argus* (Dundee), 24 May 1900, p. 3.

22

The Manx lady (**1, 16**) was equally appalled:

The Boers did not try to fight our soldiers. Oh dear, no! They did not fire on our defence works, nor yet did they come out of their hiding places and fight as Englishmen do, but kept under cover, and tried to kill defenceless women and children, and otherwise starve them to death, while they fed on the fat of the land.

'Horrors of the Siege', *Isle of Man Weekly Times*, 16 June 1900, p. 5

23

Equally frustrating was the limited ability of the defending artillery to counter the bombardments. Corporal U. W. J. Jones (Royal Garrison Artillery) admitted that

All our guns ran short of ammunition, and if it had not been for De Beers Company making some we should have had to give in long ago, and would, perhaps, have been dead by this time.[19]

'Letters From The Front. An Artilleryman on the Kimberley Siege', *Western Morning News*, 20 March 1900, p. 8

Sorties from Kimberley

As the Boers had the freedom to move their gun emplacements, the garrison could only respond by despatching armed reconnaissance parties to detect and harass these positions. If due north or south, the armoured train was still a viable means of drawing enemy fire, although the train absorbed considerable damage in the process.

---

19 Initially there were only 2,600 rounds or fewer than 200 for each piece of artillery, so the shells manufactured by De Beers were vital. Altogether the British 7-pounders fired 2,141 shells in defence of Kimberley, Maurice, *War in South Africa*, vol. 2, p. 50 and Kekewich, Evidence before the Elgin Commission, vol. 2, p. 560.

24

A. W. Newsham, continuing his letter (7), described how 'Our armoured train has done good service, and has had some rough usage, both north and south. It was at Spytfontein, and got battered with bullets and shells. One shell struck the door of the footplate and split it. The driver told me he did not know until he got back.'

'A Sheffield Man in Kimberley', *Sheffield Daily Telegraph*, 21 March 1900, p. 5

25

The experience for colonial mounted riflemen was both challenging and exhilarating. Trooper Pattrick (Kimberley Light Horse), writing on 15 December as part of letter 9, encountered

> My first smell of powder . . . at a place called Kenilworth, where the Boers came to try and sneak cattle, but that was a very small affair, and the afternoon was very much warmer . . . we had to go right to the opposite side of the town, and we ran into a very strong force of Boers who made it very warm for us. I saw my first man brought down there. He was galloping along quite close to me when he was bowled over; he was a Cape Policeman . . . Several times since then I have been lying down in the veldt firing with bullets striking all around and singing over my head but I did not notice it so much; after the first time you get used to it.
>
> You will see by the papers that the K.L.H. have lost more men than all the other troops so that will tell you that we have not been in the rear all the time . . . You cannot think how wild it makes you feel when you see your comrades bowled over. You do not stop to think that you are taking life, you simply delight in doing the best to kill the first one you can . . .
>
> I never thought when I came to South Africa that I should be living under canvas for two or three months in a military camp, constantly under arms, and sometimes in the saddle for twenty-four hours at a stretch, with scarcely a day passing without being shot at, and shooting back at the enemy.

'At the Siege of Kimberley with the Light Horse', *Essex County Standard*, 24 March 1900, p. 6

26

One of the young Boers besieging Kimberley also found these engagements exhilarating; he later became a prisoner of war and wrote to his cousin in Europe, describing how he had participated in the defence of a position to the south of the town on 11 November, when

> we had our first bit of a fight. Fifty of us were guarding two small kopjes below one of the British forts, and about 1,500 yards [1,371.6 m] distant, when we were attacked by a superior force of the besieged. We managed to hold out for an hour and a half until reinforcements arrived. We had then lost two men killed and three wounded. The fight was kept up for four hours, when the British retired to the town. Well, we had it rough there. The Maxims (four of them) were playing on us in grim earnest all the time. On account of our bad rifles – Martini-Henrys – we were not able to reach the Maxims, which were out of range.[20]

'With Cronje on the Modder', *Western Mail*,
27 December 1900, p. 3

27

Writing in December 1899 Dr G. E. Heberden, who was later mentioned in despatches for his services as the surgeon-captain of the Kimberley Light Horse, confirmed that his regiment had borne a heavy price in the early exchanges:

> The Boers have removed themselves to some distance, and are not teasing us any more. We occasionally go out; and stir them up; it is rather like taking a wasp's nest. When the place is relieved our force may be disbanded; if so I shall come home, if not I shall follow the fortunes of the war, and stick to my regiment, which is the Kimberley Light Horse. I am very proud of it, as it has distinguished itself greatly. Alas! 150 have been killed and wounded.

'The Defence of Kimberley', *Bradford Observer*,
23 January 1900, p. 6

---

[20] The letter confirms that not all Boers were equipped with modern smokeless-powder magazine rifles. The British had first used Martini-Henry rifles in 1871 and had employed them against the Zulus, but this single-shot rifle, with a punishing recoil and effective range of about 400 yards (365.8 m), was no match for Maxim machine guns.

Carter's Ridge (November 1899)

The most severe fighting occurred during the two engagements at Carter's Ridge, where the Boers had established a gun emplacement and entrenched defences. The first sortie, on 25 November, was intended to ascertain the strength of the Boers. In a co-ordinated assault, with the armoured train acting as a decoy, and the flanks protected by Royal Engineers at Otto's Kopje and a combined artillery/infantry force under Lieutenant-Colonel G. D. Chamier, RGA,[21] Scott Turner[22] led mounted forces in a surprise assault on Carter's Ridge. This reportedly killed between 50 and 60 Boers, captured 33 prisoners and a quantity of arms and ammunition, for the loss of 6 killed and 29 wounded. With bad weather precluding the use of the heliograph to call for reinforcements, the column withdrew.[23]

28

Commenting on this assault, Pattrick in his letter (**9**, **25**) recalled that

> Only in two engagements did we lose heavily, and in both of them we had to rush some very strong redoubts and were at times at very close quarters, with the enemy potting us from behind stone walls. When we got right into their forts with bayonets fixed they all ran like sheep. I can assure you they did not all get away, a good many of them had a prick from a bayonet. I think I struck one or two myself. One little lot we cornered, and they very soon had a white flag out, but we took no notice of that till they dropped their rifles and we made sure they could not shoot again. There were thirty-three in all, they are still in gaol here.
>
> 'At the Siege of Kimberley with the Light Horse',
> *Essex County Standard*, 24 March 1900, p. 6

---

21 Major (local Lieutenant-Colonel) George Daniel Chamier, RA (1860–1920), who served in the Royal Horse Artillery, the Royal Field Artillery and the Royal Garrison Artillery, commanded the artillery during the siege of Kimberley. He was promoted lieutenant-colonel on 11 January 1907 and placed on the half-pay list on 11 January 1912.
22 Brevet Major (local Lieutenant-Colonel) Henry Scott Turner (1867–99) was educated at Clifton College and entered the Black Watch in December 1887. He served in Matabeleland (1893–4 and 1896), when he was adjutant and paymaster to the Matabeleland Relief Force. Promoted captain and brevet major on 24 May 1898, he entered Kimberley as a special service officer. Wounded at Carter's Ridge on 25 November, he was killed in the engagement on 28 November 1899.
23 Downham, *Red Roses on the Veldt*, pp. 47–50; A. J. Beet and C. B. Harris, *Kimberley Under Siege* (Kimberley: Diamond Fields Advertiser, n.d.), p. 78.

More problematic was the second assault on 28 November, only three days after the Boers had reoccupied the position. On this occasion Kekewich sought to relieve pressure on Methuen's relief column by drawing off and holding as many Boers as possible in the vicinity of Kimberley.[24] He was willing to commit 1,800 men, more than a third of his entire garrison, in three columns: Scott Turner with 633 mounted men on the right, Chamier with the bulk of the artillery, Maxims, five companies of infantry and a detachment of sappers (960 men) in the centre, and a left-hand column under Major J. R. Fraser (Loyal North Lancashires) with detachments of the Kimberley and Beaconsfield Town Guards (300 officers and men). Much smaller detachments occupied Otto's Kopje and a forward position on the Kimberley–Barkly West road. With the armoured train, steaming first north and then south, to draw off the enemy's fire, the columns advanced at about 3.30 p.m. While the centre column engaged in a long-range artillery and rifle duel at 2,000 yards (1.8 km) without casualties, Scott Turner led the assault on Carter's Ridge. Advancing in rushes of 50 yards (45.7 m) under the cover of Maxim fire, and later artillery fire from the Diamond Fields contingent, they seized three redoubts before facing a fourth, 'practically a stone fortress, with loopholes and splendid head cover', that commanded the other three.[25] Only safe lying down, Scott Turner still hoped to seize the gun but when he raised his head, he was shot dead instantly. At nightfall the remnant of the force on Carter's Ridge returned to Kimberley. When they were allowed to collect the dead on the following day, the losses amounted to 22 dead and 28 wounded.

29

Of the two sorties, Leon Adlam, a town guardsman, described the 'one in which Major Scott Turner was killed . . . [as] the most important. We were away on the left preventing the Boers from attacking his flank. It was a well conceived attack, and the Boers must have lost heavily.'

'Neath Man's Experience at Kimberley', *Western Mail*,
29 May 1900, p. 7

'The worst experience was at Carter's Ridge', wrote Private David Nixon (Loyal North Lancashires), 'where we had to rush them at the point of a

---

24 Beet and Harris, *Kimberley Under Siege*, p. 41.
25 Ibid., p. 79; see also O'Meara, *Kekewich in Kimberley*, pp. 74–7.

bayonet. They cried for mercy when they saw the cold steel. There were 23 killed that day and about 50 wounded.'[26]

'News of Lancaster Men', *Lancashire Daily Post*,
29 March 1900, p. 4

30

H. A. Oliver, continuing his letter (**6**, **13**, **18**) on 8 December, described how

> We attacked an entrenched position, where they had a big gun mounted which was damaging the town. We carried the first three trenches at the point of the bayonet, and should have taken the fourth and last only for Col. Scott Turner being shot. On losing their leader our men retired. We lost 22 killed and 28 wounded. Another day we attacked the same position, and drove them out, capturing 28 prisoners, besides wounded. We brought them all into Kimberley;[27] their loss that day was very heavy, ours was slight.

'The Siege of Kimberley', *Derby Mercury*,
4 April 1900, p. 2

31

Another eyewitness to the final debacle was Albert Clucas, serving with the Kimberley Light Horse. In his letter (**19**), he described

> how Scott Turner and his brave men charged the fort, but were met with a perfect hail of bullets. About 20 or 30 of our men went down. The rest had to lie flat on the ground, while bullets rained down on them. It was just then that Scott Turner was shot. He put out his hat on the point of a rifle, and in a second it was shot through. He tried again, and the bullets flew through it. He then popped up his head to try and see what was going on when he was shot right through the head, and another young officer near him just missed being killed, a bullet shaving out a groove right along the top of his head. Our men then crawled back and came in to camp.

'Experiences of Kimberley Siege', *Isle of Man Weekly Times*,
31 March 1900, p. 1

---

26 This is a confused account in which the numbers of wounded from the two engagements may have been added together.

27 One of Oliver's horses was grazed by two bullets while he was bringing in the wounded, 'Reminiscences of the Siege of Kimberley', *Lancashire Lad*, no. 2 (1908), pp. 15–16, at p. 16.

32

A long-term resident of Kimberley recounted how

> Our men went right up to the fourth redoubt with fixed bayonets, hoping to get the gun, when a perfect hail of bullets poured on them, darkness came, and they were obliged to retire, bringing twenty-seven wounded with them. In the morning they went back for the remaining wounded, and found the fiends had been out and murdered them all. One man had forty bullets in him; many had eight or ten.[28]

'The Siege of Kimberley From Within', *Birmingham Daily Post*, 22 March 1900, p. 5

33

'The loss on our side was severe', acknowledged Jessie Guild, continuing her letter (**17**),

> the commander of the troops being killed, with about twenty others. I witnessed a scene I never wish to see again – the funeral of twenty-five men. There were twelve ordinary waggons, with two coffins placed on each. They had just a piece of canvas thrown over, and the coffins were of plain wood, painted black. The commander's coffin (Lieutenant-Colonel Scott Turner) was placed on the gun carriage. The band played, and about 800 soldiers followed these poor fellows to their last resting place.

'Life in Kimberley Story of the Siege. Wormit Lady's Experiences', *Courier and Argus* (Dundee), 24 March 1900, p. 4

34

The funeral was one of the most memorable events of the siege. The Manx lady, continuing her letter (**1, 16, 22**), recalled how

> I, along with my children, went to see the funeral, and I pray heaven I may never see such a sight again – hundreds of people (or rather thousands I should say) lined the streets from the hospital to the cemetery, and as the funerals passed along, the coffins on the gun carriages, each one wrapped in the Union Jack, and followed by their

---

28 A local doctor confirmed that 'they were so smashed up that there was some ground for the rumours [of atrocities]' but as they had all fallen very near the Boer fort 'that might account for the severity of the wounds . . . nobody knows except the Boers'. Ashe, *Besieged by the Boers*, p. 68.

officers and comrades with reversed rifles, there was scarcely a dry eye in the crowd. It was almost dark before the burial service was read, the volley firing and sounding of trumpets over, and we turned away with heavy hearts, wondering how it was all going to end.

'Horrors of the Siege', *Isle of Man Weekly Times*, 16 June 1900, p. 5

35

A Darlington family perceptively observed that

Now the greatest drawback of all to the defence here has been the total lack of competent officers. The officer commanding, Col. Kekewich and Major Chamier of the R.A., were the only officers of any standing in the place.[29] Col. Kekewich could not take the field and lead the men, and Major Chamier is an artillery officer, and evidently could not be sent out in charge of the other arms. Major Scott Turner, who usually went out, was brave enough, but, it is clear, did not possess the genius for handling Horse, Foot, and Artillery, otherwise a different tale than that of patient endurance might have added glory to the history of Kimberley. Our men, Horse and Foot, have shown plenty of true grit, and properly led, would have pushed the Boers far enough back to give us elbow room.

'Kimberley Siege. A Darlington Family's Experience', *Northern Echo*, 20 March 1900, p. 2

36

Opinions divided sharply over the late Scott Turner, who had been slightly wounded on 25 November but remained on duty. It was not the case, as Dr Ashe claimed, that his men 'all felt that he was reckless, and likely at any time to endanger their lives . . . Turner always seemed to go in for unnecessary risks, and the men naturally did not like it.'[30] Clucas, who served under Scott Turner, disagreed,[31] and, in his letter (**19, 31**), claimed

---

29   The official historian agreed: 'It is a truism that the less instructed are the men the better their leaders should be, but including one officer of the Army Service Corps, one of the R.A.M.C., and one recently retired from the infantry, Kekewich had but twenty-two professional officers under his orders, of whom by the 28th November four had been killed or permanently incapacitated for the remainder of the siege.' Maurice, *War in South Africa*, vol. 2, p. 48.
30   Ashe, *Besieged by the Boers*, p. 69.
31   Several citizens endorsed his view, see Brander Dunbar on 'poor Scott Turner' (**14**) while Mrs William Haddock described Scott Turner as 'a very brave dashing

that 'Scott Turner was a fine chap. He led our men (the Kimberley Light Horse, who were mostly young chaps who joined a few days previously), along with our volunteers . . . Scott Turner was a great favourite.'

'Experiences of Kimberley Siege', *Isle of Man Weekly Times*, 31 March 1900, p. 1

37

Mrs Rochfort Maguire, a close friend of Cecil Rhodes, observed:

In Major Scott Turner the Kimberley garrison sustained an irreparable loss, and the people of the town felt that in losing him they lost their most gallant defender, a man who was always ready to risk his life in order to keep the enemy at a safe distance from their town. He was beloved by his men, and, as organiser of the Kimberley Light Horse, he deserved all the praise for his untiring energy, and for the patience with which he drilled what were in many cases absolutely untrained men.

'The Defenders of Kimberley', *Graphic*, 31 March 1900, p. 462

38

While O'Meara affirms in his biography that Kekewich warned Scott Turner not to make an assault on Carter's Ridge unless it was either unoccupied or so slightly occupied that there was 'every prospect' of success,[32] Kekewich, despite making a similar point in his diary, was more generous:

Colonel Scott Turner was killed when most gallantly leading his men to the attack of a redoubt. The very best of officers; he is indeed a great loss.[33]

LIM, Kekewich diary, 28 November 1899, p. 81

---

officer much beloved by his men, but too daring', National Army Museum (NAM), Acc. 1985-11-12, Mrs W. Haddock, letter of 2 March 1900.

32 O'Meara, *Kekewich in Kimberley*, p. 75.

33 The citizens of Kimberley had the final word on this debate by choosing the fifth anniversary of Scott Turner's death (28 November 1904) as the date to dedicate the Honoured Dead Memorial – 'Designed by Herbert Baker and fashioned out of stone from the Matoppos where Rhodes was buried, the monument rises on a circle at the junction of five roads . . . Beneath the blue Kimberley sky, the monument stands like some ancient terracotta-coloured tomb or temple. Many regard it not merely as a symbol of the siege, but of the town itself' (Roberts, *Kimberley*, p. 338).

Chapter 2

Relief Force: Advancing to the Modder River

Assembling a Relief Force

At the outset of the South African War the invading Boers outnumbered the British forces in Natal and Cape Colony. The investments of Mafeking and Kimberley (and later Ladysmith), coupled with limited incursions into the British colonies, provided the impetus for the British authorities to dispatch an army corps of three divisions to Cape Town. For British soldiers in Cape Colony, these reinforcements were needed desperately, and for soldiers travelling to South Africa, there were plenty of new experiences to recount.

39

Writing from the Orange River near Kimberley, in letters dated 9 and 10 October, Private F. Blackburn (Loyal North Lancashire Mounted Infantry) informed his parents that

> We expect an attack at any time of the night, and we have to be out every morning at 3.30, saddled up ready to mount at any time till five when we go out, if our turn, and be in the saddle for six hours without a rest. We only get two nights sleep a week, and then we are in full dress . . . We have made a start close to the Orange River, about nine miles [14.5 km] out at a place called Belmont. Our flank was fired on, but when we advanced the Boers turned back. We were in the saddle over 12 hours, and I can tell you we are sore.
>
> 'Twelve Hours in a Saddle', *Lancashire Daily Post*, 30 December 1899, p. 6

40

Private P. H. Moore (Loyal North Lancashires) confirmed that

> Kimberley was attacked yesterday (Sunday the 15th), and our four companies, G, H, A and B, are now fighting there. The remainder are here. The armoured train is here. No trains came down here since Saturday night, and I saw the last train go up. The wires were cut late on the 14th, and the rails were pulled up ten miles [16 km] this side of Kimberley. We have ceased sending mounted patrols out from the camp . . . Many refugees come from the Transvaal.[1] The weather here is splendid. My heart is in the work, and everything speaks to me that God is with us.

Writing on 22 October from Orange River, Private Moore stated that

> the Boers seem to be nobody [*sic*] and are shooting badly. You will have heard of our success. A German regiment and Irish artillery were cut off at Dundee[2] . . . The 9th Lancers are here, and the Northumberlands and Munsters, and some six regiments arrive here next week . . . General Buller[3] expects to have his Christmas dinner in Pretoria. They have been rather slack in not sending troops out sooner.

'Bolton and the War', *Bolton Chronicle*,
2 December 1899, p. 7

41

Of the soldiers sent from Britain as part of the Army Corps, Private J. Gray (1st Battalion, Scots Guards) described a horrendous sea journey to his parents:

---

1 D. Cammack, *The Rand at War 1899–1902: The Witwatersrand and the Anglo-Boer War* (London: James Currey, 1990).
2 The battle of Dundee (Talana Hill) on 20 October 1899 was a Pyrrhic victory for British forces in Natal. They cleared Boers off the hilltop but at great cost to themselves.
3 General Sir Redvers Buller, VC (1839–1908) was the scion of Devonian gentry. He had a distinguished military career, earning his Victoria Cross in the Anglo-Zulu War (1879), prior to his arrival in Cape Town as commander-in-chief of the Army Corps, South Africa. He lost this command after some costly reverses in Natal, and incurred withering criticism in the press, particularly from Leo Amery of *The Times*. He still retained the affection of his troops and of many people in the West Country. G. Powell, *Buller: A Scapegoat?* (London: Leo Cooper, 1994).

The passage [on the *Nubia*] was pleasant and uneventful, until we reached Cape de Verde, then our troubles began. The sea was dreadfully rough – everyone more or less sick . . . The charger of our gallant Colonel died – a splendid animal who had carried his master safely through the Egyptian Campaign.[4] I can tell you it grieved us fellows to see the tears swelling into our Colonel's eyes when we saw the animal he loved so well committed to the stormy deep. Then from this point our provisioning was something scandalous. The grub they gave us to devour was not only disgraceful but disgusting. We were only served with bread twice a week – other days hard ship biscuit . . . On Tuesdays and Saturdays we had salt junk, and one day the men almost mutinied, as the meat served up to them fairly stank – it was putrid.[5] The doctor was sent for, who, as soon as he saw it ordered it to be thrown overboard in his presence . . . At last, on the 13th November, we reached Cape Town with a cleaner health sheet than might have been expected after the putrid food . . . On 14th November we disembarked, and no man regretted walking off that ship, and after a most enthusiastic reception, entrained for Orange River 572 miles [920 km] up country. We camped there until 21st November.

'A Perth Scots Guardsman's Letter Home', *Perthshire Constitutional and Journal*, 22 January 1900, p. 3

42

With the railway crucial to the forward movement of units and reinforcements from Cape Town, John Nightingale, a Boltonian, wrote from Indwe, Cape Colony:

At Sterkstroom, where our line joins the main line, the Volunteers are encamped; various points of the line, such as culverts and bridges, are watched night and day; and a corps of the Frontier Mounted Rifles, increased by about 20 to 30 Cape Police, are under canvas in case the town is attacked . . . There are large numbers of Dutch here, who have friends and relatives among the Boers . . . I wish I could hear something definite of Kimberley; we are awfully anxious.

'Bolton and the War', *Bolton Chronicle*, 2 December 1899, p. 7

---

4 This was fought in 1882, with the Scots Guards participating in the decisive victory at Tel-el-Kebir (13 September).
5 This was not unique: the meat on the *Kildonan Castle* was pickled in tins dated 1872 and 1882 'and went black when cooked'. 'The Voyage to the Cape', *Somerset County Gazette*, 13 January 1900, p. 3.

43

In a letter from a principal railway junction, De Aar, Cape Colony, a Bathonian informed his parents that

> We left Capetown on Sunday at two o'clock, and we did not get out of the train until Tuesday night at ten o'clock. I was put straight to outpost duty until the Scots come up, and then we are to push forward to Kimberley. Everything is burnt up here with the sun. Through not getting a wash, you can imagine we are a tasty-looking lot, and our faces and hands are burnt browner than khaki. There is a splendid country all the way up, and in the train we were all the time passing flocks of ostriches, goats, and springbok. Here everything is dear . . . Some of our chaps bought a bottle of beer, about a half-a-pint, 1s. 9d. [9p]. Kruger has made the biggest mistake in his life, and will lose the number of his mess[6] and his country too, before we are done.
>
> 'A Bath Boy at the Front', *Bath Daily Argus*, 6 December 1899, p. 3

44

Armed reconnaissance patrols were still undertaken but one composed of Loyal North Lancashire Mounted Infantry and 9th Lancers led to an ambush at Belmont (6 November). As Private Hill (Loyal North Lancashire Mounted Infantry) recollected:

> there were only mounted troops taking part in it. They were too strong for us, and we had to retire. There were thousands of bullets whizzing around us . . . It is a funny sensation the first few minutes, but you soon get used to it. I am trying to get a paper with an account of it, but I cannot. It was fought at Belmont . . . We were out three days before the engagement on a day and a half's rations. We went out on Monday, and came in on Thursday at 4 a.m. . . . I was against Lieutenant Woods [*sic*: Wood] when he fell. He had just told me to fire at one of them, who, he said, was in command of the Boers . . . He had just put down his glasses when over he went . . . Becon [*sic* Beaton] and Thomson [*sic* Thompson] were the two privates wounded, and they belong to London. They are doing very well. There were some narrow escapes . . . One of the Lancers was shot

---

6   Naval idiom: to 'lose the number of his mess' means to die or be killed.

right through the heel of the boot without the bullet touching him. There were a few wounded besides ours.

'Loyal North Lancashire Regiment', *Preston Herald*, 16 December 1899, p. 5

Methuen's Relief Force

When Sir Redvers Buller arrived at Cape Town on 30 October, he found that the military situation had worsened dramatically. The British defeats at Lombard's Kop and Nicholson's Nek in Natal – 'Mournful Monday' (30 October 1899) – had left 12,500 soldiers under Sir George White besieged in Ladysmith. Faced now with three sieges, and with fears that the Boers of Cape Colony might rise in revolt, Buller abandoned plans to drive north via the railway through Bloemfontein to Pretoria and split his force into three separate divisions. While he accompanied a relief division to Natal, he sent one division under Major-General Sir William Gatacre to the railway junction at Stormberg (to secure the Cape Midlands district from Boer raids and local rebellions by Boer inhabitants), and another under Lord Methuen to relieve Kimberley.

Methuen's division (about 10,000 men) included a Naval Brigade; the 1st Guards Brigade (1st and 2nd Battalions, Coldstream Guards, 3rd Battalion, Grenadier Guards, and 1st Battalion, Scots Guards); the 9th Brigade (1st Battalions, Northumberland Fusiliers and Royal Munster Fusiliers[7] and part of the Loyal North Lancashires, and the 2nd Battalions, Northamptonshires and King's Own Yorkshire Light Infantry); Highland Brigade (1st Battalions, Highland Light Infantry, Gordon Highlanders and Argyll and Sutherland Highlanders and 2nd Battalions, Black Watch and Seaforth Highlanders) initially held in reserve; four batteries of Field Artillery (17th, 18th, 62nd and 75th), the 65th Howitzer Battery and G Battery, Royal Horse Artillery; the 9th and 12th Lancers; Volunteers, including New South Wales Lancers, and Rimington's Guides. Though heavily criticized in subsequent histories, especially for the inadequate cavalry,[8] Methuen was delighted with his force: as he informed his wife,

---

7   Although two companies of Munsters reinforced the 2nd Battalion, Coldstream Guards, in the battle of Belmont, the Munsters were mainly employed on lines of communication and escort duties, Brigadier A. E. C. Bredin, *A History of the Irish Soldier* (Belfast: Century Books, 1987), p. 373.
8   Pretorius, *A to Z of the Anglo-Boer War*, p. 280; S. M. Miller, *Lord Methuen and the British Army: Failure and Redemption in South Africa* (London: Frank Cass, 1999), p. 86; R. Brooks, *The Long Arm of Empire: Naval Brigades from the Crimea to the Boxer Rebellion* (London: Constable, 1999), p. 220.

'no general has for years had such a beautiful command',[9] and, writing on 19 November, exuded confidence that 'I shall breakfast in Kimberley Monday.'[10]

Aware of the likely advance of Methuen's division by the railway, General Jacobus Prinsloo, with 1,500 Free Staters, had moved south to join J. A. P. van der Merwe's men near Belmont on 20 November to form a united force of 2,950 men with four guns. As a large number of these men remained behind in the laagers, Prinsloo could only employ 1,500 of his men in a firing line,[11] spread along a series of small kopjes (isolated rocky hills), irregularly disposed to the right and left of the Kimberley line. They thereby exploited the only high ground on the veld, which afforded them a good line of sight towards the approaching enemy, some protection against British fire, and places of concealment for their camps and horses from which they could retreat rapidly if necessary.

The Battle of Belmont (23 November 1899)

45

Having arrived at camp, five miles (8 km) north of the Orange River, on 18 November, Private J. Levi (Grenadier Guards) described how

> We stayed there three days, till the division was complete. Then we started to look for trouble. We marched to a place called Fineham's Farm, about five miles [8 km] from Belmont, on the night of the 22nd. We halted till midnight, then we extended for attack on the Boers' position, and advanced. The Grenadiers formed the firing line.[12]
> 'Letter from a Darlington Man', *Northern Echo* (Darlington), 22 January 1900, p. 3

46

'Everything was as silent as death as we crept along', wrote Lance-Corporal Robert Rea (Grenadier Guards), 'Bye and bye we came to

---

9   Wiltshire and Swindon History Centre (WSHC), Methuen Mss., Lord Methuen to his wife, 15 November 1899 in letters 14–21 November 1899.
10 This was presumably Monday, 27 November. WSHC, Methuen Mss., Methuen to his wife, 19 November 1899 in letters 14–21 November 1899.
11 F. Pretorius, *Life on Commando during the Anglo-Boer War 1899–1902* (Cape Town: Human & Rousseau, 1999), p. 196.
12 While the Grenadiers, with the Scots Guards to the left of them, led the assault on Gun Hill, the Northumberland Fusiliers led the assault on Table Mountain.

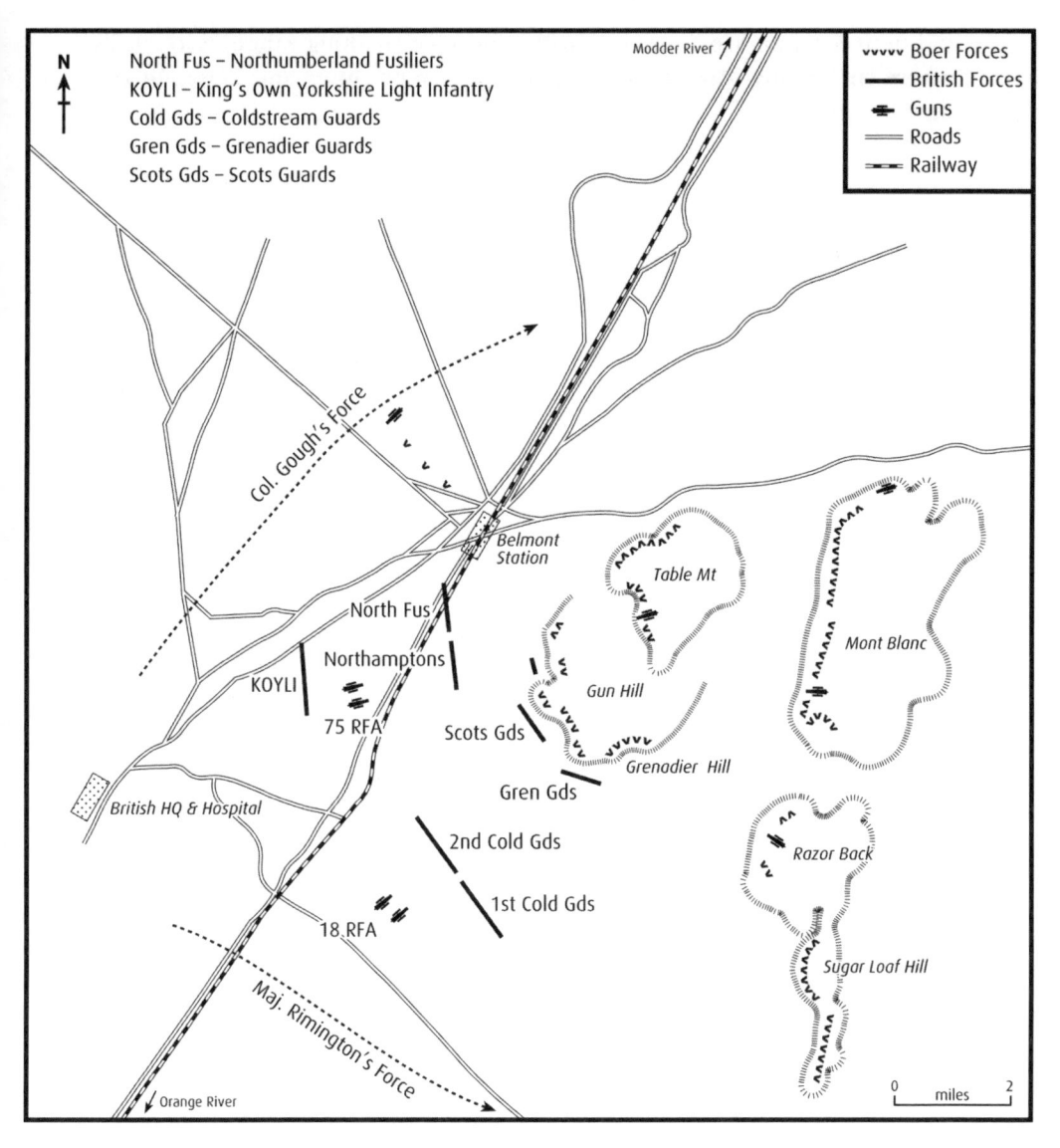

Map 3 Battle of Belmont, 23 November 1899

Belmont Station. We could see in the distance the long range of low hills where the enemy was supposed to be. We crept closer and closer in the dark – still silence.'

'A Belfast Soldier's Description', *Belfast News-Letter*, 20 December 1899, p. 5

'It was a splendid moonlight night', added Private P. Doyle (Grenadier Guards),

> and the advancing column looked awe-inspiring as it moved along in silent majesty . . . At each halt all the officers and men sank upon one knee. Every order that was given to the troops was given by movements of the hands of the commanders, no word being spoken. Here and there a few men whispered, but the light breeze hushed the men's quiet voices . . . The faint flush in the sky at the end of the Boer position told us that the enemy would see as well as hear us, and at that moment we saw a golden rim of light above the farthest kopje, and in a moment our men were moving in many thin lines, near two miles [3.3 km] long. They just looked like sportsmen stalking game birds, as each held his rifle ready in both hands and all crouched as they strode along with frequent haltings. In a few minutes there ran along the crest of the great southernmost kopje a thin line of fire jets. It was the flame of a volley from the Boers fired at the nearest English. This was the beginning of a fearful fight . . .

'Letters from the Front', *Bristol Mercury*, 30 March 1900, p. 6

47

'Our battalion', stated Sergeant John Bryson (Scots Guards),

> had to attack the position. We got within about 100 yards [91 m][13] of the Boers when they opened fire on us. We received the order to charge the position, and as it was a big long hill with nothing but boulders, we had our work cut out for us. For about twenty minutes or half an hour the bullets rained round us like hailstones. It was awful to see the men dropping on every side and to hear the groans of the wounded. Once we shifted the Boers from off the kopje we could

---

13   Most accounts of the battle indicate that the firing began rather sooner, at about 350 yards (320 m) from the hill, L. Childs, *Kimberley: Belmont/Graspan/Modder River/Magersfontein* (Barnsley: Leo Cooper, 2001), p. 33.

get a shot at them when they were retiring, but before that they were too well sheltered with boulders.

'Interesting Letter from a Hamilton Man', *Glasgow Herald*, 26 December 1899, p. 6

48

Just as inadequate reconnaissance had left the advancing columns short of their targets, so thwarting any surprise and exposing them to enemy fire, it had failed to detect that the hill was concave, rising to a peak on the right.[14] Accordingly, as Private R. Mercer (Scots Guards) recalled, the guardsmen 'all ran along quite unconcerned of the danger we were running to as the Boers had now commenced firing from a trench about seven hundred yards [640 m] to our left, but we kept running up the hill, the bullets striking the rocks all around us'.

'Writing Home', *Weekly Standard and Express* (Blackburn), 10 March 1900, p. 6

Private J. H. Owens (Grenadier Guards) found the cross-fire quite bewildering: 'The Boers firing from the right drove us into another party firing from the left, then we "faced about" and received another terrific fire from the front. Thus, you see, we were exposed to a terrible onslaught from three sides, and up to this we had not fired a shot.'

'Best Cold Sheffield!' *Morning Post*, 22 December 1899, p. 3

49

In continuing his letter (**46**), Private Doyle recounts how the hill was stormed:

> For protection and retort we could only shoot almost straight above our heads, without ever seeing our foe hidden behind the topmost boulders.
>
> We were advancing in too close formation, giving the bullets little chance to miss the mass we formed. We were being mowed down in butchery, but still we climbed upward and onward, never dreaming of another course. Some of the Northamptons dashed up after us, and altogether we drove the Boers from their position, and saw them leaping down the other side of the hill and across a valley to the hills beyond. In my battalion we lost something like 120 men in a few

---

14 Childs, *Kimberley*, p. 33.

minutes, and some very severe work was done by the Scots Guards, the 'Fighting Fifth',[15] Northamptons and Yorkshire Light Infantry . . . The battle opened at 4.20 a.m., and it was precisely three hours[16] later that an explosion of British cheering proclaimed the capture of the last of the hills. The artillery and naval guns, which had not been brought into action until five o'clock, silenced the last of the two Boer batteries at the moment of cheering, and the rest of the drama was made up of the flight of the Boers over the open veldt and the ineffectual pursuit by the 9th Lancers.[17]

'Letters from the Front', *Bristol Mercury*, 30 March 1900, p. 6

50

Confusion had occurred as the Grenadiers lost their direction in the dark. Sergeant Walsh, a Derbyshire police constable, who was serving as a reservist in the Grenadier Guards, found his section, while charging the right of the hill,

> pushed off by the Scots Guards on our left. Anyway, the adjutant, who happened to be with me, told us to take cover in a ditch. The remainder of the battalion rushed the hill . . . Understand, that we were in safety where we were, and could pick off the Boers on the top, but at the same time we were cut off from the battalion, who were safe, too, but the adjutant, poor fellow, thought we should join the others on the hill, so said, 'Come on, lads, to the hill.' We went, and I shall never forget that run of two hundred yards [190 m]. The bullets hailed round us like a storm. The adjutant was killed outright, and I lost 11 men of my section and two missing, leaving me with 12 men out of 25. I am sorry to say that 11 out of the 13 were Reserve men.[18]

'With the Grenadiers', *Sheffield and Rotherham Independent*, 18 January 1900, p. 6

---

15   The Northumberland Fusiliers.
16   The fighting actually continued until about 10 a.m., Maurice, *War in South Africa*, vol. 1, p. 227.
17   Several infantrymen complained about the tardy artillery support, see 'A Belfast Soldier's Description', *Belfast News-Letter*, 20 December 1899, p. 5, and 'A Bolton Guardsman at Belmont', *Bolton Chronicle*, 23 December 1899, p. 6; and about the ineffective cavalry pursuit, 'A Salford Guardsman with Lord Methuen', *Manchester Weekly Times*, 2 February 1900, p. 5, and Fusiliers Museum of Northumberland (FMN), Lt H. T. Crispin, diary (on Belmont), p. 34.
18   In his army reforms as secretary of state for war (1860–74), Edward Cardwell had introduced 12-year enlistments, whereby soldiers could leave the colours after 7 or 8 years and join the Army Reserve for the remainder of their enlistments.

51

With the Grenadiers coming under fire so early in their approach, this left the Northumberland Fusiliers and Northamptons even more exposed as they advanced towards the more northerly target of Table Mountain. 'I was supporting Captain Ripley's Company in the firing line', noted Captain L. G. Freeland (Northamptons),

> and were about 1,000 yards [915 m] away when the Boers really discovered they were attacked in force. You could only see the smoke puffing out of the rocks; we really ought to have waited till the right had been taken by the Guards, but we had no cover and moved slowly on, and reached the first line of kopjes, hardly firing a shot ourselves.
> 'Interesting Letter from Captain L. G. Freeland',
> *Essex County Standard*, 30 December 1899, p. 6

'When we got to the shelter of the hills', wrote Private W. Gray (Northumberland Fusiliers), 'we made them fly like chaff before the wind. In fact, for half an hour it was like shooting rabbits. Then commenced the most serious part of the business, that of driving them out of the kopjes. This continued upwards of five hours before we routed them.'
'A Stockton Man's Experiences', *North-Eastern Daily Gazette*,
27 January 1900, p. 3

'The bullets', recalled Private Turnbull (Northumberland Fusiliers), 'were flying like hailstones at Belmont. We drove them out of the kopjes at the point of the bayonet. They used the white flag – that is how our captain [Captain Edward Boaz Eagar] got killed and three men of my company.'[19]
'Fifty-Three Heroes in One Grave', *Leeds Mercury*,
13 January 1900, p. 8

52

Of all the units serving under Methuen, only the Northamptonshire Regiment had previously fought the Boers, in 1881. In a letter written immediately after the battle, Private W. James indicated that some of this experience had been passed on in regimental lore:

---

19 There were several white flag incidents in one of which E. F. Knight of *The Morning Post* was seriously injured. They were all resented bitterly by British soldiers, see 'A Guardsman's Miraculous Escape', *Rotherham Advertiser*, 27 February 1900, p. 3; 'A Goole Guardsman at the Front', *Leeds Mercury*, 21 December 1899, p. 6; see also FMN, Private F. Smith, diary, pp. 24–5; and Lloyd, *Boer War*, p. 11.

We fought a big battle at Belmont on the 23rd of November, and we were victorious after four hours' hard fighting . . . The enemy were all behind rocks about 300 feet [90 m] high, and we had to advance for 700 yards [640 m], all in the open ground, and then came my first experience of active service. The rocks they were hidden behind were horse-shoe shape, and we had to advance on these rocks in extended order, all exposed to their fire, although we could not see them until we were quite close to them, and then we could only just see their heads. The bullets were flying in all directions, and the worst part of it is that you see your comrade fall at the side of you either dead or wounded, and you think it is your turn next . . . We managed to get under cover after we had advanced for a considerable distance. Then there were shots fired on both sides with serious effect, and we had been fighting like this for about an hour, when the artillery worked round the enemy's flank, and then the Boers suffered severely. You could see horses and men going down like ninepins, but it did not finish at that, for we kept at it for another two hours, and then the Boers showed the flag of truce, but we were not having 'any' this time . . . they showed it in 1881, and when our fellows exposed themselves they fired again, so we had to be careful this time. They could talk English as plain as we could, and we shouted to them to come out and give up their arms, and they came leering out like a lot of thieves and gave us their arms one by one. I could not tell you the number exactly, but out of 2,000 we captured 40 or 50 prisoners and killed about half their number. In our regiment we had one officer and one private seriously wounded and about 14 wounded, but none killed.[20]

'The Battle of Belmont', *Leicester Chronicle and Leicestershire Mercury* (hereafter *Leicester Chronicle*), 23 December 1899, p. 3

Reflections on the Battle of Belmont

53

As Methuen intended to drive north along the railway, his soldiers had little time to recover and reflect upon the battle. Private J. Lazenby (2nd Battalion, Coldstream Guards), though, managed to write on 24 November, admitting that the victory had come

---

20 Boer losses appear to have been 36 captured, 30 wounded and 15 killed, Pretorius, *A to Z of the Anglo-Boer War*, p. 32, but the regimental losses are about right: 1 officer and 14 men wounded, Miller, *Lord Methuen*, p. 119, n. 49.

at such a great sacrifice! We have such a lot killed and wounded: it makes me sick to think of it; but, thank God, I came safe out of it . . . The Guards' charge was the first I have ever experienced. I was in the support line, and I tell you the bullets were flying about me like peas. We lost a lot of men. The sight of the battlefield is horrible, but it cannot be helped. We have got to do our duty.

'A Goole Guardsman at the Front', *Leeds Mercury*, 21 December 1899, p. 6

54

Even a month later, Trooper Robert Buckley (9th Lancers) remembered the sights and sounds of the wounded after Belmont,

who had been shot and were in the greatest pain. They were saying, 'Oh, my poor wife', 'Oh, my poor parents!' and some of them cried, 'Shoot me and put me out of my pain.' No one has any idea what war is only those who have been there. The sights you see on the battlefield are something fearful.

'Fearful Sights: Halifax Trooper's Account', *Bradford Observer*, 19 January 1900, p. 6

55

The casualties were often concentrated in particular units: Private Lees (Grenadier Guards) reckoned that 'There were 38 killed and wounded in my company alone, so you can tell what it was like.'

'Bolton and the War', *Bolton Chronicle*, 13 January 1900, p. 7

'As far as is at present known', wrote Corporal W. Longthorn (2nd Battalion, Coldstream Guards),

our side have lost about 50 killed and 200 wounded.[21] It was a sad sight to see the killed being buried at night. They were nearly all smashed in the face with Martini Henry bullets[22] . . . I never would say that I was a coward, but I can tell you I don't care much about this sort of butchering work. You don't think much about it when you

---

21   The amended list of casualties was 50 killed and 260 wounded, with 21 killed and 105 wounded in the Grenadier Guards, Miller, *Lord Methuen*, p. 119, n. 49.
22   However severe the facial injuries, some of them were almost certainly caused by bullets from Mauser rifles.

are on the job; it is when the battle is over, and you see the killed and wounded lying in all directions, bleeding and moaning . . . The Boers are smart at picking out the officers. In this battle we have had three killed and several wounded.[23]

'Bolton and the War', *Bolton Chronicle*,
23 December 1899, p. 6

56

The first encounter with the Boers was hardly auspicious. In the opinion of Lance-Corporal J. Walton (Northumberland Fusiliers),

They have acted like barbarians to us, firing on our ambulance, which you know in civilized warfare (as this is supposed to be) is allowed to gather killed and wounded. At Belmont one of the Boers came out with a flag of truce. A captain of my right [Captain Eagar] went eager to see what he wanted when a proper hailstorm of bullets was put into him. Our G.O.C. has since sent a message to G.O.C. Boers that a flag of truce will not in future be recognised.

'An Eldon Lane Youth's Experience', *Auckland Times and Herald*,
5 January 1900, p. 8

57

Writing to friends in Rotherham, Private J. T. Hirst (1st Battalion, Coldstream Guards) admitted:

You will think it strange that we should lose such a lot of men. But the Boers have strong positions, and it is like marching a soldier to his grave in attacking them . . . I am pleased to belong to the Coldstreams. It made a good name at Belmont in charging the Boer position. My company was told off to find the dead and wounded, and we were out all day with nothing to eat or drink.

'Has Fought in Six Battles', *Rotherham Advertiser*,
10 March 1900, p. 8

---

23 Four officers were killed and 19 wounded despite Methuen insisting that 'No officer has a sword, all rifles, no marks on their tunics, and putties like the men', WSHC, Methuen Mss., Methuen to his wife, 19 November 1899 in letters 14–21 November 1899.

58

The post-battle predicament was keenly felt: as Private Stockwin (Northamptonshires) explained, 'It's not the fighting we don't like, it's after – the sights are something hideous: and then when we get a rest there is no water, scarcely anything to drink, and what we have got is like mud. We've not shaved for a fortnight or washed for a week . . .' His comrade Private John Kersley added in the same article that 'One thing I don't like – we can't get enough to eat. We are being served out with water now.'

'Letters From The Front', *Northampton Mercury*, 22 December 1899, p. 3

59

Private Booth (2nd Battalion, Coldstream Guards) was even more blunt:

> We are starved to death nearly. They cannot get the stuff up here; it is so hilly. It is awful marching. We have only what we stand in – one suit, one shirt, and one pair of socks. We had to leave everything else behind. It is very hot in the daytime, but at night it is as cold as England. The water we get is dirtier than the River Rother, and we have some long marches for it . . . You would not know me now. We have all got whiskers; I look a treat – I am nearly as black as the niggers.

'A Rotherham Soldier at the Front', *Rotherham Advertiser*, 23 December 1899, p. 13

The Battle of Graspan (Enslin), 25 November 1899

As he drove the 1st Division north towards Kimberley, Lord Methuen encountered 2,300 Boers (Free Staters under Prinsloo and 800 Transvaalers under General Koos de la Rey brought from the forces besieging Kimberley), with six guns and two machine guns behind the hills at Graspan (also called Enslin). Deployed on positions across the railway line, they were only 11 miles (18 km) from Belmont. Once again British reconnaissance through the armoured train and mounted escorts underestimated the number of Boers manning the hills.[24] Lord Methuen ordered the combined forces of 9th Lancers and mounted infantry, under the commands of Lieutenant-Colonel Bloomfield Gough and Major Percy

---

24 Maurice, *War in South Africa*, vol. 1, p. 231; but only 1,300 Boers were in the firing line, Pretorius, *Life on Commando*, p. 196.

W. A. A. Milton respectively, to move forward, covering the advance for three miles (5 km) on either side of the railway, and planned to engage the enemy with artillery before rolling up their positions from east to west. He accorded the recently arrived Naval Brigade the honour of leading the flanking march, with the King's Own Yorkshire Light Infantry, two companies of North Lancashires and a field battery in support. The Naval Brigade, a composite of companies from various ships, as well as five officers and 190 Royal Marines, was delighted to 'have a "show" all to herself'.[25]

60

'It was six o'clock of the 25th', wrote Private P. Doyle (Grenadier Guards) in continuation of his letter (**46** and **49**)

> that fire was opened on a party of Rimington's scouts, who were in front of us. Then our troops marched into position facing the larger kopjes, and half-an-hour later our batteries opened fire on the rocks which hid the enemy. The Naval Brigade in the centre at 5000 yards [4.6 km] joined with short range artillery in bursting shrapnel with unvarying accuracy over the enemy. The Boers shot beyond and behind our guns. They seemed to have guns everywhere, for they were on almost every hill.
>
> A bit after seven o'clock the good marksmanship of a Boer gunner attracted the attention of our gunners, and the Naval Brigade undertook to silence him. Then began the duel. The Boer gun was hidden, and the only thing that our men had for a target was the thin smoke which arose over the Boer gun, and into this little cloud we planted shot and shell until at the end of the day we had given them 210 projectiles.
>
> 'Letters from the Front', *Bristol Mercury*, 30 March 1900, p. 6

61

With artillery engaged from the outset, Private L. Jackson, Royal Engineers, described his exhausting and dangerous activities 'as supports to the naval guns':

---

25 Surgeon T. T. Jeans (ed.), *Naval Brigades in the South African War 1899–1900* (London: Sampson Low, Marston & Co., 1902), p. 22.

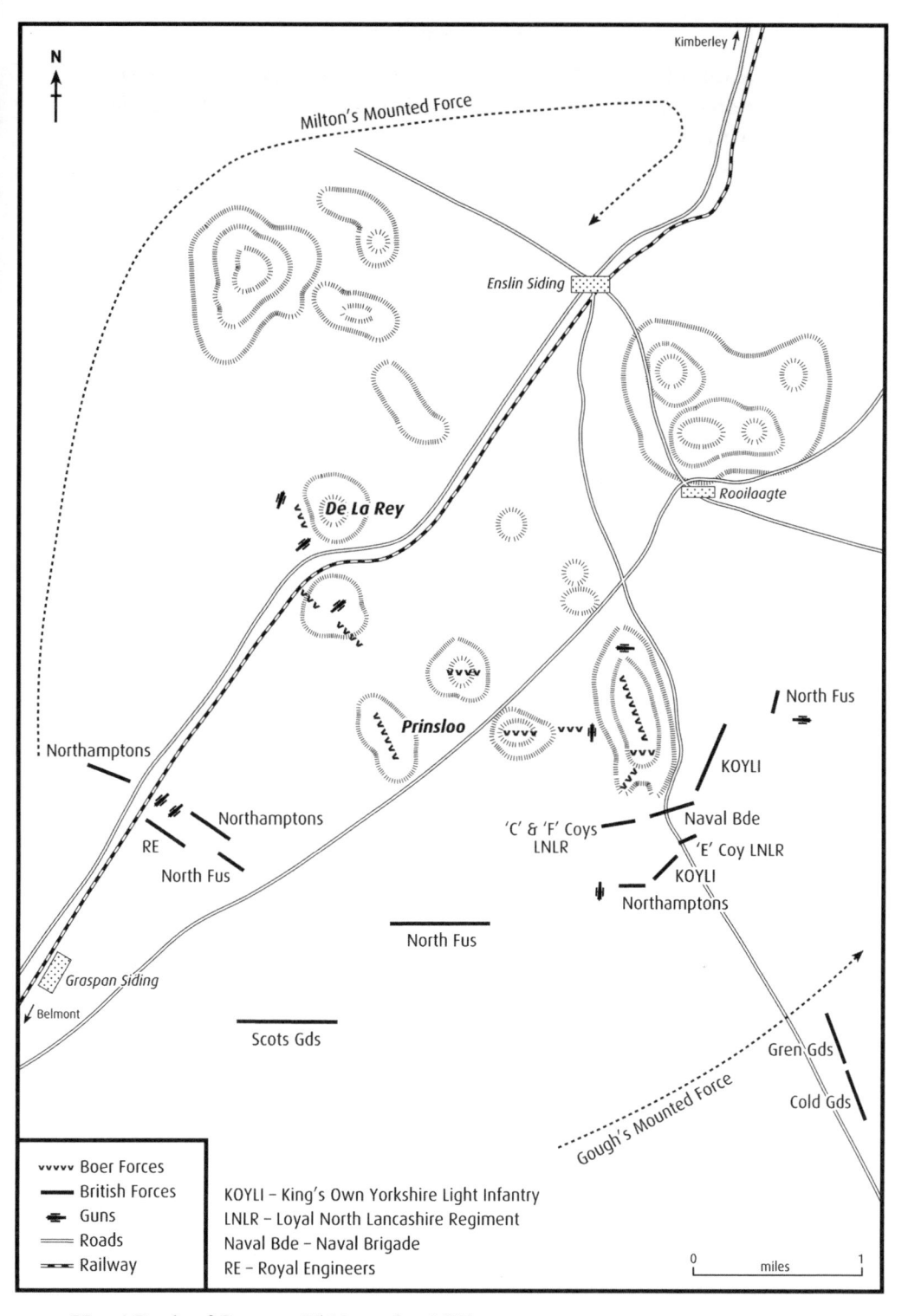

Map 4 Battle of Graspan, 25 November 1899

the naval officers took us too near the hill where the Boers held their position, and they waited until we got on the flat. Then they opened fire with their artillery. I was laid close to the gun, and we dared not raise our heads for about three hours. Then nearly all the gunners got picked off the guns. Then my section had to get up and feed the guns with shell. I was against the waggon when a shell dropped beside me, killing two and wounding two. The other troops were getting round them while we were engaging them in the front.

'Artilleryman's Thrilling Experience', *Leicester Chronicle*, 13 January 1900, p. 2

62

It was only 'two days after [Belmont]', added Trooper William Nobron (9th Lancers), that

we attacked them again. They were up on the hills, and we had to shell them out. The 9th Lancers were under fire for seven hours. We were shelled, and if the shells had burst there would only have been a few of us left. Then we ran in [to] an ambush, and some of our scouts were wounded. Before the day was over we thought we were going to have a charge. My horse fell down dead, throwing me over his head, and fell across me. We were shelled all the time, and I should have been taken if a comrade had not dismounted under fire and given me a lift on his horse.

'Letters from Sheffield Soldiers', *Sheffield and Rotherham Independent*, 6 January 1900, p. 8

63

Major Michael Rimington[26] had a near escape when his scouts crossed the barbed wire fence of the Orange Free State. 'I was lucky yesterday', he informed his family on 26 November:

and probably won't be in as hot a corner again for some time. My orderly, a steeplechase jockey, saved me by charging a barbed wire

---

26 Major (later Lieutenant-General Sir) Michael F. Rimington (1858–1928), who joined the 6th (Inniskilling) Dragoons in 1881, was one of the more successful cavalry commanders during the South African War. Having commanded an irregular cavalry corps, known as Rimington's Guides or Scouts, nicknamed 'Rimington's Tigers', during the first year of the war, he later commanded a regular regiment and a cavalry brigade. In the First World War, he commanded the 1st Indian Cavalry Division, and later the Indian Cavalry Corps, before retiring in 1916.

fence when we were close under a heavy and unexpected fire. He broke the fence and fell, and his horse cleared. Then I got him up on my pony, and we got out.

'A Jockey who saved Major Rimington's Life',
Lancashire Daily Post, 29 December 1899, p. 2

64

Yet the Naval Brigade, 'huddled together',[27] bore the brunt of the battle. As a Royal Marine from HMS *Powerful* described,

Our Naval Brigade of 230 Marines and 40 Bluejackets had to attack the Boers' main position on Gras Pan under two cross fires.[28] We suffered horribly, losing 112 killed and wounded[29] and most of our officers. But we stuck to it, and carried it in a bayonet charge.

'Royal Marine's Experience', *Morning Post*,
27 December 1899, p. 3

65

Understandably survivors dwelt upon their near escapes and the casualties incurred, as another Marine, Private A. G. Edwards, reflected, 'there were 105 killed and wounded. I thought my time was come when the bullets came down like a hailstorm. You could feel them touching your clothes, but I didn't get hurt.'

'A Taunton Marine on the Modder River Battle',
Devon and Somerset Weekly News, 18 January 1900, p. 6

---

27   J. Ralph, *Towards Pretoria: A Record of the War Between Briton and Boer to the Hoisting of the British Flag at Bloemfontein* (London: C. Arthur Pearson, 1900), p. 174. Criticism of the 'shoulder to shoulder' charge (FMN, diaries of Privates J. Porteous and F. Smith; and by Methuen in his despatches), was countered by the claim that it focused on the peak-shaped kopje with each sailor taking 'the summit as his point of direction', Jeans, *Naval Brigades*, p. 34.
28   The mobility of the Boers had enabled them to reinforce the eastern flank, turning it into the 'main position', and the naval assault into a frontal attack. The cross-fires came from Boers who had occupied positions among the lower ridges, from which they could enfilade the attack with devastating effect from flat-trajectory rifle fire.
29   Officially the Naval Brigade suffered 44 per cent casualties, namely 13 killed and 90 wounded, Miller, *Lord Methuen*, pp. 102 and 120, n. 73. The gallantry of the Naval Brigade became 'the subject of general eulogy' at home, Creswicke, *South Africa and the Transvaal War*, vol. 2, p. 95.

66

One of the wounded sailors, Gunner A. Foster of HMS *Monarch*, described how

> It was about 6 a.m. when we started firing at the Boers, but not before they fired on us. We were about 1,000 yards [914 m] distant, and we advanced towards the hill. We had not got 200 yards [183 m] before our Marine officers were killed.[30] Of course we had to carry on without them and get to the top of the hill the best way we could ... We did not have the least chance even of seeing them until we had got to the top of the hill, and to do that we had to advance under a heavy fire. In fact the bullets were falling as thick as hailstones.
>
> 'A Sailor at Graspan', *Yorkshire Herald and The York Herald* [hereafter *Yorkshire Herald*], 17 February 1900, p. 15

67

Fighting in more extended order, the Yorkshire and Lancashire units assisted in the successful assault. Private George Hewitt (2nd Battalion, King's Own Yorkshire Light Infantry), writing on his twenty-sixth birthday, described how

> We had a big affair yesterday, and got about 50 killed and wounded; and two days before that we only had five wounded ... The Boers are a poor lot to fight against. They get all amongst the hills, and when we get to the hills they show us the white flag and run away ... Yesterday we took a hill, after crossing a plain for about a mile [1.6 km], and I can tell you it was a very hot place to get across. It is a marvel that half of the brigade was not shot in some way or another; but we drove them out of it at the finish, and then the artillery gave them 'socks' as they were going across the plain.
>
> 'Ossett and Horbury Men in the Transvaal War', *Ossett Observer*, 23 December 1899, p. 8

---

30 'Nearly all the petty officers and non-commissioned officers were killed or wounded. Nearly half the line were down before they reached the foot of the kopje.' Amery, *Times History of the War in South Africa*, vol. 2, p. 338. After Graspan, Captain A. E. Marchant (Royal Marines) assumed command of the Naval Brigade.

68

Private S. Whitehead (King's Own Yorkshire Light Infantry) recalled that

> Both our officers fell at Graspan,[31] but we did not lose heart, as it would not do on this job. The Boers are a cowardly lot. They blew the bottom of one of our ambulance waggons but they will have to suffer for it before long. They cannot understand being driven out of a hill by the bayonet . . . they do not care for our cheese knives.
>
> '"Don't Care for Our Cheese Knives"',
> *Leicester Chronicle*, 6 January 1900, p. 2

69

Supporting the Naval Brigade on its left were the Loyal North Lancashires of whom Private J. Snape, of 'C' Company, wrote

> We lost one killed of our regiment and 20 wounded, all of my company. The reason we had so many wounded was we had to charge them off a big hill with the bayonet. The General says all England is talking about the gallant Loyal North Lancashires. We are glad we have done something to be proud of at last, for it shows people there are as brave men in Lancashire as anywhere else.
>
> 'Lancashire Men at the War', *Lancashire Daily Post*,
> 30 December 1899, p. 6

Reflections on Graspan

70

Corporal H. Smith (King's Own Yorkshire Light Infantry) reckoned that the Boer powers of concealment had proved crucial: 'The Boers we are fighting are all up on the hills, and they get behind rocks. That is why we are losing so many of our men; but we are beating the Boers all ends and sides.'

'With the Yorkshires', *Leeds Mercury*,
29 December 1899, p. 3

---

31 Actually three officers of this battalion were wounded: Captain C. A. L. Yate, Lieutenant H. C. Fernyhough and Lieutenant C. H. Ackroyd.

71
The Boers agreed. In his letter (**26**) the young Boer, who had initially served with burghers besieging Kimberley, had been sent

> to Graspan. There I fired my first shot in a real battle. There again we were beaten. My horse was wounded by a shell in the ribs just below the saddle bags, and I had to carry the saddle and ran for a mile, before a friend of mine picked my saddle up, and I got a seat on a water-cart with three mules in front and another wounded mule at the back of us. All was confusion, everything was muddled up. The generals in command were inexperienced, the burghers disobedient, and the whole blooming show had to clear again. How I got out of that is a miracle. When we got the order to retire the enemy were at the bottom of the kopjes. Shell upon shell was dropped on all sides, some exploding, the majority, however, quite ineffectual. We lost a good lot of men and very many horses. Many wagons had to be left behind. I was disgusted.
>
> 'With Cronje on the Modder', *Western Mail*,
> 27 December 1900, p. 3.

72
Once again Methuen found himself unable to exploit his victory: as Private A. E. Crossley (Scots Guards) observed, his force was 'sadly in need of cavalry, for there were only two squadrons of the 9th Lancers[32] against 2,000 Boers, so they had to retire, or there would not have been one left to tell the tale'.

'Letters from the Front', *Lancashire Daily Post*,
9 March 1900, p. 5

73
Lieutenant Hugh T. Crispin, then serving with the mounted infantry of the Northumberland Fusiliers, admitted that

> Though we got right round in rear we did not do much good except that we stopped them breaking away W[est] tho. they probably never intended to go that way. We were too weak to harm them in any way,

---

[32] Disappointed in the performance of his cavalry, Methuen relieved Gough of his command of the 9th Lancers. Gough later committed suicide. The Marquess of Anglesey, *A History of the British Cavalry 1816–1919*, vol. 4: *1899–1913* (London: Leo Cooper, 1986), p. 80.

and were extended at intervals sometimes of 100 or more yards with gaps of ¼ to ½ a mile between sections, lying flat down in the open. The Boers eventually retreated in a NE [north-east] direction, they were in great numerical strength compared to our mounted force and we shd. have been rolled up badly if they had gone for us.

FMN, Lt H. T. Crispin diary,
25 November 1899

74

Another wounded sailor, Arthur Gosling, dwelt on the losses incurred and the horrific aftermath of the battle. Writing from De Aar Junction on 3 December, he informed his parents:

> I must tell you that the Naval Brigade suffered great loss – about 20 killed and 93 wounded – and it is a great wonder that ever [*sic*] one of them was left to tell the tale. The charge down was a splendid thing. We had 5 officers killed and 2 wounded out of 8. The captain of my Company was shot right through the heart while he was standing by the side of me . . . When I was shot I shook hands with myself and said I was a very lucky man.[33] Our troops suffered a great deal through hunger and thirst while on the march . . . It was sickening to see the dead, dying, and wounded lying around on all sides of you. We had a little red Marine drummer, barely 18 years old, and he sat down and cried like a child when he saw our men shot down around him.

'Exmouthians at the Front', *Devon Weekly Times*,
5 January 1900, p. 5

75

Nevertheless, many were in good spirits and highly confident after their second victory: Private Hewitt, continuing his letter (**67**), affirmed that

> We are on the road to Kimberley. I think we shall be there in four or five days,[34] and then I think we shall go somewhere into the Orange Free State, and wipe them all out if they don't give in soon. You will

---

33   Gosling's confidence proved misplaced as he later had three fingers amputated.
34   This was too optimistic, not least personally, as Private Hewitt was shot in the arm at the battle of Modder River and had to be sent home. 'Wounded Barnsley Soldier Home Again', *Barnsley Chronicle*, 24 February 1900, p. 6.

see that we are in a very good division, under the command of Lord Methuen.

'Ossett and Horbury Men in the Transvaal War',
Ossett Observer, 23 December 1899, p. 8

76

Writing to his parents on 26 November, a Northamptonshire soldier was even more ebullient:

> we kill and wound twice as many of them as they do of us, and we have caught no end of prisoners, so you see we are giving them 'sock' this time.[35] But it is terrible. No matter where you look you can see dead and dying ... We have done some good work, and no mistake. We have got to advance at six o'clock to-night to get ready for another 'go in'. I like it very much. It is such good sport, and I hope I shall be able to go right through it.

'Bullets Buzzing Like Bees', *Leicester Chronicle*,
23 December 1899, p. 4

The Battle of Modder River (28 November 1899)

Just as the British soldiers who survived the carnage of Belmont and Graspan were buoyed by their success, so the Boers, despite inflicting casualties and delaying the British briefly, became somewhat demoralized by the ease with which they had been swept off their kopjes. Once the British forces had reached the hillsides, they gained the protection of the steep sides ('dead ground') while endangering any Boer riflemen who leaned forward to fire. Meanwhile the crests had proved a clear target against the skyline for artillery bombardments. Koos de la Rey not only perceived these tactical weaknesses but also realized that the Boers at ground level during the battle of Graspan had maximized the effects of flat-trajectory rifle fire. He exhorted his fellow burghers to adopt revolutionary ground-level positions, by using the deep banks of the Riet River, which flowed across the British line of advance at the confluence with the Modder River. As the riverbed was a huge trench made by nature, the Boers could

---

35 Only by comparison with 1881: at Graspan, the Boers probably suffered 103 casualties (of whom 19 were killed, 41 wounded and 43 captured), Pretorius, *A to Z of the Anglo-Boer War*, p. 164. Initial reports gave 23 British dead and 165 wounded, Miller, *Lord Methuen*, p. 103, but the Official History, which claimed that 23 Boers were buried after Graspan, gave the 1st Division's casualties as 18 killed, 143 wounded and 7 missing, Maurice, *War in South Africa*, vol. 1, p. 242.

conceal themselves and fire at veld level under the protection of the banks. 'De la Rey's magnetic personality' swept aside reservations and persuaded General Piet Cronjé, who had arrived with his Klerksdorp and Potchefstroom commandos from Mafeking, to join in the riverside deployments.[36]

After the arrival of Cronjé's forces, the Boers had some 3,500 to 4,000 men, with six Krupp 75-mm guns and at least four pom-pom 1-pounders. About 2,100 Boers took positions on the southern side of the Riet along a front of 4 miles (6 km), split either side of the railway line and the blown-up railway bridge.[37] Whitewashed stones were placed as range markers for the riflemen and gunners on the approaches, and de la Rey concealed further men and guns in trenches on the northern banks and fortified a few buildings.

Unaware of these new tactics, Methuen believed that the bulk of the Boers had retreated to Spytfontein, north of the Modder River. Initially he had planned to march east and conduct another flanking movement, despite his inadequate body of mounted troops and reliance on a map, prepared by O'Meara before he became besieged in Kimberley, which proved utterly erroneous. The map not only showed an inaccurate course for the Riet River but also indicated that the Riet and Modder rivers were fordable almost everywhere. When Methuen received intelligence from a local English-speaking station master that the Boers were in force in the nearby village of Rosmead and were 'digging themselves in like rabbits',[38] and from the 9th Lancers that some 4,000 Boers were near the village, he still doubted that these forces constituted anything more than a rearguard left to delay his advance. Unwilling to leave this enemy force on his flank, and desperate to reach the water for his men and animals, he changed his plan and decided to advance northwards on both sides of the railway line. With the armoured train, Rimington's Guides and the 9th Lancers leading the way, the Guards followed on the right and the 9th Brigade, bolstered by the newly arrived Argyll and Sutherland Highlanders, on the left.[39]

---

36 J. Meintjes, *De la Rey – Lion of the West: A Biography* (Johannesburg: Hugh Keartland Publishers, 1966), pp. 114, 117–19; Amery, *The Times History of the War in South Africa*, vol. 2, pp. 341–3.
37 S. Lunderstedt, *From Belmont to Bloemfontein: The Western Campaign of the Anglo-Boer War, February 1899–April 1900* (Kimberley: Diamond Fields Advertiser, 2000), p. 32; Pretorius, *A to Z of the Anglo-Boer War*, p. 286.
38 Maurice, *War in South Africa*, vol. 2, p. 246; see also W. Baring Pemberton, *Battles of the Boer War* (London: Pan Books, 1969), ch. 3.
39 S. M. Miller, 'Lord Methuen and the British Advance to the Modder River', *Military History Journal*, vol. 10, no. 4 (1996), pp. 121–36; Pemberton, *Battles of the Boer War*, pp. 55–7; Phillipps, *With Rimington*, pp. 24–5.

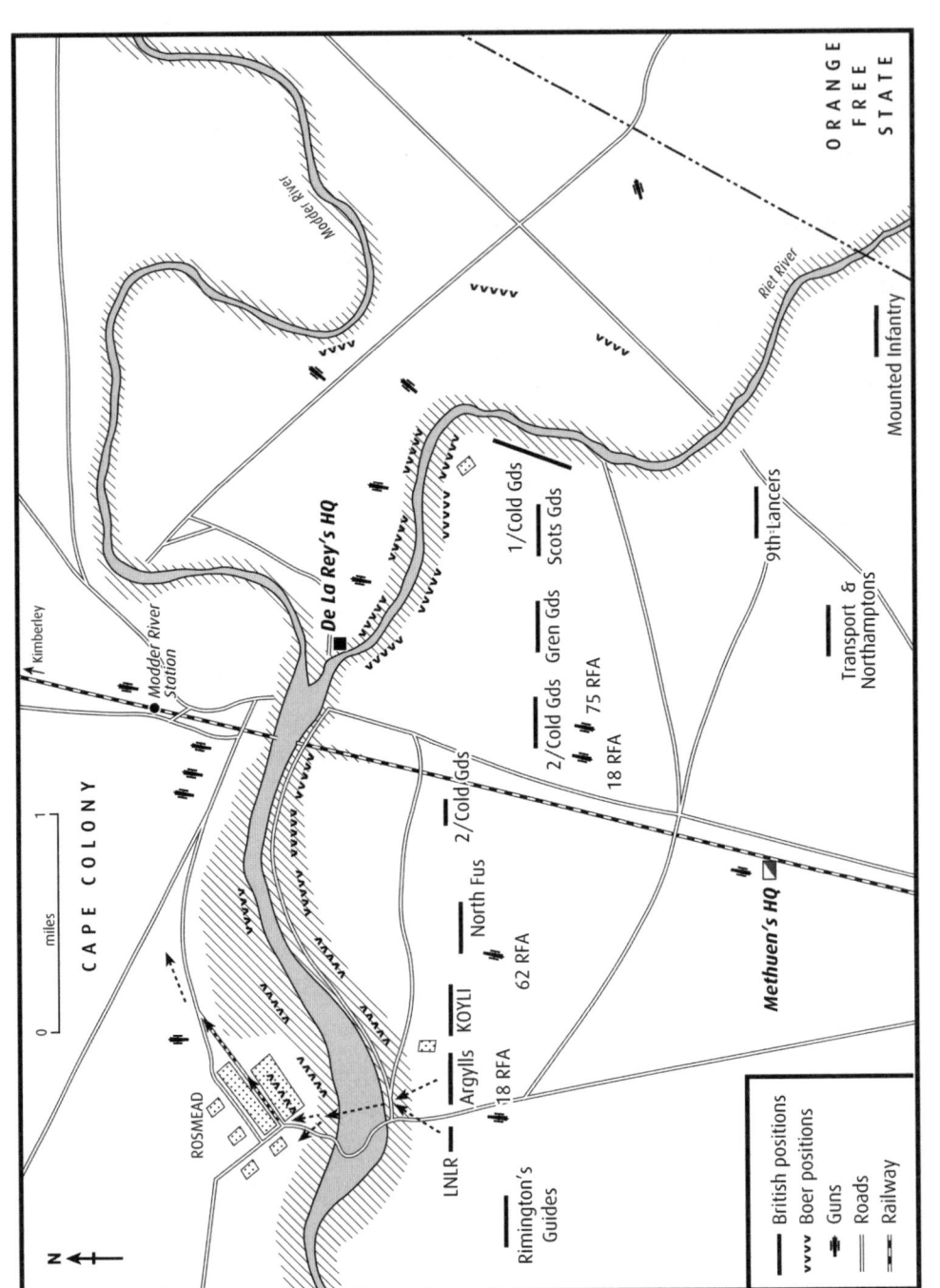

Map 5 Battle of Modder River, 28 November 1899

77

Like the armoured train which came under fire and had to retreat,[40] the cavalry units had to abandon their reconnaissance duties. As a sergeant-major of the 9th Lancers informed his mother,

> We started at 3.30 a.m., and the Boer artillery was too strong, having completely demoralized our naval battery, which was our only one . . .[41] There is another battle yet to be fought, and that is the taking of Kimberley. I have had a lot of narrow squeaks, having had my horse shot in the head, but not killed. The two days upon which we were fighting for this place was the most terrible I ever experienced. The two days and half [*sic*] without food and thirty-six hours without water.
>
> 'A "Human Slaughterhouse"', *Leicester Chronicle*,
> 6 January 1900, p. 2

78

Having suffered three slight bullet wounds at Belmont, Lance-Corporal R. M. Rea (Grenadier Guards) (**46**) was again in the firing line:

> We moved on towards the Modder River, silent as ghosts, and just about daybreak the enemy opened fire. We found they had the position carefully marked off, and they were all entrenched, and so we were out in the open. Of course we could see nothing to fire at. Well all we could do was to lie down, and take snapshots if anything rose up . . . We lay all day, ten hours, without anything either to eat or drink . . .
>
> 'Graspan and Modder River', *Belfast News-Letter*,
> 29 February 1900, p. 5

79

'We were peacefully sleeping, not expecting to march that morning', recalled Lance-Corporal W. H. Atkinson (2nd Battalion, Coldstream Guards),

---

40   'Sapper Champion's Account of the Modder River Fight', *Crewe Guardian*, 20 January 1900, p. 4.
41   The war diary claims that the march began at 4 a.m. but confirms the abrupt withdrawal of the Lancers, Brevet Lieutenant-Colonel F. F. Colvin and Captain E. R. Gordon, *Diary of the 9th (Q.R.) Lancers during the South African Campaign, 1899 to 1902* (London: Cecil Roy, 1904), p. 32.

when we were suddenly aroused by the Commanding Officer himself, and told to get ready to move at once. We marched two miles [3.2 km], and then came in sight of a village, which we were informed we had to attack. I never feared for a minute as I fancied there would only be a handful of Boers to play with. Our company had the fortune (or rather the misfortune) to be in the firing line, dead in front of the position. We never troubled at the time, and when the word was given to advance, we did so quite merrily.

It was all open country, with not sufficient shelter for a mouse, and our leaders were such idiots that they marched us straight towards the position, as if we were at Pirbright practising. We did not know exactly where the enemy were, as they took no notice of us, and so we never wondered at all when we were ordered to turn round and retire 50 yards [45 m]. No sooner did we turn, however, than the Boers opened fire, and in less time than it takes me to write, we were in a veritable death trap.

'Letters from the Front', *Northampton Mercury*, 19 January 1900, p. 5

80

Another Coldstream Guardsman, Private J. Sharples, remembered the surprise and shock of the attack:

We were advancing in attacking order, never dreaming that we were marching into the Boers' nest. Our colonel had just said that he believed that the village was deserted, and gave the order that the men might smoke, when a cannon from the enemy sent one of their shells amongst us and dropped at the feet of our commanding officer,[42] bursted [*sic*], and killed him dead on the spot. That put our men on their mettle when they heard of the death of their commanding officer. We were ordered to advance, but the fire from the enemy was so strong that we had to get down on the ground and fire in a lying down position, and it fairly sickened our men to be fired upon and not to be able to fire on them, for they were in pits in the ground and hidden from view.

'"Put up with it and kept smiling"', *Blackburn Times*, 6 January 1900, p. 3

---

42 Lieutenant-Colonel Horace R. Stopford (1855–99) had not previously been on active service.

81

Continuing his letter (**46**, **49**, **60**), Private Doyle (Grenadier Guards) recalled that

> In the course of the morning Lord Methuen led a movement of Guards to flank the Boers. The General's attempt was gallantly seconded, but the fire was too hot and the river too deep, so that his plan had to be abandoned. It was an awful sight to see our wounded limping and crawling back or being carried through a fire so thick and hot that only those who were there can imagine what it was like.
>
> 'Letters from the Front', *Bristol Mercury*, 30 March 1900, p. 6

82

The Boers had certain obvious targets, as described by Private George Mullineaux (Scots Guards),

> Our Maxim was on the right of our company. The officer in charge of it was wounded, along with his horse, the sergeant had half his head blown away with a shell, the armourer-sergeant was shot through both legs, six men were wounded, the only one escaping being the corporal, and he was kicked in the stomach by a mule; and four mules were riddled with bullets. If the Maxim hadn't been there, very few of our company would have escaped.
>
> 'In the Firing Line of Every Engagement', *Lancashire Daily Post*, 4 January 1900, p. 5

83

Similarly after four hours 'our ammunition gave out', wrote Private Washington (2nd Battalion, Coldstream Guards),

> Then came a terrible suspense, for all the ammunition bearers were shot as they attempted to bring up, and we could not advance and charge because of the river. It was during this hour that many of our men fell . . . I was the extreme left man of our brigade, in the firing line. Eventually they sent the Argyll and Sutherland Highlanders to strengthen us, but, poor fellows, they got more shot in reaching us than we got all the time we were there. The Boers had all the distances marked, so they knew exactly how to adjust their sights. There was seven hours' more fighting in front of us. Lord Methuen

was wounded charging up the hill at the head of about 30 of our battalion.

'A Normanton Reservist', *Pontefract Telegram*,
6 January 1900, p. 5

84

In desperate circumstances, there were inevitably calls for the guns. As Driver J. Pipes (18th Field Artillery) observed,

The Coldstreams were losing a few men, and they soon called for the Artillery to fetch the Boers out of the rocks. The coward curs will not come out in the open field to fight, so our battery, which was the only battery there, advanced right between the two fires. The bullets were like hailstones around our heads, and they did ping, I can tell you.[43] However, we got them out somehow, but I never saw them go.

'A Derby Artilleryman Under Fire', *Derby Mercury*,
10 January 1900, p. 2

85

Initially the artillery had taken up positions '1,500 yards [1,370 m] from the Boer trenches', and then, as an artillery officer commented,

We then advanced past our own infantry, and came into action, about 900 yards [825 m] closer than artillery had ever taken up position before. After severe loss on our side we managed to silence the Boer guns . . . [after retirement] up rode an orderly giving us instructions to go and relieve the Guards. Our major advanced . . . We took up our position 800 yards [730 m] from the Boer trenches, and, by Jove! the Boers let us have a fearful reception. Before I got my horses out they shot one of my drivers and two horses . . . and brought down my own horse. We then got my gun round on the enemy, when one of my gunners was shot through the brain, and fell at my feet. Another of my gunners was shot while bringing up shell . . . At last we had a look in, our shells began to tell. We were firing six rounds a minute, and were at it until it was too dark to fire any more.

'An Officer's Experience', *The Star* (Saint Peter Port),
13 January 1900, p. 1

---

43 The 75th Battery suffered in similar fashion. As a bombardier recalled, 'they knocked some of us down like ninepins: 23 wounded, two killed, and about 15 horses dead', 'Living Like Kings', *Sheffield Daily Telegraph*, 12 January 1900, p. 6.

86

On the left side of the railway, companies of Yorkshire Light Infantry and North Lancashires pressed the Boers on the southern bank of the Modder River. Lieutenant Edward Brooke (King's Own Yorkshire Light Infantry) noted that, after noon,

> we were ordered to charge the position, and charge we did, and how I escaped is an absolute marvel. When we got down there was a large river flowing between us and the enemy. However, we found some cover and about 130 got across by a ford, only to be shelled by the enemy. Night found us lying in a ditch uncertain whether it was victory or defeat. All night we lay in the ditch. Fortunately, some men had looted some houses, so we got some food after dark, and you can imagine how welcome it was.
>
> 'Archdeacon Brooke's Sons at the Front', *Sheffield Daily Telegraph*, 3 January 1900, p. 7

87

As the Boers fell back across the river to Rosmead and the northern bank, a section of the 18th Battery on the extreme left entered the fray as Major S. Jackson (Loyal North Lancashires) recalled:

> I sent my adjutant to the nearest artillery officer to ask for guns, and after a long time two came up. Before they could unlimber or fire a shot, the Boers ran for it, mounted their horses, and went for their lives. I then rushed the ford, which was on my right front, losing one officer slightly wounded, and several N.C.O.s killed and wounded. I got my men over the river and was joined by crowds of men – Highlanders, Guardsmen, all sorts. We were then ordered to advance against their right, and started. The roar of the guns all this time was deafening. After about 400 yards [365 m] a shell burst among our men, and the ground was covered with dead and wounded.
>
> 'Major Jackson's Experiences', *Preston Herald*, 6 January 1900, p. 6

88

Quartermaster Sergeant Bennett had followed his Argyll and Sutherland Highlanders with the first ammunition cart some 200 yards (183 m) in the rear. He was convinced that

The Boers knew all the ranges, as it was all marked off on the railway, and they peppered us with artillery . . . The heat was terrible and we couldn't get water till two o'clock. Men were falling fast all the time. As they came to where we were we bandaged all we could, and gave them what water we had in our own bottles, and put them under cover till they could be removed . . . Our regiment had to turn the flank, and we had hardly any cover, consequently we lost very heavily – 2 officers wounded, 15 men killed, 92 wounded, and 2 missing.[44] Up to date [2 December] 1 missing man has rejoined, and 4 of our wounded since died, so our dead now totals 19, and I'm afraid there will be fully 6 or 8 more, as some of them were terribly wounded. The sun was awfully hot, and as we were laying there 12 hours . . . it punished our poor legs – blistered them awful at the back, and we can hardly walk. It was lying in the one position so long that's done it.

'Interesting Letter from Modder River Camp',
Chronicle (Doncaster), 5 January 1900, p. 8

89

Another English Argyll, Private Thomas Walter Barnard, writing to his parents, reckoned that

We lost out of 800 men 130 killed and wounded and out of the whole division of 12,000, 300;[45] so that will tell you how our regiment suffered. I was in F company, who were the first to charge the river. I came out on the other side dripping with water and blood; a lot of dead horses and men had fallen in. One of my chums got half his foot blown off, two were shot in the river, and one of Mac's chums lost an arm.

'A Chelmsford Man's Experiences in the Battle of Modder River',
Essex County Standard, 30 December 1899, p. 5

---

44 The Argyll and Sutherland Highlanders bore the brunt of the British casualties, see Miller, *Lord Methuen*, p. 122, and another eleven died of their wounds subsequently, P. J. R. Mileham, *Fighting Highlanders! The History of the Argyll & Sutherland Highlanders* (London: Arms and Armour Press, 1993), p. 73.
45 Again an estimate that is far below the total of 483 British casualties (of whom 4 officers and 66 men died) compared with 82 Boer casualties (of whom 16 were killed or died of wounds), Pretorius, *A to Z of the Anglo-Boer War*, pp. 287–8.

90

In the decisive crossing of the river, Private J. Hayes (Loyal North Lancashires) remembered that 'We drank the water till we nearly burst, and we dipped our rifles in the water to cool them.'

'In Three Battles', *Blackburn Times*,
13 January 1900, p. 3

Friendly-fire incidents occurred, as recalled by Sapper W. C. Chalmers, 'Our artillery was at one time firing upon some of the Argyll and Sutherland Highlanders, who had taken some of the Boer trenches, but happily they soon found out their mistake.'

'A Perth Sapper on the Battle of Belmont', *Strathearn Herald*,
13 January 1900, p. 2

As Free Staters under Prinsloo came under pressure on one flank, de la Rey mounted a brief counter attack with his Transvaalers on the other, which Private Doyle (Grenadier Guards) described in his letter (**46, 49, 60, 81**):

> In the afternoon the Boers flanked us and poured a tremendous volley into our ambulances and ammunition train, which frightened the Kaffir drivers and their mules into a panic, and yet they did not profit by this, as they retired[46] as soon as our boys appear[ed].

'Letters from the Front', *Bristol Mercury*,
30 March 1900, p. 6

91

The young Boer from Bloemfontein, who had fought at Kimberley and Graspan (**26, 71**) had been 'determined to make a stand' at the Modder River after the 'two last fights'. Like the British soldiers, the Free Staters found the sun 'baking us, and although only fifty yards [45.7 m] from the river we were nearly perishing from thirst'. The crucial moment had come

> Towards the afternoon one party, the Argyll and Sutherland Highlanders, crossed the river at a point not far from our guns. Instead of coming to the rescue most of the burghers began to scoot . . . The burghers seemed to get mad. Some of them were seized with a great desire for sprinting, others were, in their excitement, executing the

---

46 They included de la Rey, carrying off his mortally wounded son, Adriaan.

most wonderful jumps over man, gate, or whatever blocked their way. Some jumped into the river, leaving guns in the running stream, everyone grabbed for a horse, heedless whose property it might be, as long as he could 'scoot' on it. Our field cornet had cleared early in the morning already.

He and his eleven friends (two of whom were wounded) retreated later at 9.30 p.m.

and not a khaki in sight! In the distance ambulance men could be seen moving about lanterns in hand, helping the wounded and burying the dead. I was very sad. One of my friends was killed by a shell . . . I was so angry with our burghers, generals, and the rest . . . The generals had no control over that fanatic [*sic*] crowd of inexperienced fighting men.[47]

'With Cronje on the Modder', *Western Mail*, 27 December 1900, p. 3

Reflections on the Battle of Modder River

After three battles in six days, the British soldiers had a week to rest and recover at the Modder River and reflect on their gruelling experiences. Some were only too keen to repeat Methuen's wildly exaggerated claim, which was expressed in divisional orders, that the battle of Modder River had been 'one of the hardest in the annals of British history';[48] others were still concerned about the surprise and costs of 'another crushing victory'.[49]

92

A Northumberland Fusilier insisted that

We never expected[50] to have to go that morning but we had not been long on the move before they were sighted, Cronje and all . . . There

---

47 This experience was not unique; see Pretorius, *Life on Commando,* p. 143.
48 'In Three Battles', *Blackburn Times*, 13 January 1900, p. 3; 'A Nether Edge Man at Modder River', *Sheffield Daily Telegraph*, 8 January 1900, p. 7; 'A Chelmsford Man's Experiences in the Battle of Modder River', *Essex County Standard*, 30 December 1899, p. 5.
49 Phillipps, *With Rimington*, p. 22.
50 What these soldiers did not appreciate was the private admission of Methuen that 'it was a surprise to me, for I thought the enemy had cleared off, as did everyone else,

is no doubt the Boers meant it this time, as you couldn't move without you got a shower of bullets or a shell of some sort at you, and what made it worse you couldn't scarcely see them. Victory seemed to come all in a sudden and not before every one was eager for it.

'Letters from Newcastle Soldiers', *Newcastle Daily Chronicle*,
3 January 1900, p. 5

Private Albert Robinson (Loyal North Lancashires) also seethed at the lack of intelligence: 'This battle would not have lasted as long as if our men knew they could have got across the river.'

'A Colne Soldier Escapes by the "Skin of his Teeth." A Murderous Fire', *Burnley Express and Advertiser* (henceforth *Burnley Express*), 6 January 1900, p. 8

93

Major Jackson, continuing his letter (**87**), dwelt on the costs of victory:

Since the battle we have been everlastingly burying the dead – a very gruesome job.[51] The field was simply covered with dead horses, and the smell yesterday was something to remember. The thing which put men off more than anything was the screams from the wounded. It was dreadful! The shellfire was more like a railway accident, men falling, howling, and screaming with pain, and mutilated most shockingly.

'Major Jackson's Experiences', *Preston Herald*,
6 January 1900, p. 6

94

However, at the Modder River, an Argylls sergeant appreciated the opportunity to rest and recover. On 4 December he conceded that

I am going sick on account of my legs; the sun has simply burned holes in them. I have struggled on so far because I am acting Colour-Sergeant, but I cannot walk, so am obliged to go sick . . . The food here is very insufficient and bad, and the water from the Modder

---

whereas Cronjé, de la Rey and 9000 men were waiting for me in an awful position', WSHC, Methuen Mss., Methuen to his wife, 1 December 1899; see also Methuen to Lord Roberts, 4 December 1899.
51 Private Taylor (2nd Coldstream Guards) added that the burying parties spent three days looking for corpses and 'have not found all the bodies yet', 'A Guardsman's Awful Experience', *Rotherham Advertiser*, 13 January 1900, p. 2.

River is strongly diluted with dead Boers and horses, and so we had to camp, or bivouac rather, three miles [4.8 km] further up.

'A Soldier's Letter from the Modder River. A Sergeant's Interesting Narrative', *Stirling Observer*, 24 January 1900, p. 3

95

Rest was even more appreciated by those who had survived three battles in six days, as Private H. Hawley (King's Own Yorkshire Light Infantry) commented:

> We are having seven days' rest after being worked so hard, and I think we need one after this last fight. We should have been two days without something to eat if we had not stolen something. We killed all the ducks, pigs, fowls, and everything we came across in the gardens.

'A Sheffielder in the Battles in the West', *Sheffield Daily Telegraph*, 3 January 1900, p. 7

A regimental comrade, Lance-Corporal James A. Green, added ruefully: 'When we came to De Aar, we had 900 men, now we have only 600, and that is probably why we don't move.'

'A Gainsbronian at Modder River', *Sheffield Daily Telegraph*, 3 January 1900, p. 7

96

The captured Boer positions also impressed the more perceptive. As a medical officer affirmed,

> The Boers had taken up their position in the riverbed, and had dug entrenchments with mounds as fortifications. It was a very strong position; and as they were completely under cover and we on the open plain, the only way to make them evacuate was to shell them. We had 24 guns and one lyddite[52] – would we had more of the latter! It was simply a bombardment . . . If the Boer gunners had been better marksmen our casualties would have been trebled. A German Boer officer was found dead with his head shattered by a shell. All the

---

52 An error as lyddite was first employed on this front at Magersfontein, Miller, *Lord Methuen*, pp. 131–2. Named after an artillery range in Kent, lyddite was a compound of picric acid used in high explosive shells. It exploded with a huge flash and emitted clouds of yellow smoke. The visual effects greatly exceeded their tactical value.

Boers are mounted, and so get away very quickly after a fight on their horses.

'After the Battle at Modder River', *Leicester Chronicle*,
6 January 1900, p. 8

97

Another Leicester soldier in Methuen's division, Private G. Gregory, admitted that 'We had a good many killed and wounded on our side' but claimed, without any evidence, that 'the enemy must have had hundreds more than we did.' He found, though, other reasons to dislike the enemy:

> It is a great shame, and would make your heart burn to see the way the Boers have treated the English homes here. They have broken everything up, and when we came here the people came back again, but they don't know what to do or where to go. Arrangements are being made to send them to Cape Town.
> 'Leicester Lad's Experiences at Belmont, Graspan, and Modder River',
> *Leicester Chronicle*, 6 January 1900, p. 2

98

The fact that 'loyalists are flocking in', argued a Newcastle soldier, continuing his letter (**92**), confirmed that

> This place is very important not only on account of the river alone, but there is a railway bridge here to be repaired, which the Boers blew . . . up at both ends and have pulled all the telegraph wire down, so that engineers have got their work cut for a while. They are making a temporary bridge.[53]
> 'Letters from Newcastle Soldiers', *Newcastle Daily Chronicle*,
> 3 January 1900, p. 5

99

Sapper J. Millard (Royal Engineers) described how

> we were working from four in the morning till eight at night. We have to work like niggers, and there are hundreds of Kaffirs with us. They, the Boers, blew two portions of the Modder River Bridge down, and

---

53 The bridge would enable Methuen to fulfil his orders to evacuate non-combatants from Kimberley, Methuen (Q. 14147), Evidence before the Elgin Commission, vol. 2, p. 120; Miller, *Lord Methuen*, p. 127.

so we put a temporary one right across in eight days, so that trains can carry on with the traffic.[54] We can signal to Kimberley every night with searchlights, so we can get to know how they are.

'A Loughborough Man with French's Column', *Leicester Chronicle*, 24 February 1900, p. 3

100

The railway had already been in use, removing the seriously wounded for treatment to hospitals such as Wynberg, near Cape Town, from where a Dundonian, Private W. Eadie (Argyll and Sutherland Highlanders), reported that

> We are well looked after, the people of Wynberg treating us like gentlemen . . . The Boers are getting quite disheartened, and are coming into our camps every day and giving themselves up. One of the Boer prisoners whom I was chaffing the other day told me that he was led to believe that the English soldier could not shoot at all, but says he knows differently now. They lost very heavily at the Modder.[55]

'Dundee Soldier's Experience', *Strathearn Herald*, 13 January 1900, p. 2

101

Another potentially significant change was the arrival of the 1st Balloon Section in early December. A sergeant recounted how 'I was up in the balloon reconnoitring this morning, and could see the Boers with the glasses bringing in stores and forage. I have been up in the balloon several times, and I could see Kimberley quite plain.'

'The Balloonists Faint', *Chronicle* (Doncaster), 10 January 1900, p. 7

102

Yet the delayed advance (which gave the Boers ample time in which to construct their next defensive position) frustrated Private W. J. Anthony (Northumberland Fusiliers): 'I can't make out why Lord Methuen doesn't go on up to the relief of Kimberley. I can't think what he is waiting for.[56] We have some fine troops up here. The [New] South Wales

---

54 According to Sapper Cookson, they also built a pontoon bridge for the troops, 'Modder River Bridge A Sight', *Crewe Guardian*, 20 January 1900, p. 4.
55 Another exaggeration, possibly based on hospital gossip and providing some solace for those who had been wounded in the battle.
56 On that date Methuen was about to launch the disastrous attack at Magersfontein,

Lancers, Canadians and the Australians are here with us, and are all eager to have a go.'

'After the Battle of Belmont', *Sheffield and Rotherham Independent*, 6 January 1900, p. 8

103

The Boers had benefited as much as the British forces from the period of rest. Within a day of the battle the young Boer from Bloemfontein (**26, 71, 91**) had retreated fifteen miles (24 km) northwards to Scholtz Nek. He described how

> The artillerists were done for. Major Albrecht[57] told me (I knew him very well) he had not rested since the day before the Battle of Belmont. His horses were either shot, lost, or worked until completely done for . . . At Scholtz Nek we ten men represented the Bloemfontein commando. In about four days the lost sheep came back. Some had cleared right away to Bloemfontein, and some were lingering in the kopjes, and were not at all game for another try. From Scholtz Nek to Magersfontein. At the latter place we entrenched . . .
>
> 'With Cronje on the Modder', *Western Mail*, 27 December 1900, p. 3

---

but some soldiers agreed with subsequent critics that he had delayed for too long at the Modder, see Amery, *The Times History*, vol. 2, p. 390. Yet Methuen, recovering from his injury, the loss of his chief of staff and 58 out of 350 officers, wanted to rest his men and animals and bring up reinforcements. As Kekewich had assured him that Kimberley was not in danger, he could also complete the rebuilding of the bridge. Pemberton, *Battles of the Boer War*, p. 78, and Miller, *Lord Methuen*, pp. 125–7.

57 Major Richard Friedrich Wilhelm Albrecht (1848–1926) was born in Potsdam, Prussia, and had commanded the Free State Artillery Corps since 1880. He had drilled it into an efficient unit on Prussian lines.

Chapter 3

Magersfontein:
Highlanders 'Marched to their Graves'[1]

Reinforcements Arrive

While Methuen rested his division on the Modder River, hoping to revive his exhausted men and horses, and enable the engineers to construct a temporary bridge across the river, he brought up reinforcements. These included the Black Watch and Seaforth Highlanders to complete, with the Argyll and Sutherland Highlanders and the Highland Light Infantry, the Highland Brigade. He also brought up the Gordon Highlanders, still basking in their triumphs from the Tirah campaign (1897–8), as line of communication troops; two more light infantry battalions, as well as Australian and Canadian contingents to guard the railway; the 12th Lancers and another 100 mounted infantry to ease the shortage of mounted troops; the 65th Howitzer Battery, 'G' Battery Royal Horse Artillery (RHA); and the long-range 4.7-inch naval gun.

104

Trooper Claude Harrison ('A' Squadron, 12th Lancers) recalled the eventful march sometimes through 'heavy thunderstorms' at night:

> We are up every morning at half-past one. We had to cross two battle-fields – Belmont and Gras Pan – and the smell from them was terrible. They had buried the dead men, but there were all the carcases of the dead horses and also blood, and with the burning sun the smell was strong. We passed the bodies of several soldiers whose deaths had

---

1 'Tommy's Treatment at the Front', *Bolton Chronicle*, 24 March 1900, p. 5.

occurred after the Boers had gone. The Squadron was very lucky, for if we had been a day later we should have had a very busy time of it coming through Gras Pan, as the Boers had been working their way there for about a week and our patrols reported about five hundred of them advancing towards us, this being the day after our arrival there. The regiment, with some artillery and infantry,[2] went back to Gras Pan, and found the Boers had taken up a position in the rocks, but it did not take long for the artillery to shift them out for us to have a charge at, and we did some glorious work.

'A Local Lancer in Camp at Modder River',
Chronicle (Doncaster), 12 January 1900, p. 6

105

The 'glorious' charge was less apparent to Private A. Middleton, who was serving in one of two companies of the 2nd Battalion, Northamptonshire Regiment, left to guard the line of communications. On 7 December he learned that some 1,000 Boers with three guns were advancing towards them:

> we hardly believed it. We, however, soon found out that it was quite true, as a short time afterwards we heard an explosion, and found out that the Boers had blown up the line of communication. We made haste to get prepared for them, and although there were only 200 of us we kept this large force of Boers busily engaged for over six hours. This was the hottest time ever I had. The rifle was bad enough, but the big guns were the worst. Four shells fell in quick succession round about where me and my chum were, but as luck happened they did very little damage . . . After about six hours heavy firing we saw reinforcements coming to our assistance, and then the Boers 'scooted' but not without leaving a few dead and wounded . . . our casualties were very light, we having eleven wounded (one since dead).

'A Plucky Little Force', *Manchester Evening News*,
28 March 1900, p. 5

106

The process of moving forward was quite systematic. Private Charles V. Priest (Gordon Highlanders) described how

---

2   This was the 62nd Battery and 2nd Seaforth Highlanders in an armoured train, Maurice, *War in South Africa*, vol. 1, p. 309.

We arrived at Orange River and relieved the Seaforth Highlanders, who proceeded to the Modder River. We stopped at the Orange River three days, and during that time train-loads of troops were continually being carried to the front. There was a large hospital at Orange River, and it was full of wounded that were sent down from Modder River. We were relieved by the Shropshire Light Infantry, and proceeded to Belmont, where a great battle had been fought . . . We stayed there two days, and during that time we were repairing the line the Boers had destroyed; and as soon as it was completed, we were sent on to Graspan – another battlefield – where we stopped; but only for a few hours, when we started again for the Modder River.

'Interesting Letters from Dumbarton Men at the Front', *Lennox Herald*, 13 January 1900, p. 3

107

Battle-hardened soldiers, like Sergeant W. Herbert Sampson (Northamptonshire) welcomed the new arrivals. Writing to his parents on the eve of battle, 10 December, he assured them that

The next fight we have with them they will 'smell hell' as we have now got a 5 in. Lyddite gun,[3] besides a Royal Horse Artillery Battery, and a howitzer battery only just come up. That is what we have wanted all along, and where, in fact, we have been handicapped, as we had to advance under their artillery fire, and could not return it . . .

'A Buxtonian's "Picnic"', *Sheffield Daily Telegraph*, 6 January 1900, p. 8

108

The reinforcements were also eager to see some action, not least the 1st Battalion, Highland Light Infantry, which had missed the battle of Modder River by arriving on the afternoon of 28 November.[4] As Sergeant William Hamilton observed,

We just came on the scene in time to be engaged, but the General kept us in reserve, so that our regiment would be fresh, as he intended us to take the position at the point of the bayonet. But as

---

3 He refers to the 4.7-inch quick-firing naval gun that was capable of firing a lyddite shell over 5,000 yards (4.6 km), Miller, *Lord Methuen*, p. 130.
4 'A Vale of Leven Reservist at Modder River', *Lennox Herald*, 17 February 1900, p. 5.

it turned out we were not called into action that day, and were very disappointed.

'"A Grand but Awful Sight"', *Glasgow Herald*,
8 January 1900, p. 8

109

Once again reconnaissance proved problematic, as an officer with the 12th Lancers wrote on 5 December:

> To-day some of our fellows went out and got shot at by the Boers, who practically surrounded us. One can always get shot at in a half hour's ride from camp, so things are fairly exciting. Almost every one here has been in three actions. We passed the scene of two battles on the way up . . . We can see the flashlight from Kimberley from here, every night. It looks like a fire behind a hill, and throws up a beam from horizon to horizon. It is about 25 miles [40 km] away.
>
> There is plenty of game about, and lots in my tent, including lizards, scorpions, spiders, three inches long, and lots of smaller bugs . . .
>
> This place is a large, healthy camp, but the water is bad, and the sand horrible.

'A Cavalry Officer's Experiences', *Daily Free Press* (Aberdeen),
10 January 1900, p. 6

110

Experienced Rimington Guides did not fare any better; on 9 December, a colour sergeant with the Argyll and Sutherland Highlanders recalled how

> My company was on outpost duty last Tuesday and Wednesday, and were fired on by the Boers, but I don't think they were aware we had so many, as the signallers were sending messages to the camp when the bullets passed over us. They were actually tackling our scouts (Remington [*sic*] Guides, a splendid and fearless body of men). One of our scouts and his horse were wounded, but one rode back and took up his wounded comrade, and the horse followed after the remainder. We could not fire, as the scouts were between us and the enemy. The Boers retired baffled, as they neither caught nor saw anything.

'A Baptism of Fire', *Glasgow Herald*,
8 January 1900, p. 8.

The Battle of Magersfontein

The Boers had used the week since Modder River to regroup, bring up reinforcements (until they had about 8,500 men for the next battle) and reconsider their defensive options. Having abandoned their first preference of holding Spytfontein lest it be shelled by the British if they took Magersfontein, they resolved to defend the latter, a large rock-bound kopje that dominated the plain, extending over a space of several miles, some 20 miles (32 km) south of Kimberley. De la Rey then persuaded his fellow commanders, with the assistance of President M. T. Steyn, that the Boers should defend the position not from the heights (as favoured by General Piet Cronjé)[5] but from concealed trenches in front of and parallel to the hills. The defensive line, with ten guns, would stretch from Moss Drift on the Modder River for 5 miles (8 km) in a north-westerly direction, past Magersfontein and beyond the railway to Langeberg. Mostly the defences consisted of earthen embankments or low stone walls (sangars), with narrow trenches, protected by breastworks of soil and camouflaged by branches and grass, constructed only in front of Magersfontein.[6] There were also gaps on either side of the hill, with the Scandinavian corps, about sixty strong, posted to guard the plains to the south-east of Magersfontein. As de la Rey was absent, seeking medical attention for his wounded shoulder, Cronjé assumed command.

Methuen knew nothing of this beyond the evidence of Boer defensive activity in the vicinity of Magersfontein. As mounted troops were unable to get within 1,000 yards (900 m) of the Boer position, he knew neither the size nor the disposition of the Boer forces. Once again he had to find a way of crossing the veld, described by one Gordon Highlander as 'quite treeless with very little water, and heathy scant grass and scrubby prickly plants on mostly horrid red sand'.[7] Accordingly Methuen resolved to repeat the tactics of Belmont, centred upon a night march by his new elite formation, the Highland Brigade under the command of Major-

---

5 General Pieter (Piet) Arnoldus Cronjé (1836–1911) had served in the Anglo-Transvaal War (1880–1), in which he secured a British surrender at Potchefstroom, and, in January 1896, captured Jameson and his men. Despite his victory at Magersfontein, he was surprised by the relief of Kimberley, and then trapped at Paardeberg, where he would surrender on 27 February 1900. He and his wife were sent to St Helena as prisoners of war.
6 Lunderstedt, *From Belmont to Bloemfontein*, p. 35.
7 Lieutenant-Colonel L. Gordon-Duff, *With the Gordon Highlanders to the Boer War and Beyond: The story of Captain Lachlan Gordon-Duff* (Staplehurst, Kent: Spellmount, 2000), p. 50.

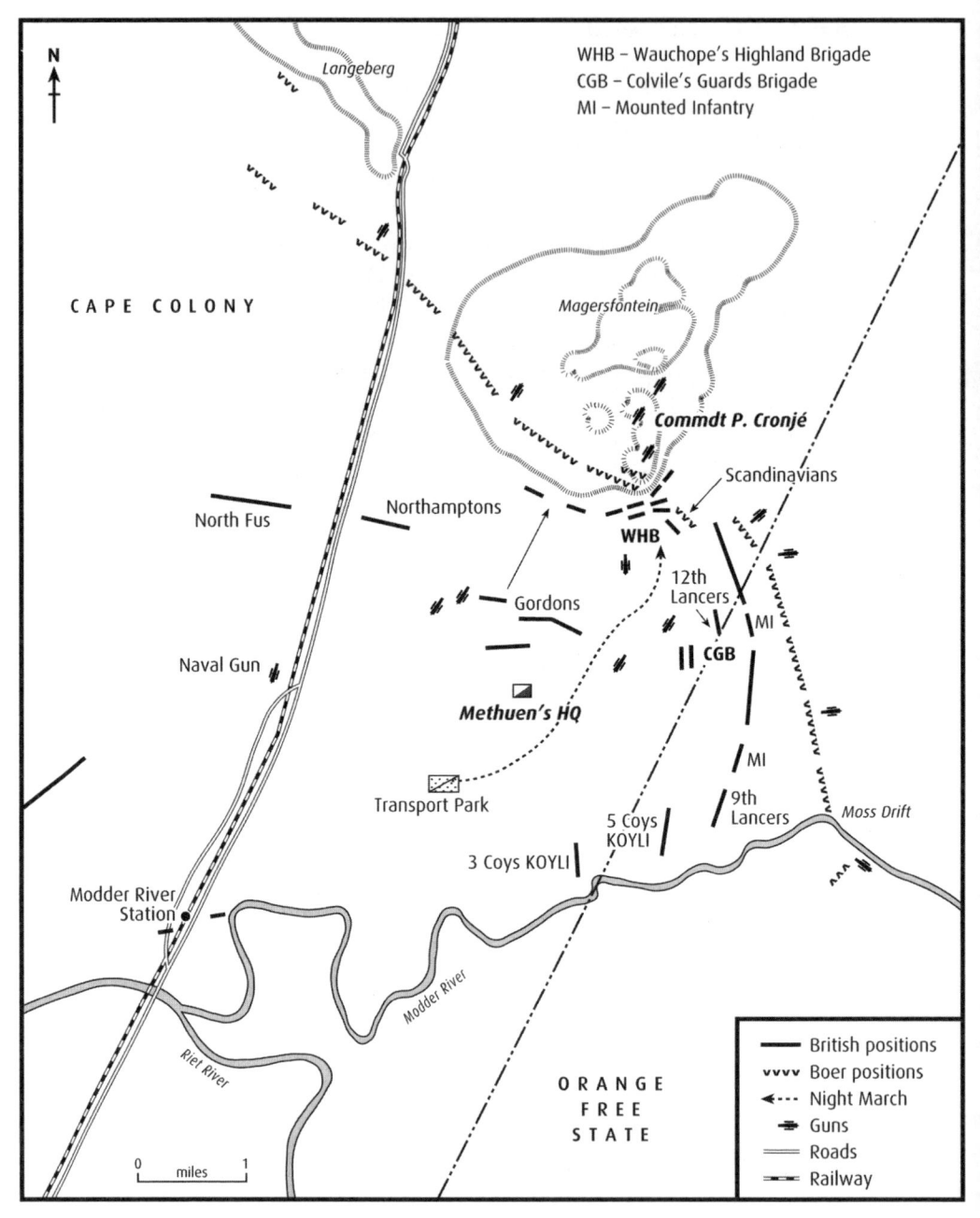

Map 6 Battle of Magersfontein, 11 December 1899

General Andrew G. Wauchope,[8] with English infantry making a feint to the left while the Guards Brigade under Major-General Sir Henry Colvile[9] remained in reserve, followed by the storming of the heights at the point of the bayonet. He also decided to prepare the assault with a massive artillery barrage,[10] aimed at the crests of the kopjes. He chose to launch this bombardment on Sunday, 10 December.

111

The choice of day, reckoned the Reverend E. P. Lawry, the Wesleyan chaplain, was inauspicious:

> It may have been one of the sad necessities of war-time, but was a fact nevertheless, deeply to be deplored, that at four o'clock on Sunday afternoon our guns, which had been silent for a fortnight, opened fire and shelled the Boers with lyddite. As I listened to the thunder and the thud of them I could not repress a wonder whether that was quite the best possible way of propitiating the God of battle.
>
>   'A Wesleyan Chaplain's Narrative', *Western Morning News*,
>   12 January 1900, p. 8

112

A sergeant-major of the Royal Field Artillery noted that

> Our Brigade Division, consisting of the 18th, 62nd, and 75th Batteries, with the 65th Howitzer Battery, G Battery, and the 9th

---

8 Major-General Andrew Gilbert Wauchope (1846–99) was a battle-scarred and highly experienced Black Watch officer, who had seen extensive service in Africa from the Asante War (1873–4) to Omdurman (1898). One of the wealthiest men in Scotland, and a staunch Conservative, he had slashed Gladstone's majority in Midlothian (1892) by over 80 per cent. He was killed at the beginning of the battle of Magersfontein.
9 Major-General Sir Henry Edward Colvile (1852–1907) joined the Grenadier Guards in 1870 and saw active service in Egypt, the Sudan, Burma and East Africa. He commanded the Guards Brigade at Belmont, Graspan, Modder River (where he assumed overall command when Methuen was wounded) and Magersfontein. After failing as commander of the 9th Division to relieve British forces at Sannaspost and Lindley (on 31 March and 31 May 1900 respectively), he was sent home and took his discharge with the rank of lieutenant-general.
10 The artillery expenditure at Magersfontein, 18,517 rounds, averaging 1,047 rounds per battery, was the heaviest of the entire war. General G. H. Marshall (Q. 18,571), Evidence before the Elgin Commission, vol. 2, p. 361.

and 12th Lancers, immediately set out to meet them. We shelled the hills, in order to prepare the way for the infantry until dusk.

'The Highland Brigade', *Cork Constitution*,
20 January 1900, p. 6

Bandmaster Harry Hope (Seaforth Highlanders) added that, 'As soon as we got within range of the hill where the Boers were, the Artillery opened fire and shelled the hill till dark, the Boers never once showing fire.'

'A Thurso Boy at the Front', *Caithness Courier*,
26 January 1900, p. 3

113

The blunder was all too apparent to the Boers sheltering at ground level. As an English farmer from the Orange Free State, then fighting for the Boers, informed his father in Kent, this bombardment simply boosted enemy morale:

> You should see our entrenchments, for we burrow under the ground, and never get hit. Millions of pounds must have been shot away by the English gunners, and you, father, will have to pay for all the waste. It made me laugh to see the firing hour after hour and not one of our men hit . . . as they always follow the same childish plan we know that they will not attack until after a day or two's bombardment.[11]

'Letter from a Traitor', *Morning Post*,
20 March 1900, p. 5

The Bloemfontein Boer (**26, 71, 92, 103**) was equally unimpressed on the 10th:

> when a fearful bombardment of lyddite, shrapnel and other shell of the most infernal kind failed to frighten us out of our senses. The lyddite shells make a terrible noise by their explosion – the very ground around you seems to shake; but it is just like the usual explosive. When it drops among a dense crowd it may kill 30 or

---

11 Three men were injured but the bombardment revealed both the target and imminence of the British assault. Pemberton, *Battles of the Boer War*, p. 85.

50 but dense crowds are seldom found for targets among the wary Boers . . .

'With Cronje on the Modder', *Western Mail*, 27 December 1900, p. 3

114
Drummer F. Gordon, writing to his parents in Leeds, described how

We got the order to advance on Sunday, December 10th, and paraded at 2.30 p.m. in the following order:– Our regiment [Black Watch] first, then the Seaforths, Argyll and Sutherlands, and then the Highland Light Infantry. On the right of the brigade came the Royal Artillery and Royal Engineers; on the left the Northumberland Fusiliers and King's Own Yorkshire Light Infantry; and in the rear the transport and a company of the Cape Medical Volunteer Corps. When all had taken their proper places, we started, the Artillery going forward and crossing to the left . . . It started to rain very heavily, and in about ten minutes we were wet through, having nothing on but thin khaki. For a time we advanced very slowly, lying down at intervals. Suddenly, as we were passing a low ridge, the Artillery opened fire. Then the ball commenced. The Black Watch went forward about 2,000 yards [1.8 km], and then . . . slowly advanced to within about nine hundred yards [0.8 km] of the Boer trenches, and opened a desultory fire on the trenches to try and find the strength of the enemy. They never answered our fire, although we kept it up till dark, when we retired to where the rest of the brigade were lying and bivouacked for the night, with no protection from the wind and rain. At twelve o'clock the officers came round to wake us, and we formed up. All orders were given in whispers, as we were intending a surprise attack . . . Owing to the darkness, which made it almost impossible to see your front rank man, we had ropes passed along the brigade to keep us together. We kept on going until about 3.20 a.m., when suddenly we all noticed a bright red light for a couple of seconds on our right. Before we had time to think . . . two rifle shots rung out as a signal to the Boers. Then began a terrible fusillade from the trenches, in which was a force of Boers estimated at 15,000[12] . . . We

---

12   Many soldiers, repeating camp or hospital gossip, exaggerated the numbers of the Boers and their casualties: Private John M. Ingham (Black Watch) claimed that the Boers 'were 23,000 strong, and . . . lost a lot over 500', *Weekly Standard and Express* (Blackburn), 13 January 1900, p. 7 and Sergeant H. Joel (1st Coldstream Guards), 'Boers . . . about 23,000 strong' and losses of 'about 5,000 or 6,000', in

got the order to lie down flat, so as not to offer such a good target. Then we were ordered to fix bayonets and charge. Having a brave leader at our head, a man whom any of our brigade, and especially my own regiment, would follow anywhere (I mean our gallant old Colonel, the late General Wauchope), we charged forward with a loud cheer, some shouting for Queen and country, until we were suddenly checked by barbed wire entanglements, in which we stuck, and were shot like sheep. Seeing we could never get through the wires, we retired to about 300 yards [275 m], leaving about two hundred lying in front of the trenches.

'When Wauchope Fell. Graphic Account of the Battle by a Leeds Soldier',
Leeds Mercury, 15 February 1900, p. 8

115

'Our whole brigade was in mass of quarter column, and we were the leading battalion', wrote Second Lieutenant the Hon. Maurice Drummond (Black Watch),[13]

we marched on till we got within 100 yards [91.4 m] of the enemy's position. One of our companies had begun to extend, when suddenly we had bullets poured in on us like hailstones. We lay down and fixed bayonets, and then spread out as best as best we could. I had only been up in the firing line for four or five minutes, and was standing up to see the best point to aim at, when suddenly I got hit in the leg, right up in the thigh. I was unable to move, so there I had to lie, about eighty yards [73 m] from the Boer trenches.

'Experiences of an Officer of the Black Watch',
Nairnshire Telegraph, 17 January 1900, p. 3

'Swindonians at the Front', *Evening Swindon Advertiser*, 9 January 1900, p. 2. The Boers actually suffered some 255 casualties of whom 87 were killed, Pretorius, *A to Z of the Anglo-Boer War*, p. 261.

13 The second son of James Drummond, eighth Viscount Strathallan, the Hon. (later Sir) Maurice Charles Andrew Drummond (1877–1957) would serve with distinction in the Great War, being awarded the Distinguished Service Order (1916) and appointed as a Chevalier of the Legion of Honour (1917).

'The Searchlight at Wesselton Mine' with soldiers of the Loyal North Lancashire Regiment.

Right: Charge of the Brigade of Guards under Colonel Paget up Gun Hill in the battle of Belmont, 23 November 1899.

Left: Lieutenant-Colonel Robert Kekewich, the commander of the Kimberley garrison.

Cecil Rhodes (front row third from right), Mrs Rochfort Maguire and defenders of Kimberley alongside artillery and a searchlight on the perimeter of the siege.

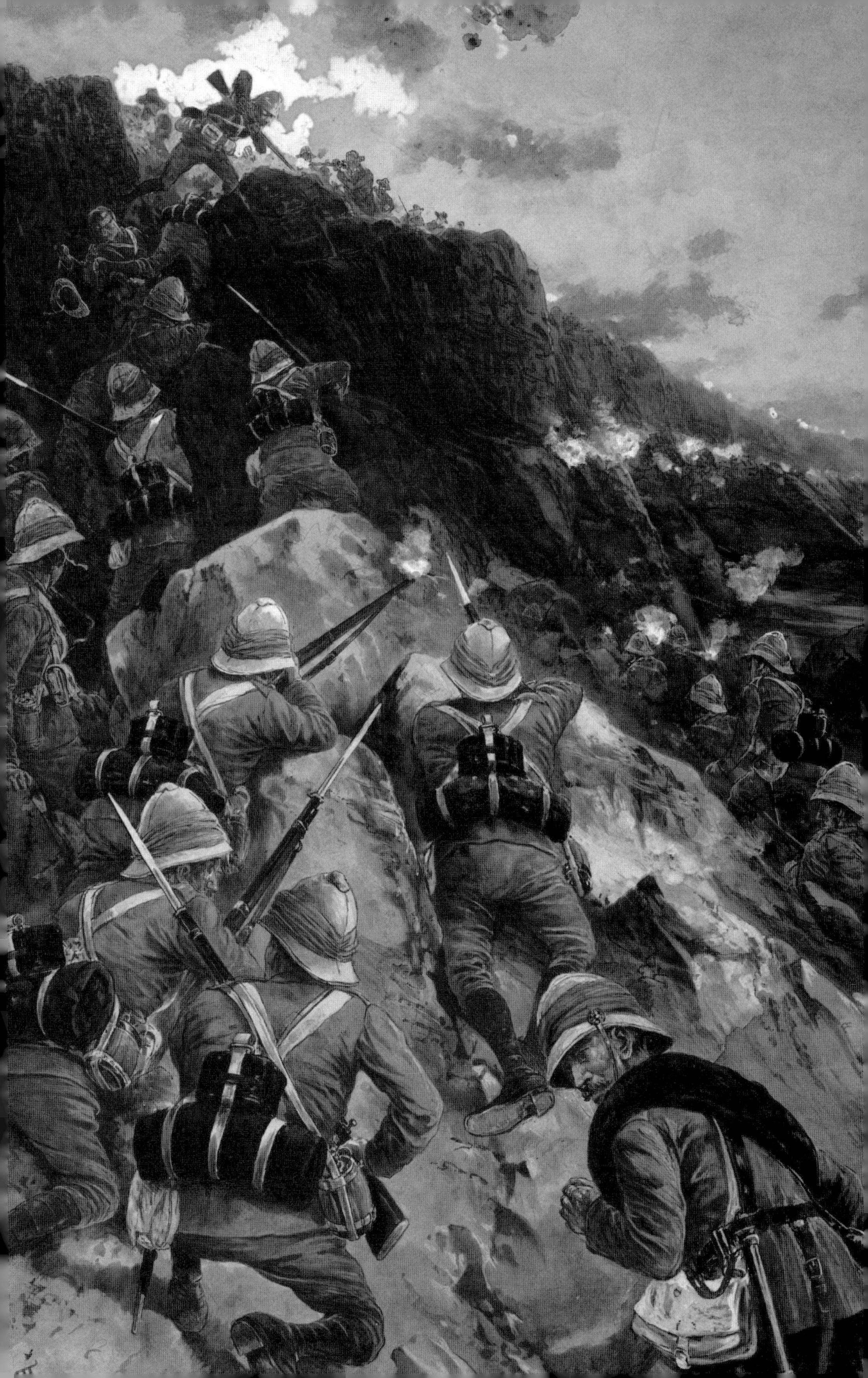

Above: Argyll and Sutherland Highlanders crossing the Modder River after the costly battle on 28 November 1899.

Left: Lieutenant-General Lord Methuen, who commanded the relief division that met with defeat at Magersfontein on 11 December 1899.

Above: Kimberley people waiting to draw their rations of meat in the early morning.

Left: 'Siege Baby', Miss Agnes Oliver with a Long Tom and an ordinary Boer shell.

Below: Women and children waiting to go down a mine after the Boers began bombarding Kimberley with Long Tom shells on 7 February 1900.

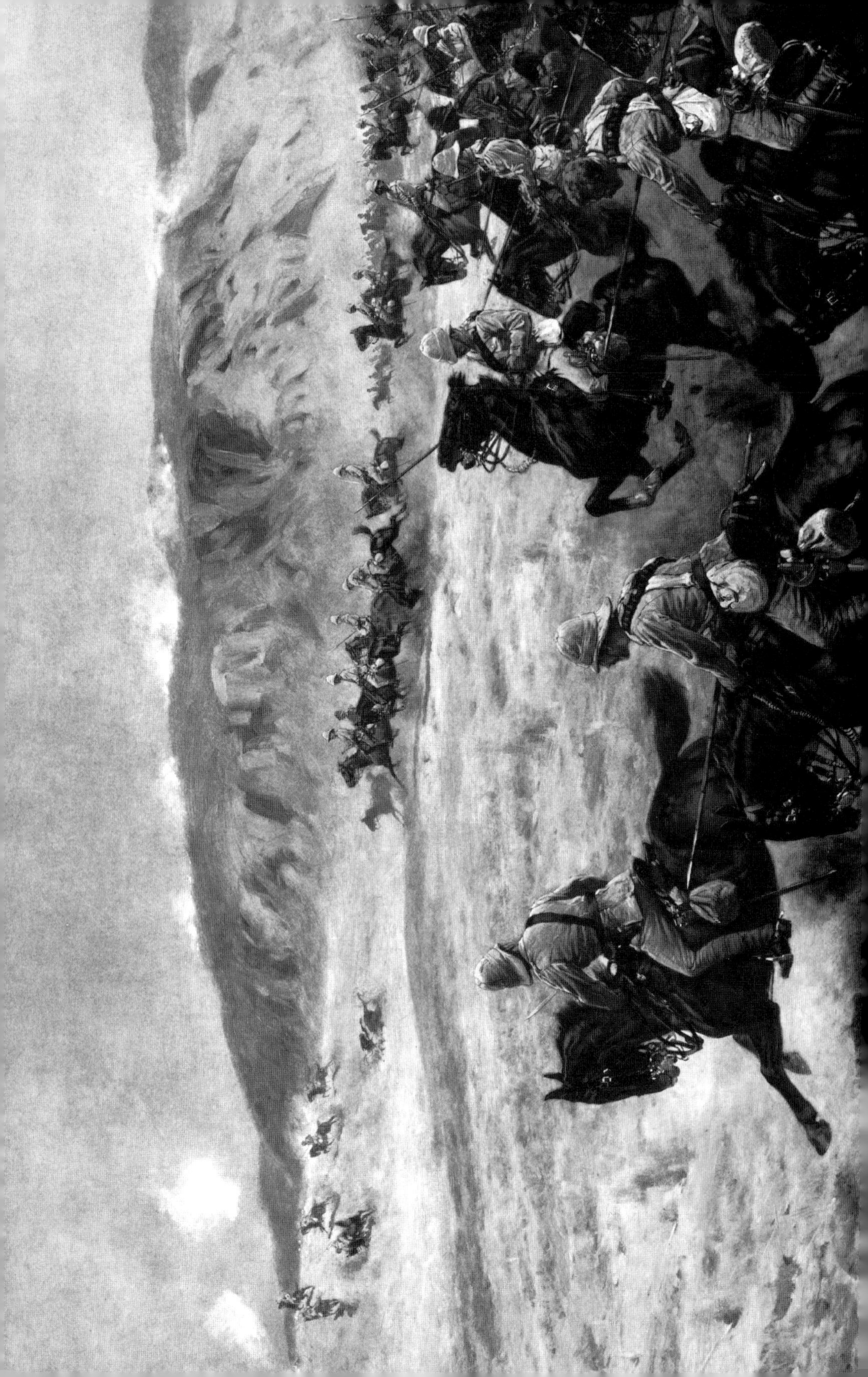

Above: 'Entrances to the underground tunnel at Kimberley', photograph by M. Bennett, Kimberley.

Left: 'Advance on Kimberley: The 16th and 17th [*sic*] Lancers at Klip Drift', photogravure after a painting by John Charlton, 1910.

Below: John Carlton, 'The Rush to Kimberley: the 10th Hussars Crossing Klip Drift' after a sketch by G. D. Giles, in H. W. Wilson, *With the Flag to Pretoria*, (1900–1).

'General French's meeting with Mr. Cecil Rhodes at the Sanatorium Hotel, Kimberley, on the evening of the relief'. From a sketch by the special artist Mr Frederic Villiers, *Illustrated London News* (24 March 1900).

'General Cronjé in Captivity'. Photograph of the defeated Boer commander after the battle of Paardeberg (18–27 February 1900) by Reinhold Thiele, *The Graphic*, (7 April 1900).

116

'Some one gave the order to retire', claimed Sergeant James T. French (Highland Light Infantry),

and it was here that most of the casualties occurred. Men were dropping all around, and I think the reason of our having so few killed was our being in the rear of the Brigade, as the Black Watch who were leading, had the most killed. We retired about 800 yards [700 m], and then up again and advanced by rushes under cover.

'Letter From The Front', *Motherwell Times*, 23 February 1900, p. 3

117

An Argyll recalled that

The dawn was just breaking, and the sight was awful. The men were panic-stricken, and horses were galloping in amongst them, knocking them down, never to rise again. I made a good sprint myself, and after going a good half-mile [0.8 km] I wheeled to the left behind a hill, and just afterwards up came ——— the piper,[14] and started playing 'The Campbells are Coming' on the bagpipes to rally the men. I could have cried when I heard him.

'The Campbells are Coming', *Evening News* (London), 13 January 1900, p. 2

118

'The General, our colonel, and most of the officers were either killed or wounded', commented Private J. M. Ingham (Black Watch) but

I heard an officer (Lieutenant Ramsey [*sic*: Ramsay])[15] shouting 'To the right.' So I rushed with a few others, and we met some of the Seaforth, H.L.I., and Argyles [*sic*]. There were about 100 of us. We got round by the right and into the back of the trenches. We rushed into the trenches and gave them the bayonet, when our own troops in

---

14 This was Pipe Major James MacKay (Argyll and Sutherland Highlanders), see Pemberton, *Battles of the Boer War*, p. 97.
15 Aged thirty-three, Lieutenant Nigel Nels Ramsay was killed in the battle.

front started firing and we were catching it all. So the officer made us retire. There were just 20 of us came out.

'Writing Home', *Weekly Standard and Express* (Blackburn), 27 January 1900, p. 2

119

Friendly fire and barbed wire, as described by Lieutenant R. B. Graham (Argyll and Sutherland Highlanders), meant that

> we had to retire, as the Boers were firing at us from the front in great numbers, and our own men were firing from behind us at the Boers, so of course could not help hitting some of us . . . it made it too hot for us. I do not think there is the least doubt we should have taken the position if it had not been for this, as also two wire fences we had to get over during our charge.

'Local News From The Front', *Gloucestershire Chronicle*, 13 January 1900, p. 7

120

For most highlanders, though, the enduring memory of the battle was lying prostrate on the veld unable to move: as a Seaforth sergeant observed,

> There was nothing for it but to lay down and pretend to be dead, and this I did about 5.30 a.m. till, I suppose six p.m., the sun pouring down on me all the time, and not a drink of water all day, and dare not stir hand or foot, and expecting every instant to be my last. I could hear nothing but the cries, moans, and prayers of the wounded all round me, but I daren't so much as look up to see who they were. Shots and shells were going over me all day from the enemy and our side, and plenty of them striking within a yard of me – I mean bullets, not shells – and yet they never hit me. I believe some of our fellows went off their heads and walked right up to the enemy's place, singing till they dropped them.

'Singing to Death', *Manchester Evening News*, 16 January 1900, p. 5

121

'Some one made a terrible blunder', wrote Lance Sergeant B. Linworth (Highland Light Infantry) 'and of course the men paid the penalty of it.' The Black Watch, he added, were in front and they charged it until they came up against a barbed wire fence 10 feet [3 m] high, and the whole of us had to run for life. We could not fire for fear of killing our own men in front, and the Boers shot us down like dogs. You may guess the way they fight when I tell you that I never saw a Boer all day. We were simply firing at the hills and taking our chance, and if we as much as showed our head up, we were saluted with a shower of bullets.

'Letters from South Africa', *Ayr Advertiser or West Country and Galloway Journal*, 11 January 1900, p. 5

122

Even those kilted soldiers who survived the ordeal felt the effects, as Private Harold Dutton (Seaforth Highlanders) affirmed: 'We were burnt something awful about the legs, and we dare not stir or we got a bullet at us. Oh! It was terrible.'

'A Frodsham Man at Magersfontein', *Cheshire Observer*, 20 January 1900, p. 7

Another Seaforth, Lance-Corporal Bourne, wished 'a thousand times I was dead, but had not any luck that way. With the Highlanders being in the kilt the backs of our knees got scorched with the blazing sun, and they lost the use of their legs'.

'"Wished a Thousand Times He was Dead"', *Birmingham Daily Post*, 10 January 1900, p. 9

123

While the artillery provided covering fire, Private George Waller, an Argyll and Sutherland Highlander from Heeley, Sheffield, recollected how

> We were scattered all over the field by this time, and it was well for us that we were, as 2,000 Boers were trying to work round on the right flank to take us in the rear, and the Guards just caught them in time, and stopped their advance. I and a lot more of our fellows, H.L.I., Seaforths, Black Watch, went to the right to try and stop the cross fire that was coming right across from the right. We found the enemy's picket here in small trenches, they were mostly Scandinavians. We completely wiped them off the map. One of them said, 'Give me a chance mate, I am a Glasgow man.' One of the Seaforths promptly

ran him through, accompanied with the remark, 'Then take that you —— traitor.'

'Heeley Man at Modder River', *Sheffield Daily Telegraph*, 20 January 1900, p. 8

124

'The Guards', confirmed Private J. H. Clarke,

> were on the right. No. 4 Company of the 1st Coldstreams; that is my company, was selected to advance in the first, or 'firing line'. Nearly all the men who have been killed and wounded belong to No. 4 company in the 1st Coldstream Guards. Major the Hon. W. Lambton was shot through the knee; he is captain of my company[16] . . . it would be about dinner time when I fell severely wounded. I lay there till dinner next day before I was picked up, covered with blood. Two Highlanders carried me on their backs . . .

'Letters From The Front', *Weekly Standard and Express* (Blackburn), 13 January 1900, p. 7

125

The 'fighting' on 11 December, wrote Private Ted Hicklin (Grenadier Guards), lasted 'sixteen hours . . . and again on Tuesday eight more, and now we have not shifted them'. Apart from entrenchments, the Boers had

> big rocks, too, with loopholes to put their rifles in to shoot at you, but you cannot see them though they see us plainly, and the moment they see us they take snap shots at you, but when we do lay hold of one we get our own back. The artillery are doing some good work, but we cannot get at them (the Boers) to do much at present.

'Letters From The Front', *Lichfield Mercury*, 19 January 1900, p. 3

126

As soon as the Highland Brigade encountered 'a very heavy fire', observed a gunner of the 75th Battery, RFA,

---

16   Major the Hon. (later Major-General Sir) William Lambton (1863–1936) had served in the Nile expedition (1898). He commanded 1st Battalion, Coldstream Guards, in 1912 and was General Officer Commanding 4th Division in 1915. He retired in 1920.

so the order came for the artillery to go in close support of them . . . Well, we trotted quite 1,000 yards [914 m], and it came 'Halt, action, front', and then we caught it . . . Our leading driver got shot through the stomach, and one of his horses was shot, and when going down dead the two centre horses fell on top of them, and the wheel horses went on top of the lot. Well, the wheel driver got up, and unhooked his horses . . . and while he was doing that he had a bullet through the helmet . . . I was serving ammunition to the gun, and I got a bullet deep in the leg. A little while after I had one go through my water bottle, and then I got another cross-wise at me; it went through my coat, and just scratched my chest. And when they brought an ammunition wagon down, and I was unhooking the horses, a bullet took a button off, and killed the horse I was standing against.

'Leicester Gunner's Thrilling Experiences', *Leicester Chronicle*, 13 January 1900, p. 2

127

While the infantry could lie down, the gunners had to fight from more exposed positions. 'We were in action for over 15 hours', recalled Private Edgar Jackson ('G' Battery, RHA), 'and fired over 1,000 shells. We had one officer and four men wounded, and had nine horses killed, besides a lot wounded. One of my horses was shot through the leg. How we escaped so easily God only knows.'

'"Mown Down Like Grass" If the Boer Shells Equalled Ours ---!' *Burnley Express and Advertiser*, 20 January 1900, p. 8

128

The cavalry performed several support roles. A 12th Lancer described how they had tried to draw the enemy's fire,

so that our artillery could locate the position of the guns. The cavalry were disappointed in this, as the Boers did not fire their big guns until they were within about 500 yards [460 m] of their trenches, which they could not see until they gained the brow of a hill . . . the Boers did not forget to pepper them with rifle fire, and the bullets were flying about in all directions. They lost four men killed, while about 25 were wounded in about 10 minutes. The artillery then got into action, and shelled them all day.

'A Cestrian at the Front', *Cheshire Observer*, 10 February 1900, p. 7

129

The 12th Lancers also operated on the right of the front. 'The ground', as Sergeant Woodhead recalled,

> was not suited to cavalry, nor the position of the enemy's strongholds either, so we galloped to a place of safety for the horses, and dismounted, and with carbines did the duty of the foot soldier. We advanced in splendid formation on the right flank, where we thought the Guards were, but only to find that they had been driven back . . . We advanced and retired several times on our stomachs, and lay there banging away until four in the afternoon, amidst groans which made you cry almost.
>
> 'The Highlanders Heartbroken', *Leicester Chronicle*, 13 January 1900, p. 5

130

Writing to his brother, Captain Francis Egerton-Green (12th Lancers) explained that

> We had to get up gradually, taking all the cover we could get, as their fire was very hot, and our orders were to hold the ridge until an Infantry Regiment could . . . relieve us. The Coldstream Guards actually took my place, and I was surprised and pleased to get out of the firing line without being hit. At one time my squadron was under a heavy cross fire, the Boers giving it us in front, and some of our own troops letting us have a dose from the left, right down our line. During that part of the show we had to lie flat and get the best cover we could behind stones and bushes. I think our work was useful, and the General complimented us and said we had saved the situation . . . The men behaved splendidly. They went out quite coolly, in spite of the retreating infantry running back through their ranks, and the many wounded carried back on stretchers, which is not an encouraging sight.
>
> 'Graphic Letter From Captain F. Egerton-Green', *Essex County Standard*, 13 January 1900, p. 5

131

The feint on the left had scant effect. Private George Hewitt (King's Own Yorkshire Light Infantry) admitted that 'We had not much to do until about eleven o'clock in the morning, when we got into it, having made good cover for ourselves. We only had 11 men wounded, which makes our total casualties 125, 25 of whom were killed.'

'Letter From An Ossett Soldier', *Ossett Observer*, 20 January 1900, p. 8

132

Meanwhile the Northumberland Fusiliers, as one of their lance-corporals observed, served as 'escort for the big naval gun':

> The 'Fifth' were under arms from Sunday, 3 p.m., till Wednesday, 7 p.m., which is, I should say, a record and a proper feat of endurance; skirmishing during the day and trying to draw their fire, and outpost duty during the night.

'The Ragged Fifth', *Newcastle Daily Chronicle*, 11 January 1900, p. 5

133

For the Highland Brigade, some of whom had reached the lower slopes of Magersfontein, Methuen only sent one unit as reinforcements: the 1st Battalion, Gordon Highlanders. Sergeant McDougall recalled that

> Our regiment was looking after the baggage, when we were ordered to reinforce the fighting line, and then the fun began. We got to about 1500 yards [1,370 m] of the Boer position, and then the bullets were coming pretty thick, but still we advanced till we got within 600 or 500 yards [550–457 m]. The Boers kept up so heavy a fire that we had to lie where we were for about four hours. Our fellows were beginning to fall, but still we had to remain for [an]other three hours, the backs of our legs being all burnt with the sun. We could not get a drop of water. It was something awful – the wounded shouting for water, and with none to give them.

'A Dundee Gordon's Letter', *Dundee Advertiser*, 12 January 1900, p. 5

134

The advance of the Gordons in broad daylight was one the more remarkable exploits of the battle. 'Our advance', claimed Corporal Wilkie,

> was conducted in a manner that pointed to previous experience. You can judge for yourself when I say that we were right up to the enemy's

position without firing a shot. The teaching we had in India[17] was that day exemplified . . . Every available cover was taken advantage of, yet there were times when we were fully exposed to the Boers' fire.

'A Good Word for Methuen', *Dundee Advertiser*,
12 January 1900, p. 5

135

A private of the Scots Guards witnessed the advance:

They opened out, and went forward bravely, some of the other Highlanders backing them up. My heart swelled with pride as I saw my countrymen enter the terrible fire zone, and push grimly on, leaving the plain behind them dotted with dead and wounded, for there was no cover, and the Boers had the range to a yard. Still onward the gay Gordons went, but the bullets fairly hailed on them now. They came to their hands and knees, and finally they lay down.

'Letter from an Ex Constable', *Hamilton Advertiser*,
27 January 1900, p. 3

136

The retirement, though, proved a disaster. Lance-Corporal W. H. Hodgson (Gordon Highlanders) explained that

Time crept on, and the casualties steadily increased, until it was about four o'clock in the afternoon. Then I suppose the General decided that something must be done. To advance without terrible losses was impossible, whilst to stay where we were was also out of the question. The 'Retire' was signalled, and as long as I live I shall never forget that retirement. We hadn't retired a dozen yards before we lost our brave colonel, Colonel Downman,[18] who fell with a bullet through his right breast. I was near him at the time, and together with a colour-sergeant, carried him out of danger. I grieve to say that he died almost two hours afterwards.

'Magersfontein: "Send Up The Gordons"',
Lancashire Daily Post, 24 January 1900, p. 5

---

17 The 1st Battalion, Gordon Highlanders, had served recently in the Tirah Campaign (1897–8), gaining fame across the empire for its storming of the heights of Dargai (20 October 1897). The 'teaching' refers to practice in hill warfare.

18 Lieutenant-Colonel George Thomas Fredrick Downman (1855–99) was a Devonian and had served in the Sudan (1884), the Nile Expedition (1884–5) and on the North-West Frontier (1895 and 1897–8).

137
Private Reg Mannion (Gordon Highlanders) confessed that once pinned to the ground,

> I was in an awful funk at first, and I wrote my diary up, and finally went to sleep. When I awoke I found a mob of all corps retiring past me, and on looking round could see nothing of my section. I got up and walked back about a hundred yards [90 m], and found the company there. We lay there until the whole line retired through us, and then retired ourselves, the brigade forming up about a mile [1.6 km] from the position. Here we piled arms, and our water-carts came up . . .
>
> 'Magersfontein. A Gordon's Account of the Battle',
> Leicester Chronicle, 13 January 1900, p. 5

138
None of the retirements were orderly affairs: Private Harry Anderson (1st Coldstream Guards) saw

> the Highland Brigade running towards us as if the devil was after them. Some had no rifles, others had no hats. They were completely demoralized. It was just like a fire at a theatre. Highlanders were dropping off by the score, all shot in the back. The Highlanders ran past us, and no wonder, as nearly half the Highland brigade lay on the field, dead and wounded.[19]
>
> 'Letters From The Front', Burnley Express and Advertiser,
> 17 February 1900, p. 8

139
The battlefield, as Sergeant Edwards (Royal Engineers) saw from an observation balloon, was one that 'I shall never forget':

> The sight was sickening. I myself saw sixty-two dead in one heap, including General Wauchope and several other officers. The Boer loss

---

19 The highlanders bore the brunt of the 948 casualties, with 15 officers and 173 other ranks killed, and 30 officers and 529 other ranks wounded and missing. The Black Watch suffered most severely: 7 officers and 86 men killed, 11 officers and 188 men wounded, Maurice, *War in South Africa*, vol. 1, p. 329.

was terrific, as we could see from the balloon the effect of the lyddite shells, and gave the batteries the result, and where they were bursting.

'A Narrow Escape for the Balloon', *Northern Scot and Moray & Nairn Express*, 3 February 1900, p. 5

140

A contrary view, explaining the scale of the disaster, was given by the Englishman fighting in the Boer trenches, whose letter home (**113**) was reprinted, as below, in provincial newspapers.

> I haven't stained myself with English blood and don't mean to. It makes me proud of my fellow countrymen, and the good class Boers regret having to kill such plucky fellows, who have come along to their death. Like the battle of Balaclava, it is not war, but it is magnificent. Poor chaps, I am sure they can never see us. One whole day of hard fighting we never showed ourselves, and I see by the papers that hundreds of English were killed, and especially the Scotchmen. Our loss was trifling. You cannot hit men with rocks protecting them all round, and who are underground when the cannons fire.
>
> 'An Englishman in the Boer Ranks', *Bury and Norwich Post, and Suffolk Standard*, 27 March 1900, p. 8

Similarly the Bloemfontein Boer (**26, 71, 91, 103, 113**) reflected upon how the fighting was largely on a concentrated front from his perspective: 'At Magersfontein we had four hours' awful work. All the time busy. Most of the fighting was done about 800 yards [730 m] away from us, round the corner of the position.'

'With Cronje on the Modder', *Western Mail*, 27 December 1900, p. 3

141

'We left most of our wounded and dead on the field that night', wrote Sergeant John Wallace, a Manxman in the Seaforth Highlanders,[20]

> every one of them [the wounded] speak in the highest manner of the kindness of the Boers. It seems that after our guns stopped fire, when it got dark, the Boers came out of the trenches to our wounded,

---

20   He himself would die at Paardeberg, 'Seaforth Highlanders killed at Paardeberg', *Northern Scot and Moray & Nairn Express*, 3 March 1900, p. 3.

brought them water, food, blankets, lighted their pipes for them, and did everything that was possible for them. It is only the scum of the Rand that fire on our sick and ambulance waggons.[21]

'A Seaforth Highlander's Description of the Modder River [*sic*] Battle',
Isle of Man Times, 27 January 1900, p. 3

142

Gathering in the dead and wounded would prove a dangerous and exhausting task. Sergeant Walter Furness (1st Division Field Hospital) found himself operating 'temporarily' as part of a bearer company:

We had many narrow escapes, as at times we were between fires. In conjunction with other bearer companies, we cleared the field of wounded, but could not reach the dense mass of wounded Highlanders near the Boer trenches, as the enemy were deliberately firing at us. We then went back, and pitched our field hospital tents . . . The battle lasted till noon on Tuesday, when our forces retired, having failed to dislodge the enemy . . . We are having a rest to-day (15th December) as we have got nearly all the sick and wounded sent down by train. From early Monday morning till Wednesday noon, however, I had but three hours' sleep. Our work has been tremendous.

'A Lincoln Sergeant at Magersfontein', *Sheffield Daily Telegraph*, 12 January 1900, p. 6

143

The burial details, as a sapper remembered, were particularly grim:

The first grave we dug was about thirty feet [9 m] long and three feet deep, and would you believe it? – we put fifty-three Scotsmen into it – thirty-four of the Black Watch alone. It was something horrible, and every man of us was crying all the time we worked; and when, after we had placed them all in, the burial service was going on before we covered them over, three or four fainted, whilst the others cried so loudly that you could hardly hear the minister.

'Laying the Brave to Rest', *Leeds Mercury*,
13 January 1900, p. 8

---

21 See also 'An Officer's Experiences at Magersfontein', *Western Morning News*, 12 January 1900, p. 8; and E. N. Bennett, *With Methuen's Column on an Ambulance Train* (London: Swan Sonnenschein, 1900), p. 82.

144

The Reverend J. Robertson, chaplain to the Highland Brigade, found the ordeal equally harrowing:

> Think of my burying 176 after Magersfontein, the great majority of whom I had to handle and identify alone, as the Boers would not allow any one else near their trenches! While the work had to be done, a sense of duty kept me up, but by the end of the year, a reaction had set in, and out of the depths I cried, literally with strong crying and tears . . . Of the seven who formed our original mess (General Wauchope's Brigade Staff) only Colonel Ewart[22] and myself remain.

'Pathetic Letter from Chaplain Robertson', *Northern Scot and Moray & Nairn Express*, 7 April 1900, p. 6

145

The sufferings of the wounded were not confined to the battlefield. When the wife of a resident at De Aar visited the hospital to write letters, address envelopes, and collect mail from the patients, she found that

> There is not a single murmur from one of the sufferers. The greater part of the men are lying on the floor, having no beds, fully dressed, with the exception of their coats, which most of them have rolled up and tucked under their heads for pillows. One man I spoke to had been shot five times, but was quite lively . . . [on the following day, Wednesday 15 December] Over 100 wounded men have come here to-day from Magersfontein. Poor things in such a plight – many of them on the battlefield were glad of a scrap of hard biscuit . . . [on the following Thursday at 9 p. m.] The ambulance train has just come in with about 130 wounded. There is no room in hospitals here (we have about 400 sick and wounded soldiers at De Aar), so they are going to take them on to Cape Town; fancy 500 miles [805 km] more in the train.

'Among the Wounded', *Cork Constitution*, 20 January 1900, p. 6

---

22 Colonel (later Lieutenant-General Sir) John Spencer Ewart (1861–1930) was a Cameron Highlander, who served in several Egyptian/Sudanese campaigns, fighting at Tel-el-Kebir (1882) and Omdurman (1898). He never forgave Methuen over Magersfontein and rose to the post of adjutant-general to the forces before resigning over the Curragh Incident (1914).

Magersfontein: Recriminations

Unlike the aftermaths of the previous battles, a wave of bitterness, resentment, and recriminations swept through Methuen's division. The feelings of highlanders towards Lord Methuen were even described as 'mutinous'.[23]

146

The highlanders were in a dreadful state after the battle: 'I did not get near my regiment until Sunday [*sic* Tuesday] morning at 5.30 a.m.', wrote Lance-Corporal W. Macfarlane (Seaforth Highlanders),

> I had been without food since Sunday afternoon, and had not had a drop of water from the Monday at 9 a.m., having given it all away to the wounded. At the roll call on Monday night, I was marked up missing, but turned up the following morning.
> 'Letter from South Africa', *Nairnshire Telegraph*, 21 February 1900, p. 3

'The worst thing about this affair', added Private Mannion in his letter (**137**), written on 16 December,

> is the lack of water. We have only the clothes we stand up in; we have given in our sporrans, and have got khaki fronts to our kilts. We've given up shaving, and get a wash about once a week . . . altogether we are about the most dejected-looking crew you can imagine. Add to this that we can't walk for blisters on our legs, and have to limp about like lame ducks . . .
> 'Magersfontein. A Gordon's Account of the Battle', *Leicester Chronicle*, 13 January 1900, p. 5

147

Many asserted that a dreadful blunder had occurred. There was 'a terrible mistake', opined Private J. Cockcroft (1st Battalion, Coldstream Guards), 'God knows who is to blame for it . . .'
Weekly Standard and Express (Blackburn), 14 April 1900, p. 2

---

23 'Lord Methuen's Command', *Elgin Courant and Courier*, 19 January 1900, p. 3.

'The thing was, of course, a blunder or a mistake', asserted a Paisley man in the Highland Brigade, 'Methuen did not expect them to be where they were, for it seems that the Boers have departed from their usual tactics of occupying the tops of kopjes and were at the bottom strongly entrenched. Our blunder was in advancing right up to their position in mass of quarter column.'

'Interesting Letter From the Front', *Paisley and Renfrewshire Gazette*, 17 February 1900, p. 3

148

A quarter-column formation meant, as a Seaforth corporal explained, that:

We were offering a front of, say, fifty yards [45 m], and immediately behind, following in double ranks, were company after company of the Highland Brigade, of, say, 3,500 men . . . Monday's work was a huge blunder, and who is to blame I do not know; but there is no doubt the Highland Brigade were led like lambs to the slaughter.

'"Like Lambs to the Slaughter"', *Birmingham Daily Post*, 10 January 1900, p. 9

149

Most highlanders absolved their fallen general: 'It was not the Brigadier's fault – I mean Wauchope', affirmed Private J. Austin (Seaforth Highlanders), 'and not a man of the Highland Brigade blames him'.

'Letter from an Aberlour Man at the Front', *Northern Scot and Moray & Nairn Express*, 13 January 1900, p. 3.

Several referred to the last words that Wauchope supposedly said (and here they were almost certainly repeating camp or hospital gossip as they could not possibly have heard them at first hand). 'Wauchope', wrote a Seaforth lance-corporal from Wynberg Hospital, 'was about the first to fall, and his last words were, "Make to your right and left men; don't blame me; it's not my fault as I had my orders."'

'With the Seaforths. Letter from a Dover Constable at the War', *Dover Express*, 12 January 1900, p. 2

Another wounded soldier, Colour-Sergeant A. J. Gray (Black Watch), writing from De Aar Hospital, claimed that Wauchope 'shouted in the vicinity of the Argylls – "Highlanders don't blame me for this; I received my orders, and had to obey them.'"[24]

'Letter by a Comrie Man on the Battle',
Strathearn Herald, 13 January 1900, p. 2

150

Whether Wauchope actually said those words (and they are disputed in some accounts and disavowed as completely out of character by his widow),[25] they testify to the depth of bitterness within the Highland ranks, accentuated by Methuen's subsequent address to his beaten army. 'Lord Methuen', recalled an Argylls private, 'gave us a very disheartening speech the following day; in fact, the truth is no man has any faith in him whatever. You can hear the men grumble every hour of the day about the way he treats the Highland Brigade.'

'Stirling Soldiers' Impressions of Campaign', *Bridge of Allan Reporter*, 13 January 1900, p. 5

151

By sympathizing with the highlanders 'on their terrible loss', and by suggesting that if someone had shouted 'forward' instead of 'retire' the battle could have been won,[26] Methuen infuriated the highlanders. As a Montrosian wrote home,

> It is Lord Methuen who is to blame for all this. He is no class; he is not fit to command troops. He gave us a speech, and they were very near hooting him.
> The men have got no confidence in him.[27]

'Mutinous Spirit in Highland Brigade. Methuen in Danger',
Dundee Advertiser, 16 January 1900, p. 5

---

24 See also 'Wauchope's Last Moments "Don't Blame Me"', *Dundee Weekly News*, 13 January 1900, p. 8, and 'The "Death Trap" at Magersfontein', *Perthshire Advertiser*, 10 January 1900, p. 5.
25 'General Wauchope's Last Words', *Oban Times*, 27 January 1900, p. 8; and E. M. Spiers, *The Scottish Soldier and Empire, 1854–1902* (Edinburgh: Edinburgh University Press, 2006), pp. 166–7.
26 NAM, Acc. 1973-10-85, Private F. Bly (Seaforths) diary, 14 December 1899; Black Watch Regimental Archive (BWRA) 0186 Captain A. R. Cameron to mother, 25 December 1899; 'Highland Brigade and Methuen: Grave Statements by a Soldier', *Glasgow Herald*, 9 January 1900, p. 6.
27 See also 'Perth Soldier's Experience at Magersfontein. Scathing Criticism of Methuen', *Strathearn Herald*, 20 January 1900, p. 2, and 'Kilmarnock Soldiers at the Front', *Kilmarnock Standard*, 24 February 1900, p. 3.

152

When news of the criticisms of Methuen in the British press reached his command, guardsmen and many English soldiers wrote in his defence, blaming Wauchope and the highlanders for the debacle. Private Clifford Rushton (Scots Guards) maintained that 'Every Guardsman you meet has the same opinion that it was not Methuen who made the mistake, but being a thorough gentleman, he prefers to take all the blame, and suffer the cruel criticism of the English people at large, rather than blame a departed comrade.'

'A Tribute to Lord Methuen', *Somerset County Gazette*, 26 May 1900, p. 3.

Sergeant T. G. Morris (12th Lancers) agreed that 'Lord Methuen was in no way to blame for this awful disaster.'

'A Wounded Lancer returns', *Burnley Express and Advertiser*, 31 March 1900, p. 8

Private J. Hayworth (Loyal North Lancashires) was more blunt: 'The Scotch Regiment proved themselves proper cowards, and that is the reason we had to retire.'

'Kruger's Whiskers. No More Soldiering for a Thousand Pounds', *Blackburn Times*, 20 January 1900, p. 3

153

Private W. O. Purnett (Scots Guards) was rather more measured in his assessment:

> It is a curious thing that the rest of the troops were opened out all right and the Highland Brigade [was] still in quarter column when they were fired upon. Our chaps think the Brigade was taken too near before the General in Command of them was aware of it . . . They have told our chaps that it was a death-trap, but we think if the charge had been made as it ought, the kopje would have been taken.[28] They, being in quarter column had soon to fall back. They lost all their prestige as Scotchmen, and you don't hear the Highlanders brag to us now, although it may not have been any fault of the men. Someone

---

28 Privately Methuen agreed: 'poor Wauchope', he wrote, 'made his plan for attack too late', and 'the Victory was a matter of minutes, for had the word "forward" been given, not "retire", the trenches were ours and the field of battle', WSHC, Methuen Mss., Methuen to his wife, 14 December 1899.

made a '——' of a mistake, but we don't think it was Methuen, for our chaps would follow him to the devil.

'Letters from Swindonians at the Front',
Evening Swindon Advertiser, 28 March 1900, p. 2

Christmas and New Year on the Banks of the Modder

None of this belated support availed Methuen much. Magersfontein followed the defeat at Stormberg (10 December) and preceded Buller's defeat at Colenso (15 December), three shocking defeats known collectively as 'Black Week' in Britain. These defeats had shattered complacency at home and prompted the cabinet to replace Buller as commander-in-chief in South Africa with Lord Roberts,[29] and send Roberts with vast additional forces, including a significant mounted arm, to assume command in the western theatre. Methuen, having resolved to dig in along the Modder and engage the enemy with long-range artillery, waited until Roberts arrived.

154

Continuing his letter (**147**) the Paisley soldier affirmed that 'Of course, I don't mean to say that we are doing nothing here. Our 4.7 naval guns keep giving them a shell now and then, and very seldom a day passes without a few of their shells falling about our trenches, although they have not managed one the length of the camp yet.'

'Interesting Letter from the Front', *Paisley and Renfrewshire Gazette*, 17 February 1900, p. 3

155

Writing home on 22 December, Private T. Smith (2nd Battalion, Coldstream Guards) admitted that 'We have a lot to do yet. The enemy are only five miles [8 km] in front of us, but I think we are going to stay here for one month . . . This is a healthy country, but is hot. We are doing nothing but digging trenches now.'

'A Pontefract Man "Through a Great Deal"',
Wakefield Express, 20 January 1900, p. 8

---

29 Field Marshal Frederick Sleigh Roberts, Baron, later first Earl Roberts of Kandahar (1832–1914) was an Anglo-Irish officer, who won the Victoria Cross during the Indian Mutiny (1857) and established his reputation in India after the march from Kabul to Kandahar (1880). He was commander-in-chief in India (1885–93) and in Ireland (1895–99) before his appointment in South Africa. After nearly a year in South Africa, he replaced Wolseley as commander-in-chief at the War Office.

156

By Christmas Eve, Sergeant Hitchcock (Loyal North Lancashires) was reporting that

> We are getting a lot of reinforcements, so by the time you get this, we might have got them through . . . I hear Roberts is coming out to take command, and Kitchener[30] with him. He will find these people different to his late acquaintances in the Soudan. My word, they can shoot. We have lost a big number of officers, as doubtless you will have read.
>
> 'A Nelson Soldier and the Boers' Shooting at Magersfontein', *Nelson Chronicle*, 26 January 1900, p. 6

157

Christmas and New Year, as described by Sergeant William Hamilton (Highland Light Infantry), were 'very quiet':

> Christmas, except for the church parade, was just like any other day. At New Year . . . Scotsmen in the Cape . . . sent the whole of the Highland Brigade a present of two sticks of tobacco, two packets of cigarettes, matches, one pint of beer per man, and also a small sum of money equal to another pint, with their best wishes . . . We have had some sports going on since Christmas, the principal events being football, tug-of-war, and cricket . . .
>
> Most of the troops, however, are anxious to get on, as they are all pretty tired of the camp life at Modder River on account of the sand. We have had a great many sand storms lately, and they are most uncomfortable . . . Although we have not made any advance we have been kept very busy digging trenches. We have erected trenches all round the camp, so that if the Boers attempt to advance on us they will get a warm reception.
>
> 'Letter From The Front', *Argyllshire Herald*, 10 February 1900, p. 3

---

30   Field Marshal Horatio Herbert Kitchener, first Earl Kitchener of Khartoum and Broome (1850–1916), saw extensive service in the Sudan from 1882 until the defeat of the Mahdists at Omdurman (2 September 1898). He succeeded Roberts as commander-in-chief in South Africa until the end of the war, whereupon he became commander-in-chief in India (1902–9) and later secretary of state for war when the First World War broke out in 1914. He was drowned in 1916 when HMS *Hampshire* sank off the Orkney Islands.

158

Whatever else would happen, though, Lord Methuen realized that 'The Highland Brigade will never wish to serve under me again, and I can see that Macdonald[31] is a regular sergeant-major, therefore I am glad to be among my original brigades again.'

WSHC, Lord Methuen to his wife,
4 February 1900

---

31 Brigadier-General Hector Archibald Macdonald (1853–1903), who assumed command of the Highland Brigade, had risen from the ranks through the Gordon Highlanders and was to become a major-general and receive a knighthood. Having served in the Second Anglo-Afghan War (1878–80) and at Majuba (1881), he later commanded an Egyptian brigade at Omdurman (1898). After the South African War, he served in Ceylon (Sri Lanka) where he incurred allegations of sexual impropriety. *En route* home, he committed suicide in Paris (1903).

Chapter 4

Kimberley: Beleaguered and Bombarded

Hopes Dashed as the Siege Intensifies

159

Understandably the residents of Kimberley had taken a keen interest in the battle of Magersfontein. W. O. Lunson, continuing his letter (7), recalled the dreadful night before the battle and then the 'excitement' when told that the balloon was visible:

> I soon made a beeline for some high ground from whence I knew it could be seen, and on arrival found I had been preceded by any amount of other folks. We could see the balloon, and hear such a cannonading from artillery, shells bursting, and in the lulls between musketry and machine guns. Little did we imagine that, early as it then was, that hundreds of poor fellows were already down in their gallant attempt for our own relief . . . although so near, it was a week before we knew of the unhappy event.[1]
>
> 'The Siege of Kimberley', *Wells Journal*, 12 April 1900, p. 5

160

W. J. Campbell, a former resident of Thurso, Caithness, who had enrolled in the Town Guard, recorded the sights visible from the conning tower:

---

1 When Kekewich received news of 'very heavy' losses at Magersfontein, he published only 'a portion of what is in the papers', LIM, Kekewich diary, 17 December 1899. He was probably fearful of the adverse effects on morale from this blow to British military prestige, Beaumont, 'The British Press', p. 9.

> I saw quite distinctly the shells from our artillery under Lord Methuen burst over the Boer positions at Spitzkop, during the battle of Magersfontein, and we noted the course of the balloon all day. But it took about ten days before we heard the result of the action . . .

He placed this in context:

> During all December, the people of Kimberley, combatants and noncombatants, have been in the position of Micawber, 'waiting for something to turn up'.[2] We have waited patiently and hopefully during November, when we had enough to eat and drink, and plenty of excitement. And we are waiting still, during hot December, patiently enough, but not so hopefully I fear, for there is little to eat, less to drink, and absolutely no excitement. The attention of our enemy has been diverted to the relief column, and shelling operations are in abeyance.
>
> 'The Siege of Kimberley', Caithness Courier,
30 March 1900, p. 3

161

However, as W. O. Lunson (**7, 159**) added, 'after a week of ominous silence we heard of Lord Methuen's check at Magersfontein. This created a new phase for us. Food stuffs were at once centralized, and served out in rations by permits, and then our siege became a more serious affair.'

'The Siege of Kimberley', Wells Journal,
12 April 1900, p. 5

162

In the second part of his letter home (**160**), William (Willie) J. Campbell reflected upon the strategic significance of the Magersfontein defeat:

> We fully realized then as potently as the War Office does now, the supreme importance of the defence and maintenance of Kimberley. For had the Boers, after Methuen's occupation of this side of the Modder River, vanquished us and possessed themselves of Kimberley, with its wealth in stores and bullion, it would have been a comparatively easy matter to out-flank Methuen's little force, cut him off from relief, advance down the Colony, with disloyalists flocking to their standard. The result of such a contingency, especially had the

---

2   Wilkins Micawber, a character in Charles Dickens's novel *David Copperfield*.

Hox [*sic*: Hex River] Valley Pass³ been occupied, would have been little short of disastrous.

'Part II of the Siege of Kimberley', *Caithness Courier*,
20 April 1900, p. 3

163

Kekewich's attempt to suppress news of the Magersfontein defeat riled citizens like members of the MacBean family (**12**), who complained

> the authorities kept us fearfully in the dark, even when they knew what was going on . . . [they] felt sore at their reverses, and, anyhow, decided that all news should be retarded, and even if bad, suppressed. I think it conceivable that this might be justifiable, but in nine cases out of ten I expect it would just have the effects it had here. We came to understand that a 'great victory; Boer losses heavy; British losses unknown' meant as likely as not a heavy reverse. It also caused all sorts of wild rumours to be spread, and they often obtained belief for a time – Such as that Ladysmith had fallen, that the Colony was everywhere in rebellion, etc. It is not too much to say that many of us suffered more through lack of news than any other single discomfort.

'A Highland Family in Kimberley', *Inverness Courier*,
13 April 1900, p. 6

164

In her letter (**1, 16, 22, 34**) the Manx lady recorded that

> they issued us permits as follows:– 2 oz. sugar per person per day, ½ oz. coffee, ¼ oz. tea, 2 ozs. rice, 2 oz. mealie meal or mealies; bread, 10½ ozs.; horseflesh, ½ lb. per adult, 2 oz. children under 12 years. That quantity of meat was not always available. Most of the grocers' stores were closed – sold out. A few of the largest stores were taken as military depots and a guard on each store guarding them day and night.

'Horrors of the Siege', *Isle of Man Weekly Times*,
16 June 1900, p. 5

---

3   The Hex River Valley Pass was the gateway between the Western Cape and the Karoo Desert, with the main road and rail lines from Worcester to Townsriver. The railway was part of the Cape Western Line from Cape Town to De Aar, and thence to Kimberley.

165

'Horseflesh', Willie Campbell described in his letter (**160, 162**),

> is invariably sweet and tough, and even when converted into soup, highly seasoned with Worcester sauce and ketchup, it tasted 'horsey'. Captain Tyson[4] hit upon a brilliant idea of forming a gigantic soup kitchen to supply all Kimberley, rich and poor, black and white, soldier and civilian. It was a magnificent success, and for many to whom horseflesh was absolutely loathsome, Captain Tyson's soup came as a boon and a blessing. The ingredients were simple: a very small quantity of ex-beef or stringy boulie beef (tinned meat), a still smaller quantity of vegetables grated into powder, a very considerable proportion of prickly pear leaves, and a great deal of warm water constituted the soup. Towards the latter part of the siege the soup grew very watery indeed, but it was always pleasant, palatable and wholesome when drunk warm.
>
> 'Part II of the Siege of Kimberley', *Caithness Courier*, 20 April 1900, p. 3

166

In his letter (**6, 13, 18, 30**) H. A. Oliver, who was elected mayor on 19 December and assumed his new office on 1 January, found that he had his 'hands full':

> the whole of the population are now served with rations – fancy 40,000 rations every day. I have about 100 men under me to arrange this . . . Wood is very scarce, no coal or oil, so many people can't cook. We have therefore opened a soup kitchen, and give one pint of soup per day, in place of meat and vegetables. We give out 8,000 pints per day amongst whites. Natives get 4 oz. Kaffir corn, 4 oz. mealie meal, 2 oz. soup. Many people can't afford to pay for the above, and we distribute over £600 per week from our Relief Committee to those destitute people. I am chairman of this and many other committees. We employ over 4,000 men on our relief works, making streets at a cost of over £2,000 per week, so you will understand how my time is occupied.
>
> 'The Siege of Kimberley', *Derby Mercury*, 4 April 1900, p. 2

---

4 Captain 'Tim' Tyson (Kimberley Town Guard) was the assistant military censor.

167

With the rationing came shortages, and attempts to reduce the number of mouths to feed by persuading blacks to leave the town; by December, as Willie Campbell indicated in the first part of his letter (**160**),

> Most of the grocer shops have been closed up, aerated waterworks stopped, and at the public houses there is neither beer, wine, nor whisky, and only a limited supply of 'F.C.', 'Dop' or Cape Brandy, a concoction drunk only by the Dutch and natives upon ordinary occasions, but now eagerly sought by the dry Briton! We have had neither fruit nor vegetables this season, owing to the scarcity of water for the gardens. Vegetables, fruit, and milk cannot be procured at any price, simply because they do not exist . . . Asiatics and natives are allowed less than half the food supply of whites. Several hundreds of natives have run the gauntlet of the Boer lines in the endeavour to get to their own provinces, glad to escape from Kimberley. The situation is fast becoming serious . . .
>
> 'The Siege of Kimberley', *Caithness Courier*,
> 30 March 1903, p. 3

168

Social strains developed within the besieged community. Writing about the scarcity of foodstuffs on Christmas Day, one resident reflected upon the lack of milk:

> Sagar, a Jewish auctioneer, had been bragging that he was not short of condensed milk by any means. This came to the ears of the Commanding Officer. The military raided his place, and found 1,000 tins, which they commandeered, and left him about six . . .

By New Year's Eve, he added,

> We are getting sick of sardines, etc., of which we have never eaten so much in our lives before. De Beers' [*sic*] are now making a 15 pounder.[5] They are also turning their niggers out of the town at a rate

---

5   The gun known as 'Long Cecil' actually fired a 29.8-pound (13.5-kg) shell. It was tested for the first time on 19 January 1900, Colonel D. E. Peddle, 'LONG CECIL The Gun made in Kimberley during the Siege', *Military History Journal*, vol. 4, no. 1 (1977), http://samilitaryhistory.org/vol041dp.html (accessed 31 May 2011).

of 200 or 300 per night.[6] They cannot feed them, and are compelled to do this. Rhodes turned all De Beers horses loose the other day, also because he could not feed them. He intends advertising for them when the siege is raised. The scenes at the butchery every morning beggar description. The crush is awful, and several ladies have had to go home minus skirts, which have been torn off getting through the door.

'Diary of the Siege of Kimberley', *Alnwick and County Gazette*, 31 March 1900, p. 2

169

'Treachery', recalled George Lunt, who served in the Kimberley Light Horse,

was rampant in the town. Supposed spies and residents believed to have given information to the enemy were often put under arrest but British justice required such absolute proof of guilt that the majority were let off. Two men, for instance, were observed signalling to the Boers, and one of them was caught. The prisoner's dress and his lame leg were accurately described but as the witness was not near enough to swear to his face the charge was dismissed.

'Birmingham Men in Kimberley', *Birmingham Daily Post*, 26 May 1900, p. 5

170

These distractions, nonetheless, failed to alleviate the prevailing monotony and boredom. 'Attempts', wrote Willie Campbell (**160, 162, 165, 167**)

were also made at recreation. The combined bands of the Kimberley regiment and the Loyal North Lancashires played at one or other of the camps on Wednesdays and Saturdays, when the ladies came up from town to visit the weather-beaten khaki clad garrison and were treated to lime juice and lemonade, till the time the sugar supply failed us about the middle of January.

'Part II of the Siege of Kimberley', *Caithness Courier*, 20 April 1900, p. 3

---

6   As Mrs Rochfort Maguire recalled, when Rhodes first proposed dispersing the black Africans, the military authorities opposed him and then the Boers turned back some 2,000 to 3,000. However, they subsequently relented and Rhodes 'managed to get rid of some 8,000 out of 10,000 natives in the compounds', 'Life in Kimberley during the Siege', *The Times Weekly Edition*, 23 March 1900, p. 183.

171

There were 'sports at Fort Rhodes', added Lieutenant W. Gordon Grant (formerly a civil engineer with the Public Works Department [P.W.D.] of Cape Colony and then with the Kenilworth Defence Force). Yet by Christmas Day he was still

> getting tired of this inactivity, and wishing that something would happen. Even an attack would be welcomed, just to break the monotony . . . I should very much like to see the accounts of those battles out here as related in the home papers. I'm sure they have been gilded up to please the folks at home, and made to appear as victories, whereas, if all things be considered, I am of opinion that the Boers have beat us oftener than we have them.

By 21 January, he was even more depressed:

> Not yet! not yet! We are still in a state of siege in this 'Diamond City', and military duties only being attended to. Still no word of our relief column turning up. In fact I begin to doubt whether they mean to relieve Kimberley before marching on Bloemfontein, which they could do most comfortably by following up the Modder (Mud) River from where the troops are now lying under command of Lord Methuen . . . I ride into Kimberley as a rule twice a week, but the town appears like a town of the dead, there being absolutely nothing doing in the way of business, and every man you meet is dressed in khaki giving everything the same sort of appearance, and by the time you have spent a couple of hours you are quite content to get out to Kenilworth for meals . . . The P.W.D. Kimberley is still in the same place, and the whole of the staff are all drawing their full pay just as if working, and drawing 5s [25p] a day besides – so am I. De Beers employees are all drawing their full pay, and doing nix but soldiering. De Beers [employees] draw their military pay of 5s, and their ordinary pay from De Beers. Isn't that liberal, seeing that they have thousands of employees?

'Besieged in Kimberley', *Northern Scot and Moray & Nairn Express*, 31 March 1900, p. 6

172

This was only one of many reasons that the residents felt hugely grateful to Cecil Rhodes. Mrs L. E. Lunt, formerly of Epping and Ongar, Essex, reckoned that

> Mr. Cecil Rhodes has personally been most liberal, and has left nothing undone for the public good . . . and had we had more men of his stamp in our Colonial Parliament, I firmly believe this present trouble would not have happened . . . Mr. Rhodes went down the mines himself on the last day the people were there and asked them to be patient for about 24 hours, as he hoped by then help would arrive, and he was not far out . . .
>
> 'The Siege of Kimberley. By an Essex Woman Who Lived Through It', *Essex County Chronicle*, 23 March 1900, p. 8

173

In her published diary Mrs Rochfort Maguire provided further detail on the scale of the public works programme:

> Mr. Rhodes had also started relief works, by which every able-bodied man willing to work could earn his livelihood. On these works 13,000 men were employed at a cost of £2,000 a week. They were employed largely in road-making, and did an immense amount of useful work in this way for the town; in fact a new quarter has been laid out on high ground at Newton, beyond the hospital, with wide roads and proposed boulevards, and Mr. Rhodes hopes that future extensions of the town will be in this direction. At the meeting of the four roads on top of the hill Mr. Rhodes proposes to erect a monument to those who fell during the siege.
>
> 'Life in Kimberley during the Siege', *The Times Weekly Edition*, 23 March 1900, p. 184

Shelling and Counter-Shelling

174

The shelling of Kimberley had continued after Magersfontein on an intermittent basis and with remarkably little effect. The perceptive Scotsman Willie Campbell reckoned that he knew the answer; in his letter (**160, 162, 165, 167, 170**), he observed that

> Kimberley is built on broad principles. In this country where there are a hundred miles [160 km] between each village, people can afford plenty of space for a town, and it is to this fact that on this occasion Kimberley owes its immunity from destruction. A few shells fell into homes and turned them into riddles – houses here

are built of corrugated iron and a lining of plaster. Several fell into the wide streets or squares, but most dropped into debris heaps and the 'gloors' – stretches of ground where the 'diamondegerous' [*sic*: diamondiferous] soil is exposed to the action of the atmosphere . . . Considering that about 3,000 shells were fired into Kimberley, the amount of damage done was marvellously small.

'The Siege of Kimberley', *Caithness Courier*,
30 March 1900, p. 3

175

In his letter (**7, 159, 161**) W. O. Lunson summed up the frustrations that were probably felt by many residents:

Of course we had a quota of shells every day, but they were small ones, and did comparatively little damage, although narrow escapes were very plentiful, both of life and property . . . Our R.A. guns were 7-pounders, mere pop-guns. We had to take to living in bomb proofs and shelter trenches. I did not have my clothes off for a week.

'The Siege of Kimberley', *Wells Journal*,
12 April 1900, p. 5

176

It was in this context that the appearance of 'Long Cecil' (a gun rifled with a bore of 4.1 inches [100 mm] and capable of firing a 29.8-pound shell over 6,500 yards [5.9 km]) made such an impact. The gun was nicknamed after Cecil Rhodes. Albert Clucas, continuing his letter (**19, 31, 36**), affirmed that 'The big gun that Mr. Labram[7] made here is a beauty. Just think of making a big gun, like that here, and the powder, and shells and all.'[8]

'Experiences of the Kimberley Siege', *Isle of Man Weekly Times*, 31 March 1900, p. 1

---

7 George Labram (1859–1900), the Detroit-born chief engineer of De Beers Company, had contributed to the defence of Kimberley by organizing the construction of the conning tower, searchlights, a telephone system, the emergency fresh-water supply system and a bulk refrigeration plant. The factory also produced munitions, train materials, and 'Long Cecil'. He was killed by a shell from a 'Long Tom'.

8 L. S. Amery agreed: 'The production of this gun must be considered one of the most remarkable events in the history of beleaguered garrisons. It was designed and constructed by engineers who had no previous experience of ordnance manufacture, without special plant or arrangements, upon designs adapted from descriptions found in a stray copy of an engineering journal', Amery, *The Times History*, vol. 4, p. 560.

177

A heliograph message from Kimberley confirmed the christening of 'Long Cecil' on 19 January, and that it shot 'capitally[9] right over the ground separating us from the Boers'.[10] In his letter (**171**) Lieutenant Gordon Grant was hugely impressed with the results:

> De Beers, as you will no doubt have heard, constructed a beauty of a cannon, 26 pounder, in their workshop here, and she fires splendidly. They fired her one day at the Boer laagers about seven miles [11 km] away, and did some beautiful shooting, making the Boers run out like the very deuce, and skedaddle over the veldt.
>
> 'Besieged in Kimberley', *Northern Scot and Moray & Nairn Express*, 31 March 1900, p. 6

Unbeknown to the defenders of Kimberley, the Boer artillery options were on the verge of a major transformation. Cronjé, aware that large British reinforcements were *en route* to the Modder River, requested additional artillery support from the 'Long Tom' gun[11] that was undergoing repairs in Pretoria after being damaged at the siege of Ladysmith. Although this 'Long Tom' was sent to the western theatre, it was originally intended to support the siege operations of General Ignatius Ferreira at Kimberley. A French colonel, de Villebois-Mareuil,[12] who had come to Kimberley from Ladysmith with his compatriot, Sam Léon, deprecated Cronjé's fondness for 'position' warfare and the possibility that the 'Long Tom' would be left in idleness at Magersfontein.[13] He persuaded the Boer war

---

9 By 1 February it had been repaired on three occasions in the De Beers' workshops but it generally fired accurately, see Meyer, *Days of Honour*, pp. 53 and 61.
10 'Kimberley Bombarded. Determined Attack. No Harm Done', *Yorkshire Evening Press*, 25 January 1900, p. 3.
11 This was one of four 155-mm Creusot BL 40-pounder guns possessed by the Boers. With a normal range of 9,880 m/6.1 miles (and a maximum of 11,000 m/6.8 miles), it fired a common shell (43 kg/94 lb) and a shrapnel shell (41 kg/89 lb). It was nicknamed 'Long Tom' by British soldiers in Natal, Changuion, *Silence of the Guns*, pp. 18–19.
12 General Georges Henri Anne-Marie Victor de Villebois-Mareuil (1847–1900) was a French colonel who volunteered to fight with the Boers. Appointed as military advisor to Commandant-General Piet Joubert, he served in Natal and Cape Colony before being killed at Boshof (5 April 1900). His diary, *War Notes* (1902), revealed shrewd comments about the Boer tactics, see R. Macnab, *The French Colonel: Villebois-Mareuil and the Boers, 1899–1900* (Oxford: Oxford University Press, 1975).
13 Georges de Villebois-Mareuil, *War Notes. The Diary of Colonel de Villebois-Mareuil* (London: Adam and Charles Black, 1902), pp. 193 and 207.

council (*Krygsraad*) that the 'Long Tom' gun could be used to induce the surrender of Kimberley.

Convinced that Kimberley was 'at its last extremity', de Villebois-Mareuil had learned from the black workers 'whom the English drive away . . . that the women and children are sometimes trampled under foot during the distribution of food'.[14] By deploying the 'Long Tom' on top of the Kamfersdam Mine dump, near the headquarters of General Sarel Petrus du Toit, the heavy gun could bombard the British field fort at Otto's Kopje on the western perimeter of the town. While the 'Long Tom', in his opinion, could ensure the capture of the fort, the burghers could attack the town from three different directions (namely, from Kamfersdam, Wimbledon Ridge and Alexandersfontein). Once the town fell, some 2,000 Boers and the 'Long Tom' could be released to join Cronjé.[15]

After an indeterminable delay while the 'Long Tom' was brought through the Orange Free State, de Villebois-Mareuil and Léon oversaw the emplacement of the gun at Kamfersdam on the evening of 6 February. On the following day, de Villebois-Mareuil noted in his diary that the 'Long Tom opened fire at eleven o'clock', and, after repairing the gun platform on the morning of 8 February, the bombardment from 'Long Tom' continued each day (other than Sunday 11 February) until the relief arrived on 15 February.[16] To his intense frustration, the Boers kept finding reasons to procrastinate. 'The Boer generals', wrote de Villebois-Mareuil on 8 February, 'who are not endowed with a genius for war, let the opportunity slip. Their prudence caused all sorts of delays.' By 10 February, he recorded that 'They are always having to deliberate with a neighbour, and it is ever the neighbour who refuses to march. I consider, therefore, that my plan is ruined . . .'[17]

178

Nevertheless the shock of the first 'Long Tom' shell, as the Manx lady recalled (**1, 16, 22, 34, 164**), was considerable:

> During the earlier part of February Kimberley was startled one morning by hearing a terrific report, then a whizz through the air, and a crash into some unfortunate building, exploding with a terrible noise. Whatever could it be? . . . We soon found out – one

---

14 Villebois-Mareuil, *War Notes*, p. 176.
15 Ibid. p. 182; Macnab, *French Colonel*, pp. 123–4.
16 Villebois-Mareuil, *War Notes*, pp. 212–25.
17 Ibid. pp. 219–22.

shell after another kept coming, each one sounding worse than the last. Soon people came hurrying along with great big pieces of shells, some weighing 10 and others 12 pounds [4.5/5.4 kg]. Presently someone came along with the startling news that he had seen a whole one which had not burst, and it measured 19½ inches [482.6 mm] in length. Then we realized that the Boers were casting forth 100 pounders, and wherever one burst, it destroyed all before it.

'Horrors of the Siege', *Isle of Man Weekly Times*,
16 June 1900, p. 5

179

The physical and psychological effects were devastating. In his letter (**7, 159, 161, 175**) W. O. Lunson estimated that

The first day's shelling from this monster did more damage than the whole of their small guns put together. If a shell struck a house it would go right through. There were several casualties, all to non-combatants, being mostly poor women and children.

'The Siege of Kimberley', *Wells Journal*,
12 April 1900, p. 5

The Reverend George W. T. Laverack, formerly of Leeds, added that

The bombardment, especially that of the last week or so before relief arrived, by the big 100-pound gun, caused considerable damage to property and some loss of life, while its effects on the nerves of the inhabitants were most serious. As a member of the Beaconsfield Ambulance Corps, I have been out with the defence forces, and experienced what it felt to be under fire.

'The Siege of Kimberley', *Leeds Mercury*,
11 April 1900, p. 6

180

Drummer Ben Nightingale (Loyal North Lancashires) was appalled by the panic that ensued. Once the enemy had their '"Long Tom" gun', he wrote (**11**),

Then the trouble commenced. They started to fire on the town with it about 10 a.m., and kept it up until General French[18] relieved us about

---

18 Field Marshal John Denton Pinkstone French, later first Earl of Ypres (1852–1925), distinguished himself in the South African War by leading the column that

seven or eight days later. It got unbearable. It set a big shoe shop on fire, and killed about five persons. One was the man who made the 28-pounder [see (**183**), below]. The shell came through the roof of the Grand Hotel where this man was staying and knocked his head off. It was pitiable to see a population of about 40,000 women and children running every time they heard this big gun fire.

'Letters from Soldiers at the Front', *Blackburn Times*,
24 March 1900, p. 3

181

In his letter (**7, 24**) A. W. Newsham admitted that

It was the 100 lbs. [shells] that put us to flight. Edward Parsons, one of my acquaintances, was in his bedroom dressing for tea, when a splinter passed through the window, and killed him on the spot. Another chum – Duncan Sinclair, of Greenock – was badly wounded, and is now in hospital.

'A Sheffield Man in Kimberley', *Sheffield Daily Telegraph*,
21 March 1900, p. 5

182

Fortunately the Boers did not use smokeless powder and so an alarm system could be devised. A Beaconsfield resident described how 'Our signal was a red flag waved from the conning tower, and then a bugle was blown, which gave us thirty seconds to take shelter.'

'Letter from the Front', *Southern Guardian*,
31 March 1900, p. 2

183

Yet the death of George Labram from a 'Long Tom' shell on 9 February (**180**) caused widespread dismay in the town, compounded by the Boer shelling of his funeral procession on the following evening. As W. T. Anderson, a prominent Kimberley merchant and town councillor, recalled,

After the death of Labram, the American engineer, maker of 'Long Cecil', whose ability and devotion had secured for him universal

---

relieved Kimberley prior to participating in the subsequent victory at Paardeberg. He had a less successful experience as the first commander-in-chief of the British Expeditionary Force in the First World War, being replaced by Douglas Haig in December 1915.

respect, we did not publish the time fixed for his funeral lest the Boers should hear of it. They had fired on funeral parties before. The time of the funeral, eight o'clock at night, merely passed from lip to lip, and yet about 1,000 mourners assembled, many driving in carriages and others walking on foot. Although every precaution was taken to prevent the Boers knowing anything of the arrangements, the first shell went over the hospital, in the mortuary of which Mr. Labram's body was lying, exactly at eight o'clock. It went right over my head, so that I have every reason to remember the incident. The hospital was about two miles [3.2 km] from the cemetery, and all along the route the Boers kept up a continuous fire, directed at the procession. We went along quietly, no lights being displayed on the carriages and the interment took place in the dark.

'An Aberdeen Gentleman on The Siege of Kimberley', *Aberdeen* (Weekly) *Journal*, 8 May 1900, p. 4

184

'Rockets', explained Mrs Rochfort Maguire in her diary (**173**), had been 'sent up in the town from Boer sympathizers (of whom there were many) to indicate the time and route of the procession'.

'Life in Kimberley during the Siege', *The Times Weekly Edition*, 23 March 1900, p. 184

A hospital nurse recollected how the mourners responded: 'Just as the funeral was leaving the hospital gates a shell fell close by, everyone instinctively lying down flat on the ground so as to avoid the splinters. This was followed by a second shell, when the same performance was gone through. Then the melancholy *cortège* proceeded on its way to the cemetery.'

'Kimberley During The Siege', *Morning Post*, 29 May 1900, p. 5

185

Even those who were not present shared the indignation. As one lady commented in her letter (**15**):

Aren't the Boers demons? Can you imagine anything more wicked, firing on a dead man. The funeral took place at night on account of the enemy shelling us during the day, and then some traitor sent up rockets to let the Boers know what was going on. That was a really terrible night. We sat underground listening for those dreadful shells.

A man was placed on one of the lookouts and as soon as he would see the flash of fire from the mouth of the gun he would blow a bugle, letting us know another shell was coming, and then we would sit still, scarcely daring to breathe, not knowing where the shell would fall; but thank God none came too near us.

'Siege of Kimberley', *Bristol Mercury and Daily Post*, 14 April 1900, p. 6

186

Although Rhodes authorized the construction of splinter-proof shelters,[19] the existing makeshift shelters offered scant protection against a 'Long Tom' shell. In her letter (**17, 33**) Jessie Guild recognized that 'The rabbit holes were no protection against them, and we women and children, through the kindness of the Hon. Cecil Rhodes, had to go down the mines, and we lived there a week, and saw no daylight.'

'Life in Kimberley', *Courier & Argus* (Dundee), 24 March 1900, p. 4

187

Tributes to Rhodes now flowed from grateful residents. In his post-war interview (**5, 10, 21**) Thomas Bennet regarded Rhodes as 'the life and soul of the besieged town', whose care for the safety of the people 'was beyond all praise'. Although he had heard and read many criticisms of Rhodes before the siege, Bennet spoke of the man 'as he found him': 'a generous-hearted, self-sacrificing man, kind to the poor, and a friend to the working man'. Once the 'Long Tom' was bombarding the town, and imperilling the women and children,

> Rhodes provided a safe refuge for them in the mines. At his own expense the underground tunnels, by which the great mines are honeycombed, were prepared for their reception. The roofs of the workings were prepared with wood and the walls with corrugated iron,[20] while partitions were fitted up here and there to divide the underground habitations into different apartments. The electric light was fitted up to illuminate the darkness and ventilation was secured

---

19   'The Siege of Kimberley', *Western Mail*, 15 May 1900, p. 6. Some of these were tunnels driven into the debris heaps, Ashe, *Besieged by the Boers*, pp. 164–5, and 'Life in Kimberley during the Siege', *The Times Weekly Edition*, 23 March 1900, p. 184.
20   In parts perhaps, but not completely: the Manx lady recalled the 'very grimy' walls and the 'damp chilly atmosphere' underground, 'Horrors of the Siege', *Isle of Man Weekly Times*, 16 June 1900, p. 5.

by openings made for that purpose. Clothing and rugs for sleeping on were provided for such as were destitute of these comforts, while cooks were employed to supply tea, coffee, and soup. As the mines were found insufficient to shelter the whole of the women and children Mr. Rhodes employed Kaffirs to excavate tunnels. Mr. Rhodes' generosity was not confined to the inhabitants alone. He was also very kind to the Boer prisoners, though they showed little gratitude to their benefactor.

'In A Besieged City', *Courier & Argus* (Dundee), 24 May 1900, p. 3

188

Willie Campbell, in his second letter (**162, 165, 170**), was just as laudatory. Cecil Rhodes, he wrote,

devoted himself to the townspeople, sent the women and children down the mines, looked after their comforts, even made them little presents of smelling salts and eau de cologne, and palm leaf fans and toilet soap. Never has a man worked harder or more unselfishly, and entirely for others than Cecil Rhodes did then. The hundred pounder, which opened fire ten days before General French's arrival was not only destructive to life and property, but also dismaying and demoralizing. Kimberley was fortunate in having a strong man in Rhodes, to look after its non-combatants – women, children and invalids.

'Part II of the Siege of Kimberley', *Caithness Courier*, 20 April 1900, p. 3

189

Nor were there complaints about Rhodes causing panic and confusion, as O'Meara subsequently alleged.[21] Alpheus F. Williams, son of the mine manager and then involved in the provision of underground facilities, including 'an elaborate water-borne system of latrines . . . a far more sanitary arrangement than existed in any part of Kimberley', and of transferring white women and children down the mines, rebutted criticisms of Rhodes 'from personal knowledge'.[22] So, too, did Mrs Rochfort Maguire in her diary (**173, 184**), where she described how

---

21 O'Meara, *Kekewich in Kimberley*, p. 122.
22 A. F. Williams, *Some Dreams Come True: Being a Sheaf of Stories leading up to the Discovery of Copper, Diamonds and Gold in South Africa, and of the Pioneers who took*

Arrangements were accordingly made, and on Sunday afternoon streams of people could be seen wending their way, some to the De Beers, some to the Kimberley Mine . . . Mr. Rhodes, his friends, and staff worked hard till the middle of the night, by which time, without the slightest confusion or difficulty, 2,600 people had been put down the mines, at depths of from 1,200 ft. to 1,500 ft [365.7–457.2 m]. Everything was done for their comfort by the De Beers staff, who worked with untiring devotion, supplying them with food and everything they wanted. The people themselves looked upon it as a picnic, and were as cheerful as possible, especially when the big gun began to boom again on Monday morning, and they expressed great thankfulness to Mr. Rhodes for having devised this plan for their safety.

'Life in Kimberley during the Siege', *The Times Weekly Edition*, 23 March 1900, p. 184

190

However appreciated, the underground conditions were unpleasant, as Albert Clucas found in his daily visits to see his family. In his letter (**19, 31, 36, 176**) he explained to his parents,

> you cannot imagine what it was to be in a level damp and chilly, with five children, and to look after them, and cook, and clean for the baby. Everything was damp and clammy, the exact extreme of what it was above ground. Well, they were there, with thousands of other people, so had to make the best of a bad bargain . . . I went down every morning at six o'clock to see how they were. We were all very kindly treated, more so as nearly every miner and boss knew me, and were Freemasons. The manager of the De Beers Mines – Gardner Williams – was very kind also. I had long conversations with him while I was at the shaft waiting to go down to see Alice.

'Experiences of Kimberley Siege', *Isle of Man Weekly Times*, 31 March 1900, p. 1

---

part in the Excitement of those Early Days (Cape Town: Howard B. Timmins, 1948), pp. 271–5; see also Roberts, *Kimberley*, pp. 331–2. Dr Ashe confirmed that the mine-heads were crowded as the women and children waited to go underground but there was not a single accident, Ashe, *Besieged by the Boers*, pp. 180–1.

191

James Rochfort Maguire, a former Parnellite MP, and a close friend of Rhodes, reckoned that these arrangements benefited the men as much as the women:

> These measures were taken to comfort the men rather than the women. Fine fellows fighting out on the thirteen-mile radius looked apprehensively at every shell that passed overhead. There was the dread possibility that it might rob them of wife or child. Our brave defenders felt ever so much more comfortable when they knew that their womenfolk and little ones were out of harm's reach. Of course the mines afforded a perfect asylum. After lowering the women and children we sent down their bedding, and at intervals supplied them with food. They were quite happy and comfortable among the diamonds.
>
> 'In Besieged Kimberley', *Daily News* (London), 21 March 1900, p. 3

Final Engagements round Kimberley

While Kimberley endured its 'reign of terror',[23] and Rhodes pressed Kekewich (and then Lord Roberts) to seek the immediate relief of the town – publicizing his views through the *Diamond Fields Advertiser* (10 February 1900) in its infamous editorial, 'Why Kimberley Cannot Wait'[24] – Kekewich resumed his aggressive defence of the town by sending snipers out to harass the Boer gunners.

192

Continuing his letter (**6, 13, 18, 30, 166**), Mayor Oliver described how 'Some of our best shots went out during the night, dug holes about 1,000

---

23 'Part II of the Siege of Kimberley', *Caithness Courier*, 20 April 1900, p. 3.
24 For an account of the row between Kekewich and Rhodes on 9 February and the subsequent editorial, see O'Meara, *Kekewich in Kimberley*, pp. 109–11, Appendix III, pp. 147–50, Green, *An Editor Looks Back*, pp. 82–6, and LIM, Kekewich diary, pp. 282–8. Pakenham claims that the protests of Rhodes, and his implied threat to surrender (never explicitly made) had distorted 'the whole strategy of the war', Pakenham, *Boer War*, p. 327, but Roberts, having briefly considered bypassing Kimberley, changed his mind and resolved to lift the siege before the exchange of telegrams on 9 February, see Roberts to Lord Lansdowne, 29 January and 6 February 1900, in André Wessels (ed), *Lord Roberts and the War in South Africa 1899–1902* (Stroud, Glos.: Sutton Publishing for the Army Records Society, 2000), pp. 45–6 and 48.

yards [914 m] from their big gun, and sniped at them all day. We killed 12 of their gunners in this way, besides peppering them with our seven-pounders and Long Cecil.'

'The Siege of Kimberley', *Derby Mercury*,
4 April 1900, p. 2

'Thank Heaven', wrote R. Hilliard from the Kimberley Club (**20**), that 'we bowled over M. Léon, their head man,[25] who was working the big gun. Our snipers shot him from the brickfields, as he was sighting the gun on top of Kamfersdam Heap.'

'Another Letter from Kimberley', *Essex County Standard*,
24 March 1900, p. 6

193

In another sortie on 14 February, a scouting party from Beaconsfield seized positions at Alexandersfontein that the Boers had largely vacated. In his second letter (**160, 162, 165, 167, 170, 174, 188**) Willie Campbell proclaimed 'But joyful news! Over forty oxen, a score of pigs and goats, and three waggon loads of provisions were captured from the Boers at Alexandersfontein[26] by the Beaconsfield Guardsmen.'

'Part II of the Siege of Kimberley', *Caithness Courier*,
20 April 1900, p. 3

194

A relief force of 300 men, including 'A' and 'H' Companies of the Loyal North Lancashires, was sent out to hold these positions.[27] 'We walked straight into their entrenchments without firing a shot', recalled Private S. Brooks of 'H' Company,

> and sent word to the column that they were retiring. The next morning we were surprised to hear the column firing at them from our front. That meant to say we had got them right in the centre of us, and I can tell you we gave them beans all that day. At night we gave them a chance to run which they did.

'A Warrington Man at the Siege of Kimberley',
Warrington Guardian, 24 March 1900, p. 5

---

25   Confirmed in De Villebois-Mareuil, *War Notes*, p. 225, but Léon survived the wound after a lengthy convalescence, Changuion, *Silence of the Guns*, p. 72.
26   The position included a well-stocked farm, Royal Engineers Museum, Library & Archive (REMLA), Lance-Corporal A. E. Togwell diary, 14 February 1900.
27   Downham, *Red Roses on the Veldt*, p. 67.

195

Private Walter Sutcliffe (Loyal North Lancashires) chose to dwell on the hazards of the operation:

> One day we had to go to a place called Alexandersfontein, about seven miles [11 km] from Kimberley. We were sent out as a scouting party, and had to cross a very dangerous place. The Boers fired three or four volleys at us, but none of us were hurt. We had to hold a position some few hundred yards to the front, and whilst we were making a cover or trench for ourselves, hundreds of bullets passed over our heads, and any amount of shells . . . We had only about 250 men against a tremendous number of Boers, who were hid behind the hills. However we kept up a heavy fire all day.
>
> 'With the North Lancashires at Kimberley',
> *Lancashire Daily Post*, 19 March 1900, p. 4

Chapter 5

Kimberley Relieved: Cronjé Surrenders

Planning the Relief of Kimberley

On his journey to Cape Town Lord Roberts, the new commander-in-chief, and his staff devised a major shift in British strategy by moving the centre of gravity of the British advance to the Kimberley front. The aim was to out-manoeuvre Cronjé's forces, relieve Kimberley, and press on to Bloemfontein, thereby easing some of the pressure on Buller's front in Natal.[1] Although Roberts would modify his plan once in theatre, he persevered with his belief that he should concentrate his forces in the west. In light of a message from Kekewich[2] (compounded subsequently by news of the rift with Rhodes), he sought to relieve Kimberley as quickly as possible. For this task he called upon the services of Major-General John D. P. French, a cavalry commander, who had already conducted energetic operations in the Colesberg region, protecting the Midland railway and covering the exposed flanks of Methuen and Gatacre after their defeats at Magersfontein and Stormberg respectively.[3] Summoned to Cape Town on 29 January, French learned of Roberts's concern about the expenditure of horses and ammunition around Colesberg, and of his plan to concentrate his army (at least 49,500 men and 110 guns) behind Methuen's position on the Modder River while Major-General Ralph A. P. Clements with a mixed force held the Colesberg area. Roberts then planned to outflank General Cronjé, enabling French with a mounted division to dash for Kimberley, whereupon the rest of the force would

---

1   Wessels, *Lord Roberts*, p. 30.
2   Roberts to Lord Lansdowne, 6 February 1900, in Wessels, *Lord Roberts*, p. 48.
3   R. Holmes, *The Little Field Marshal: A Life of Sir John French* (London: Jonathan Cape, 1981), p. 80.

move eastwards towards Bloemfontein, the capital of the Orange Free State, outflanking Cronjé's army.

Although French never received the entire 8,500 horsemen promised by 11 February, he would command the largest mounted division that the British army had ever assembled.[4] It included three cavalry brigades, two brigades of mounted infantry (MI) and seven batteries of Royal Horse Artillery (RHA) with forty-two 12-pounder guns. The plan was to conceal the operation by moving 22 miles (35.4 km) south to Ramdam on 11 February, where the mounted infantry at Belmont and other units in the neighbourhood of the Orange River station could join French's column, then strike east to the crossings of the Riet River, and wait for the infantry to arrive. Thereafter the cavalry would advance north over 25 waterless miles (40 km) to the Modder River drifts east of Magersfontein and again wait for the infantry, before dashing over the remaining 20 miles (32 km) north-west to Kimberley. Pressed by Kitchener, the new chief of staff, to 'relieve Kimberley at all costs', French promised to relieve Kimberley 'at six on the evening of the 15th if I am alive'.[5]

In assembling these forces south of the Modder River, which included raising large bodies of Roberts's Horse in Cape Colony,[6] Lord Roberts benefited immensely from the passivity of the Boers under Cronjé and the demoralizing idleness of the forces besieging Kimberley. De la Rey and Christiaan de Wet, then in command of the Free State burghers at Magersfontein, asked if they could take 1,500 men and advance in the direction of Hopetown and De Aar, with a view to breaking Methuen's line of communications but Cronjé adamantly refused unless the Free State government compensated him with another 1,500 men. 'There was no moving him', recalled de Wet, 'Thus our plan came to nothing.' Even worse, there was nothing to do and, in his daily inspections along the line of entrenchments, stretching over fifteen miles (24 km), all de Wet

---

4 The exact size of the division remains a matter of dispute, with estimates ranging from about 4,000 or 5,000 men to nearly 8,000, see Holmes, *The Little Field Marshal*, p. 87; Anglesey, *British Cavalry*, vol. 4, p. 127; and S. Badsey, 'The Boer War (1899–1902) and British Cavalry Doctrine: A Re-Evaluation', *Journal of Military History*, vol. 71 (2006), pp. 75–97, at p. 90.
5 C. S. Goldmann, *With General French and the Cavalry in South Africa* (London: Macmillan, 1902), pp. 72–4 and 85.
6 A policy that infuriated Lieutenant-Colonel Douglas Haig: 'The Colonial Corps raised in Cape Colony are quite useless, so are the recently raised Mounted Infantry. They can't ride and know nothing about their duties as mounted men. Roberts's Horse & Kitchener's Horse are good only for looting and the greater part of them disappear the moment a shot is fired', National Library of Scotland [NLS], Haig Mss., Ms. 28003, Haig to Henrietta, 16 March 1900.

had to listen to were 'constant complaints'.⁷ Just as the Boers had failed to exploit their early successes in Natal, the lack of forceful action in Cape Colony left them demoralized and exposed to assault from the vast imperial forces that were now assembling, as well as the more imaginative tactics that the British were about to unleash.⁸

Relief Mission

196

French commanded a mixed force, including three cavalry brigades under Brigadier-Generals Thomas C. Porter, Robert G. Broadwood and James R. P. Gordon, and two MI brigades under Colonels Ormelie C. Hannay and Charles P. Ridley. Serving in these units were both veterans from the Colesberg operations and men who had just arrived in Cape Colony. 'R' Battery of the Royal Horse Artillery had been blooded at Colesberg, from where Private Sidney White wrote to his brother:

> Several of our horses were killed, some with their legs blown off, but when we had finished we came out of action with only two men slightly wounded. The General formed us up and told us we were lucky to come out alive and gave us great praise for our coolness and good work in action. I am in General French's column. I am getting quite used to bullets and shells now . . .
> 'Another Ryder at the Front', *Isle of Wight Observer*,
> 24 February 1900, p. 2

197

Conversely, Harold C. Ingram, son of Colonel Ingram, Penarth, enrolled as a trooper in Roberts's Horse, 'then between 400 and 500 strong', only a day after his arrival at Cape Town on 23 January, 1900. He recalled that

> A large proportion of the horses had not been broken to the saddle, and the men had to train them.⁹ In spite of this, the regiment was

---

7 C. R. de Wet, *Three Years War (October 1899–June 1902)* (London: Archibald Constable, 1903), pp. 36–7.
8 Wessels, *Lord Roberts*, p. 29.
9 Despite the fact that the dash to Kimberley took place over flat veld – ideal cavalry country (apart from the lack of water) – the horses were not in good condition: some were suffering from overwork in the Colesberg area, while others were barely acclimatized, Anglesey, *British Cavalry*, vol. 4, p. 127.

able to proceed to Orange River in a couple of days. Here they had to go through some stiff training, and on Monday, the 5th of February, they commenced the march which eventually brought them, after numerous hardships, to Kimberley.[10]

'The Relief of Kimberley. Penarth Trooper's Experience. Interview with Mr. H. C. Ingram', *Western Mail*, 19 April 1900, p. 6

198

A trooper of the Royal Scots Greys remembered that, before leaving the Modder River,

> the order went forth that the carrying weight of the horses was to be made as light as possible. The outcome of that order was . . . that we left camp in the clothing we stood up in, each man carrying 300 rounds of ammunition, 50 of which were in our bandoliers and 50 in our haversacks, with 6 lbs. of oats in wallets as forage for our horses.

'What the Scots Greys have been doing', *Edinburgh Evening News*, 12 April 1900, p. 4

199

E. Hill of 'U' Battery, RHA, described how the cavalry and mounted artillery 'left Modder at 1.30 in the morning, leaving our camp standing,[11] and marched back towards Belmont again. We did a 33-mile journey the first day . . .'[12]

'Letters From The Front', *Somerset Standard*, 12 April 1900, p. 6

200

The journey to Ramdam, wrote Captain Cecil W. M. Feilden (Scots Greys), was

> frightfully hot and dusty. Owing to our convoy being with us we did not reach our destination till 7 p.m., just in time to make ourselves as comfortable as we could till 2 o'clock the following morning, when the whole cavalry division started off again for the Rut [*sic*: Riet]

---

10 Ingram was one of the unlucky ones, being shot in the shoulder on the final charge into Kimberley. He had to lie under a bush for three hours until the firing ceased and he could be brought into Kimberley for medical treatment.
11 This was part of the deception strategy to conceal the movement of the column, Anglesey, *British Cavalry*, vol. 4, p. 128.
12 The mileage is exaggerated by about 50 per cent.

River. I happened to be with the advanced squadron, so we had a capital view of the whole day's fighting. Our first view of the Boers was a long straggling line of about 250 horsemen, just as it was becoming light, and they really had a certain amount of cavalry formation about them, so that at first in the dim light we thought that they were part of another brigade, but very soon a few bullets and a shell or two convinced us otherwise. We had a good view of the whole battle, and it really looked very much like an Aldershot field-day. We finished the day by driving the Boers[13] over the river and encamping on the far side ourselves for the night. The next day we pushed on to Modder River and crossed at Klip Drift, a point some 25 miles [40 km] east of the original Modder Camp that we had left. Here we surprised and took a Boer laager and a good deal of loot of sorts, but nothing really worth having, principally food, biscuits, etc, carts, and all kinds of clothing, generally old and shabby, but all very clean, and a good quantity of ammunition. We remained here one day . . .

'In Pursuit of Cronje', *Weekly Standard and Express* (Blackburn), 21 April 1900, p. 6

201

As Hill (**199**) recollected,

this being the first time English troops had marched in the enemy's country. We had not gone far before the Boers opened fire on our cavalry, but our guns soon drove them out. The next day we came on their camp by surprise, and sent half-a-dozen shells amongst them, captured their convoy and several prisoners. We then had a day's rest, as men and horses were almost done up. Fifteen horses fell dead, and seven men were shot. We lost no men in the Artillery during the three days; but our day was to come.

'Letters From The Front', *Somerset Standard*, 12 April 1900, p. 6

---

13 General Pieter (Piet) Daniel de Wet (1861–1929), the younger brother of Christiaan de Wet, commanded this small body of Boers trying to block the first incursion into the Orange Free State. Although he would win a famous victory at Lindley (31 May 1900), Piet de Wet surrendered at Kroonstad (26 July 1900) and later served with the British forces, becoming despised by the *bitterenders* for the rest of his life.

202

Gunner H. Hubbard confirmed that as we 'moved in an easterly direction into the Free State',

> Here an incident happened that I shall never forget. Our colonel was riding with General French, and we orderlies in the rear, when a Boer gun opened fire on us, the shell passing just over our heads . . . We at once sought shelter behind a small kopje, but they must have had the range of us well, for a shrapnel shell burst over us, the bullets dropping between the horses' legs yet not harming one of us[14] . . . Our guns and cavalry in the meantime came up, and opened fire on the Boers. This proved a bit too warm for them, for they skedaddled across the plain to the Riet River where a hot fight took place, which ended in the full retreat of the Boers, taking their dead with them. Our casualties were light. The next day was a very trying one, marching on to the Modder River. We had not gone many miles when we were fired on, but we fought our way through.[15] We lost about 100 horses with fatigue or thirst. On arriving at the Modder another fight took place, our batteries shelling the enemy in splendid form.[16] They retired and we had a fine capture, for they had no time to take their laager with them, in which we found loads of flour, clothing, etc. etc. We were very grateful for the flour, as we were on half rations – 2½ lbs. of biscuit ½ lb. of meat per day. We also captured hundreds of heads of cattle, sheep and goats. We made fine gippaties with the flour – they were a treat after hard, dry biscuit . . .
>
> 'Our County's Share in the War', *Somerset County Gazette*, 28 April 1900, p. 3

---

14 See also Goldmann, *With General French*, p. 76. French had used his superior numbers to make feints at various crossings before getting across at De Kiel's Drift.

15 The mounted column left its baggage at Ramdam until the crossings were secured, but the bullock transport then became mixed up with the transport of the following 7th Infantry Division. French, nonetheless, advanced without his transport wagons northwards in line of brigades covering a front of five miles (8 km), with the right flank encountering the first Boer resistance. Anglesey, *British Cavalry*, vol. 4, pp. 129–31.

16 Although Haig emphasizes that the cavalry reached the Modder first, NLS, Haig Mss., Acc. 3155/34, Cavalry Division, Diary and Orders, vol. 1, November 8th 1899 to 13th March 1900, p. 160, Major Allason's battery was soon in action, as letters **200** and **201** confirm, Goldmann, *With General French*, p. 80.

203

Trooper T. Simpson (Inniskilling Dragoons) reckoned that the loss of horseflesh had been heavier as

> this march was the worst I ever experienced, being on the road from seven one evening until seven the following evening, crossing about 27 miles [43.5 km] of veldt without water, and about 20 miles [32 km] of that in a burning heat. We lost about 160 horses from exhaustion, not having any water all that time.
>
> 'An Auckland Man's Letter', *Northern Echo* (Darlington), 21 March 1900, p. 4

204

On the fateful 15 February, the whole mounted column began its final advance from Klip Drift without knowing the strength of the enemy ahead of them. 'We heard all sorts of numbers given from two to ten thousand', wrote Captain Feilden (**200**), but

> On Thursday the 15th, we started off early for Kimberley carrying our forage with us on our horses (they were getting only 6 lbs. of oats per horse per diem). Soon after starting we thought we were in for a hard day, as our brigade (the 1st) was in 'mass,' two batteries being in action, one in front of us, and one on our left, and the shells soon began falling pretty thickly into the guns and limbers. [T]he Boers shot so well that nearly every shot fell amongst the guns and only odd ones came near us, we had only one man hit, but the gunners had thirty casualties in the first twenty minutes. However, after this our artillery got the range and very soon silenced the Boer guns. From here to Kimberley we got on very quickly . . .
>
> 'In Pursuit of Cronje', *Weekly Standard and Express* (Blackburn), 21 April 1900, p. 6

205

The horse artillery bore the brunt of the casualties. As Private Hill (**199** and **201**) recalled, once the 3rd Brigade (King's Dragoon Guards and the 9th and 12th Lancers), leading the advance, came under fire,

> we came into action at the place where the shells were bursting. For three quarters of an hour we stood there, bullets flying all around us, and if their shells had only burst five yards further up every man would have been hit. As it was we lost one officer and two men killed,

and eight wounded, but eighteen more were hit with spent bullets. Thirty horses were killed in our battery alone. Mine was shot and the fellow holding it wounded.

'Letters From The Front', *Somerset Standard*, 12 April 1900, p. 6

206

As the artillery galloped 'splendidly and steadily into action at a range of about 2,000 yards [1,800 m]', one Scots Grey (**198**) described how

> the order was given for A (Major Middleton's) Squadron of ours[17] to take a kopje on the right, but before our objective was reached a smart and dashing gallop of nearly a mile and a half [2.4 km] over open plain had to be covered, nearly the last 1000 yards [900 m] of which were ridden under a heavy rifle fire from the Boers. Dismounting, we opened a steady fire on the defenders of the kopje, which continued for two hours, and eventually forced the Boers to retreat . . . Luckily for us, this engagement under the trying and exposed circumstances was, so far as I observed, attended with only one casualty, that of a man of ours having his jaw shattered by an explosive bullet.[18]

'What The Scots Greys Have Been Doing', *Edinburgh Evening News*, 12 April 1900, p. 4

207

Upon entering an amphitheatre about two and a half miles (4 km) wide, French launched his column in an extended-order 'charge' (with from five to eight yards between the files), covered by the fire from the horse artillery batteries under escort from the mounted infantry. Captain Francis Egerton-Green (12th Lancers) recalled how

> We crossed a plain under a cross fire of guns and rifles on our way to Kimberley. It was a glorious sight; a sort of Balaclava with the whole Cavalry Division. It took about seven minutes . . . The Boers funk the 'Lance' or what they call 'the pointed stick,' and generally give us plenty of room.

'Another Letter from Captain F. Egerton-Green', *Essex County Standard*, 24 March 1900, p. 5

---

17 Some Inniskilling Dragoons were also engaged in this dismounted action.
18 More commonly known as a Dum Dum bullet; allegations of their use were a source of controversy and recrimination during the war.

208

The 3rd Brigade, including the 9th and 16th Lancers, had led the charge and, as Trooper H. Duffield ('D' Squadron, 16th Lancers) commented,

> It was on that relief that I experienced my first charge, and I tell you it was a bit hot, but we managed to get out of it all right, with the loss of one officer and one private killed and nine wounded.[19] When we got near Kimberley the Boers fired about four shells into us, but as soon as our artillery came into action they cleared off.
>
> 'Letters From The Front', *Jackson's Oxford Journal*, 26 May 1900, p. 3

209

While engaging the Boer artillery, where 'we lost several men, one whole gun team being hit from a bursting shell', Gunner Hubbard (**202**) observed that 'The 16th Lancers made a charge on a party of Boers, and on the left flank I saw a Lancer put his lance through a Boer, breaking it off as the horse dashed forward.'

'Our County's Share in the War', *Somerset County Gazette*, 28 April 1900, p. 3

210

Corporal Callendar, who had served under French in the Colesberg region, reassured his parents that

> We succeeded in relieving Kimberley with very slight losses, although I don't know how we managed to swing clear, nor nobody else. We had to ride to a valley two miles [3.2 km] long, which was filled on all sides with Boers who fired on us all the time with both rifle and big guns. I can tell you it was a ride for life or death, when we got through this particular valley, we had it much easier and drove the Boers back. When the enemy saw us nearing Kimberley, they got out of their trenches, dropped their heads and ran for dear life.
>
> 'An Auckland Man at the Front', *Auckland Times and Herald*, 30 March 1900, p. 5

---

19 This may be a conflation of casualty numbers for the relief as a whole; some reports record a mere twelve casualties for the charge, Anglesey, *British Cavalry*, vol. 4, p. 135. The casualties of the 9th Lancers were only one dead and two wounded in the charge, Colvin and Gordon, *Diary of the 9th (Q.R.) Lancers*, p. 68.

211

John Mackenzie, who was among the civilians supporting the Loyal North Lancashires after they had seized Alexandersfontein, some seven miles (11 km) south-east of the town, was one of the first to see the relief column. He reckoned that it was about three o'clock in the afternoon, when

> a large body of horsemen was seen away in the distance tearing across the long sloping plain that stretches towards Jacobsdal. At first we thought it was Boers, and that it was all up with us, but when they came nearer we could see it was regiments of cavalry in echelon formation riding to us – the long-looked for column. The Boers evidently saw them, too, for all of a sudden the firing ceased, and they crawled like snakes on the ground and scooted for all they were worth . . . As for us, we got on the highest stones we could see, and cheered again and again. To have stood on the same place only a short ten minutes before must have meant certain death.

'A Birnie "Loon" in Kimberley', *Northern Scot and Moray & Nairn Express*, 7 April 1900, p. 8

212

Captain Feilden (**200**, **204**) described how 'Just before arriving we shelled a small laager outside of the town; but after a few shells at our line of scouts the whole laager beat a hurried retreat. We were all very tired, as the heat was dreadful: the horses had not had food or water all day.'

'In Pursuit of Cronje', *Weekly Standard and Express* (Blackburn), 21 April 1900, p. 6

213

Yet it was a splendid reception in Kimberley: 'Everyone shaking hands with you. They nearly went mad with joy', claimed Trooper G. Fitches (6th Dragoon Guards).

'Letters from Bury Men at the Front', *Bury and Norwich Post, and Suffolk Standard*, 3 April 1900, p. 8

'The enthusiasm with which they received us was tremendous. The men were cheering, and crying too, to say nothing of the women, as we burst victoriously through. It was grand!' recalled Trooper Arthur J. Wardill (6th Dragoon Guards).

'War Letters', *Sheffield and Rotherham Independent*, 28 April 1900, p. 7

Corporal Callendar (**210**) was another early arrival, who saw 'people shouting and jumping for joy. After being shut up for four months, it was like coming out of prison they said. They nearly pulled us off our horses when they got to us, and they said they had been long looking for us. I never saw such a sight . . .'

'An Auckland Man at the Front', *Auckland Times and Herald*, 30 March 1900, p. 5

214

While French on his arrival was lavishly entertained by Rhodes in the Sanatorium Hotel with champagne and other delicacies preserved for this occasion,[20] one of his divisional staff sergeants enjoyed a very different repast after 'a very hard week'. On arrival in Kimberley, he wrote, 'I was so tired I just fell off on the sand and went to sleep. I afterwards had supper at the sergeants' mess of the Cape Police, and though it consisted only of fresh bread, horse soup, and stewed mule and Indian corn, I never enjoyed a meal like it in my life . . .'

'Letters from Barnsley Soldiers', *Barnsley Chronicle*, 14 April 1900, p. 6

215

Impressions of Kimberley and the state of its citizens varied widely. Some shared the opinions of Haig and a Rimington scout[21] that neither the town nor some of its townsfolk had suffered too severely from the siege, with Captain Feilden claiming (**200, 204, 212**) that 'the inhabitants . . . did not look nearly in such a starved condition as we had expected'.[22]

'In Pursuit of Cronje', *Weekly Standard and Express* (Blackburn), 21 April 1900, p. 6

---

20   Described as a 'master stroke of tactics on Rhodes' part', Green, *An Editor Looks Back*, p. 87, this was the occasion when Rhodes briefed French against Kekewich. A tense interview between French and Kekewich followed, with the latter removed from his command two days later. Gardner, *The Lion's Cage*, pp. 182–3; Holmes, *The Little Field Marshal*, p. 93.
21   NLS, Haig Mss., Acc. 3155/334(e), Haig to unidentified colonel, 2 March 1900; Phillipps, *With Rimington*, pp. 63 and 71.
22   A correspondent who accompanied French to the Sanatorium for a dinner of 'soup, horse, chicken, sweet, and champagne' reported that 'They all looked well enough, and we learned there was actual food enough for some weeks; though they were reduced to horse-flesh', 'The March on Kimberley', *The Times*, 6 April 1900, p. 13.

Conversely many troopers, who were not so lavishly entertained, reported on the sufferings that the besieged had endured. 'We were only just in time' claimed Private J. Upstone ('C' Squadron, 12th Lancers), 'as the people in Kimberley were half starved.'

'Bad Time for the Troops', Jackson's Oxford Journal,
26 May, 1900, p. 3

'The people', wrote Gunner Hubbard (**202, 209**), 'were almost starving, they had been living on horseflesh and rough meal.'

'Our County's Share in the War', Somerset Standard,
28 April 1900, p. 3

Trooper Simpson of the Inniskilling Dragoons (**203**), another of the advanced scouts, explained the ecstatic reception – one that 'beat all I ever saw' – by virtue of the fact the local citizens had had

> a very bad time here for four months, shut off from everybody, and the Boers dropping 100 lb. shells into the town, killing women and children. They used to sleep in the mines and the forts made for the purpose. They had not had any meat but horse meat since Christmas, so they were indeed glad to receive our relief column.

'An Auckland Man's Letter', Northern Echo (Darlington),
21 March 1900, p. 4

216

Adam Henry, a telegraph engineer in Kimberley, endorsed these sentiments. He described how he had lived on two meals a day since the New Year: 'the rations', he reckoned, had been '6 ounces Indian meal for porridge; 10¼ ounces of bread, 2 ounces horse beef; so you know how fat we are . . . I am, well, about as thick as a walking stick.'

'A Harris Academy Boy in Kimberley', Courier & Argus (Dundee),
21 March 1900, p. 3

The widow of Troop Sergeant-Major Macdonald (Diamond Fields Horse), who would be killed in the Dronfield engagement on 16 February, added that:

> I have not yet recovered from the effects of the awful siege, and I have not been able to do much. Our nerves were completely shattered by the severe strain consequent on the long bombardment, and the effect upon the system of protracted scarcity of food cannot be readily

shaken off. I spent three days with the children in a culvert (for carrying the water away after rain) during the 100 lb. gun shelling.[23] Thereafter we were ordered down the mine, and I, with the children, was 1500 feet [460 m] underground from February 11th till the 15th.

'The Death of a Peterhead Trooper. Pathetic Letter from a Soldier's Widow', *Aberdeen* (Weekly) *Journal*, 17 May 1900, p. 5

217

The soldiers, though, were all too aware of the price paid in horseflesh for the relief of Kimberley. Trooper Jenner (Inniskilling Dragoons) asserted that 'it was hard for the men and horses. We lost a lot of horses from exhaustion; they were dropping down every 100 yards [90 m].'

'With General French. A Perthshire Trooper's Experiences', *Strathearn Herald*, 21 April, 1900, p. 3

And Private Frank James (Loyal North Lancashires), one of the Kimberley garrison, described how

Men and horses were fairly done up. Some of the men could not speak, but only make motions with their hands to their mouths for a drink of water. Some of the men consumed two bottles of water, so done up with fatigue were they. Their horses were almost dead. It is a mystery how the poor animals pulled the guns and carried the men.

'Letters From Kimberley', *Essex County Chronicle*, 23 March 1900, p. 3

Reflections on the Charge

For contemporaries, the relief of Kimberley was one of the epic events of the war: as the official historian affirmed, 'It was the most brilliant stroke of the whole war.'[24] By contrast Pakenham, who criticized Rhodes for implicitly threatening Kimberley's imminent surrender, denounced the 'Klip Drift Charge as a quite unnecessary dash to self-destruction across the veld'.[25] However, the fact that Kimberley could have held out longer was beside the point: Roberts had resolved to relieve Kimberley

---

23 Even Kekewich admitted that the shelling from the 'Long Tom' impeded the daily drawing of rations as 'people really preferred to stop in their bomb-proof shelters'. Evidence before the Elgin Commission (Q. 21,906), vol. 2, p. 563.
24 Maurice, *War in South Africa*, vol. 2, p. 36.
25 Pakenham, *Boer War*, p. 327.

before the protestations of Rhodes were known, and French certainly did not know that the dash was unnecessary. He had his orders and followed them in a way that displayed all the qualities of the cavalry in mounted, dismounted, and combined-arms actions. He had also relieved Kimberley on the day that he forecast.[26]

While this exploit undoubtedly vindicated the notion of 'cavalry spirit', and would be upheld as such by cavalry theorists after the war,[27] it was not a cavalry charge in the sense of a shock assault by mounted troops in massed knee-to-knee formation with the *arme blanche* (that is, steel weapons in the form of lance or sword). The 9th and 16th Lancers, leading the charge with gaps of five yards (4.6 m), possibly killed and captured 15–20 Boers but, as the *Times History* observed, this was neither a sudden charge upon an enemy already engaged nor upon troops retiring from the field (as at Elandslaagte on 21 October 1899): in brief, 'It was no instance of shock tactics, for there was nothing opposed to it on which shock could take effect.'[28] The Boer fire proved 'ineffective', added the *Times History*, producing a minimal number of casualties even among the advanced units[29] because of the speed of the charge, the open-order formation, the massive cloud of dust raised by the galloping horses, and the supporting fire of the horse artillery in the rear.[30]

218

Nevertheless, Sergeant Harry Butler (12th Lancers) reflected the widespread elation at the relief. This 'great success', he wrote,

> shows what a division of cavalry is capable of doing when worked by such a brilliant general as French. On our third or fourth day's fight we were in a pretty tight corner, getting shelled very heavily, and the kopjes on the right were lined with Boers. We were beginning to think our march was to receive the first serious check, but French ordered the Division to trot, and then to gallop, and, by Jove it was

---

26 Anglesey, *British Cavalry*, vol. 4, p. 136; S. Badsey, *Doctrine and Reform in the British Cavalry 1880–1918* (Aldershot: Ashgate, 2008), pp. 102–3.
27 Goldmann, *With General French*, pp. 410–11.
28 Amery, *Times History*, vol. 3, p. 395; see also NLS, Haig Mss., Acc. 3155/34, Cavalry Division Diary, p. 190; Anglesey, *British Cavalry*, vol. 4, pp. 135–6; and Holmes, *Little Field Marshal*, p. 92.
29 One dead and two wounded in the 9th Lancers; four killed and six wounded in the Scots Greys; and possibly 20 dead overall; see Colvin and Gordon, *Diary of the 9th (Q.R.) Lancers*, p. 68; 'War Letters', *Cheltenham Chronicle*, 14 April 1900, p. 4; Badsey, *Doctrine and Reform*, p. 103.
30 Amery, *Times History*, vol. 3, p. 394.

glorious. The Boers went like 'old Harry' before us, and only the 1st Brigade had a chance at them . . . French deserves all sort of praise. He specially mentioned our regiment for crossing the river in such a gallant way and capturing their laager.

'Letters From The Front. With French to Kimberley',
Lancashire Daily Post, 30 March 1900, p. 4

219

Private W. S. Redgrave (6th Dragoon Guards) agreed: 'I have been with General French all the time I have been out here', he noted, 'and he is a very good general, and very cool in his head. Our regiment has only had about four killed and eleven wounded, and we have been under fire as much as any cavalry regiment out here.'

'More Interesting Letters from the Front',
Kentish Mercury, 20 April 1900, p. 3

220

However tired they were on reaching Kimberley, men and horses were pressed into service early next morning, with critics of Rhodes condemning the offer of a £1,000 reward to the cavalry division if it could capture the 'Long Tom' gun.[31] While the offer has been deprecated for compounding the exhaustion of the horses, Kekewich had already tried and failed to seize the gun at Kamfersdam, and Roberts had also sent a telegram to French, stating that 'It would be a glorious finish if you can get the 6-inch gun . . . and if you could also catch Cronje.'[32] As the Boers had moved the 'Long Tom' during the night, the next day would be spent harrying a rearguard of about 200 burghers under General du Toit.[33] As Corporal V. Sivell (14th Hussars) recalled,

> on the following morning (4 a.m., Friday) we moved off again, my squadron going on in advance. We were attached to the 6th Dragoon Guards (Carabineers). So when we got a few miles away we came in contact again. We had another battle. It was a hard fight. Seventeen

---

31 Gardner, *Lion's Cage*, p. 183; Pakenham, *Boer War*, pp. 328–9.
32 Printed in Maurice, *War in South Africa*, vol. 2, p. 88. This contradicts Gardner's claim that Roberts could hardly 'spare his Cavalry Division for such purposes', Gardner, *Lion's Cage*, p. 183.
33 Somewhat fewer than the 2,000 Boers claimed in early British accounts of the battle, but they were well positioned on the rising ground east of the railway and, in a rearguard action, the Boers were at their most formidable. Compare Goldmann, *With General French*, p. 87, with Changuion, *Silence of the Guns*, pp. 78–9.

hours I was in the saddle. I was out on patrol with two men when we came across the Boers. Retiring they chased us, and then fired at us off their horses, but never hit us. We were only 150 yards [137.2 m] away. They were bad shots, but we drove them off. There were several wounded. Sergeant-Major Ayres, of my squadron, was shot in the thigh; one man shot through the helmet. That was all of ours. We have been lucky.

'The Relief of Kimberley', *Manchester Evening News*,
21 March 1900, p. 5

221

The defenders of Kimberley had readily joined in the pursuit of the enemy. Mayor Oliver (**6, 13, 18, 30, 166, 192**), who had welcomed French and his column 'at the barricade' on the previous day, now relished the opportunity of going out 'on horseback with them, when they attacked the Dutch. It was rather exciting being on the battlefield. I was in the saddle for ten hours.'

'The Siege of Kimberley', *Derby Mercury*,
4 April 1900, p. 2

Lieutenant W. Gordon Grant (**171, 177**), who had seen the Boer guns limbering up while the relief column arrived, fought alongside the cavalry, Queensland MI,[34] New Zealanders and horse artillery. The Kenilworth Defence Force sought to

clear the Dronfield Kopje where the Boers used to shell our fort from, and the fight lasted the whole day, and we had three soldiers killed. We found six dead Boers, and took some 30 prisoners . . . [and later, after finding two subalterns of the Scots Greys shot in their legs, he and Lieutenant Lawson, another Scots Grey] went out under the cover of darkness and brought them some six miles [10 km] into safety.[35]

'Besieged in Kimberley', *Northern Scot & Moray and
Nairn Express*, 24 March 1900, p. 6

---

34 Captain Harry Chauvel (Queensland MI) described it as 'a pretty hard day's fighting', R. L. Wallace, *The Australians at the Boer War* (Canberra: The Australian War Memorial and the Australian Government Publishing Service, 1976), p. 122.
35 The two subalterns were Lieutenant William Bunbury (1880–1900), heir of Lord Rathdonnell, who would die from wounds to both legs, and Lieutenant R. D. Fordyce from Aberdeenshire.

222

Private Alexander Groundwater (Scots Greys) confirmed that this engagement had proved utterly exhausting, especially without ambulances to bring back the wounded:

> We never had a drop of water that day from the time we started until 11 o'clock at night, and the horses were worse off than we were for they never had a drop from the night before, and what made it worse that day was that we had to carry two wounded officers about five miles [8 km] . . . when we got to the De Beers mines some Kimberley boys volunteered to carry them in, and we got some water at their troughs, my horse got down on her knees to it, so you may guess what they were like . . . The Kimberley people were very kind to us while we were there, they sent down bread, and Rhodes got soup made and sent down to us through the day. The fellows that were left behind with done up horses got woollen rugs given to each of them that would cost a good bit to buy at home.

'Letters from a Wells Man from the Front',
Wells Journal, 26 April 1900, p. 5

223

Casualties mounted at Dronfield among the regular and colonial troops engaged. Private W. Price (9th Lancers),[36] who had served in every battle in this theatre since Belmont, and had had one horse shot dead at Graspan and another wounded in the neck riding past Alexandersfontein, gained 'the satisfaction of killing one Boer with my lance while charging at Dronfield. You know we are such large targets for the devils, and they throw showers of bullets into us, and sometimes we can't even see a man of them.'

'A Steeple Bumpstead Man in Eight Engagements',
Essex County Standard, 5 May 1900, p. 7

224

After being down a mine for four days (**216**), Mrs Macdonald recalled that 'My dear husband came down to see us on the morning of the 15th, and that was the last time I ever saw him until next day in the mortuary.

---

36 The 9th Lancers lost 1 officer killed and 9 officers and men wounded. They also had another 40 horses either killed or died of exhaustion. By 17 February the 9th Lancers had only 105 fit horses out of the 422 it had in service on leaving the Modder River, Colvin and Gordon, *Diary of the 9th (Q.R.) Lancers*, p. 70.

It was a terrible experience, the end of the siege being to me more awful than all the horrors of the bombardment by which it was preceded.'

'The Death of a Peterhead Trooper. Pathetic Letter from a Soldier's Widow', *Aberdeen* (Weekly) *Journal*, 17 May 1900, p. 5

Reactions in Kimberley

225

However harrowing, Mrs Macdonald's reactions were rare as the citizens of Kimberley revelled in their deliverance. Sergeant Harry Haygarth (Kimberley Rifle Volunteers), a master tailor, wrote back to his father in Keighley, Yorkshire:

> I suppose there would be great rejoicings at home when the news reached you that General French's flying column had relieved us. I had the honour of presenting arms to him on his arrival. It was a splendid sight, I can assure you, and he came just at the right time. The Boers' 6 in. gun . . . was driving the women and children crazy . . . All business places were closed up, and the streets deserted, but I was down at the shop nearly every day, and I seemed to be dodging the shells all the way down, but fortune seemed to favour me, as I have come off without a scratch. The Boers round Kimberley seemed to be panic-stricken when they knew General French had arrived, and they cleared for their lives.

'Letters on the War', *Bradford Observer*, 20 March 1900, p. 5

226

Even after Magersfontein, wrote Willie Campbell (Town Guard), 'we were determined . . . to keep the Dutch out of Kimberley':

> I have not slept on a bed since the 5th day of October. For weeks we slept in the trenches with our rifles as pillows and the sky overhead, watching and waiting for an enemy that came not, but shelled us at a distance . . . But now that it is all over I would not forego it for anything. It is an experience of a lifetime and I think it always makes a man a better man to have undergone such an experience.

'Letters From Kimberley', *Caithness Courier*, 23 March 1900, p. 3

227

As ever the Manx lady (**1, 16, 22, 34, 164, 178**) was not lost for words. Having said farewell to 'her numerous acquaintances of our underground siege residence', she left the mine shaft cage and saw

> one of our brave soldiers, a Scot's [*sic*] Grey, on his fine English horse (one of the relief column), surrounded by a crowd of women, who . . . were giving him a hearty welcome; and getting into a cart, we were quickly driven through the streets (where crowds of people were singing 'God Save the Queen' and 'Britons never shall be slaves') to our homes . . . We felt as though we had been months from our homes, and so ended the siege of Kimberley.
>
> It gives me great pleasure to let my home friends know of the very great and good work done to the people of the town by the Hon. Cecil J. Rhodes from the beginning of the siege to the finish, assisting in every way, not only by his kindly advice, but financially, and looking after the minutest details for people's welfare. He caused new roads to be constructed on the outskirts of the town, simply to provide work for the natives and the labouring classes, who would otherwise have been a terrible drain on the relief fund. In fact, only for De Beers' Company the people of Kimberley would have been in a bad state. They formed town guards of their own workmen, and for five months paid them full wages; erected searchlights, which swept the country for miles around, which no doubt saved Kimberley from being attacked during the night; provided water from the Wesselton Mine; fed thousands of people who took shelter from the bombardment both down the mine and in tunnels on the surface; and, to their credit, there was not a single accident. From the highest official to the lowest, there was kindness and courtesy shown to everybody. There were very few people in Kimberley during the siege who will ever forget what Mr. Rhodes did for them. Not only was his kindness extended to his own people, but also to the Boer prisoners in the Kimberley gaol, by providing them with new clothing, pipes, tobacco, etc.
>
> I must not forget our gallant Colonel Kekewich, who commanded the garrison during the siege, who undoubtedly displayed great tact and judgment by the manner in which he superintended the defence works of the town, and the untiring vigilance with which he looked after our safety.
>
> 'Horrors of the Siege', *Isle of Man Weekly Times*, 16 June 1900, p. 5

228

Councillor Anderson (**183**) was just as emphatic in explaining how Kimberley had survived the siege:

> Had it not been for the De Beers Company, and more especially Mr. Rhodes as head of that corporation, we would not, in my opinion, have been able to defend Kimberley for a fortnight. The De Beers Company made all the forts and put up all the barbed wire and other barriers under the supervision of Major McGinnis [*sic*: MacInnes][37] of the Royal Engineers.
>
> 'An Aberdeen Gentleman on The Siege of Kimberley',
> *Aberdeen* (Weekly) *Journal*, 8 May 1900, p. 4

229

There were plenty of similar tributes from the residents in Kimberley, including those already quoted (**187, 188**) and more besides,[38] but the sappers, who rapidly followed the Cavalry Division towards Kimberley, had more immediate priorities. As Lance-Corporal C. Green (Royal Engineers) reported,

> The 31st and 8th companies R.E. repaired the rails right up to there, laying and repairing 28 miles [45 km] in four days, which is not bad work, considering there were several culverts blown up. The Boers have a way of putting a charge in the centre of a rail, and blowing it up, so it means putting new rails and sleepers in their place. In other places they simply cut the bolts at each end, and then hitch on a team of oxen and pull the sleepers and rails into the veldt. They are also very attentive to points and crossings, and take the tumblers and switches right away out of them. In repairing, one Company works during the day, and the other during the night, so that the work is soon completed. A few are kept back for the bridge which will be

---

37   Lieutenant (later Brigadier-General) Duncan Sayre MacInnes (1860–1918) was a Canadian soldier and engineer who served in the Asante expedition (1895–6) before acting as a principal staff officer to Kekewich in Kimberley. Before and during the First World War, he played a key role in establishing the Royal Flying Corps and was accidentally killed while visiting the front on 23 May 1918.

38   NAM, Acc. 1985-11-12, Mrs William Haddock letter, 2 March 1900; 'Letters on the War', *Lloyd's Weekly Newspaper*, 1 April 1900, p. 2; 'In A Besieged City', *Courier and Argus* (Dundee), 24 May 1900, p. 3; 'Part II of the Siege of Kimberley', *Caithness Courier*, 20 April 1900, p. 3; 'The Siege of Kimberley', *Western Mail*, 15 May 1900, p. 6.

completed in a few days from now . . . They have got nine trains of supplies up in two days.

'A Marlburian at Modder River', *Evening Swindon Advertiser*, 20 March 1900, p. 2

230

Gunner W. F. C. Pugsley (38th Battery, RFA) arrived in Kimberley on 9 March *en route* to Mafeking. Writing to his wife in Totnes, he observed that

> the place seemed to have withstood the bombardment very well. Things are frightfully dear here, which is only natural considering the inhabitants and garrison had been living on a few ounces of horseflesh or soup before the relief . . . The jewellers are coining money by making brooches out of the copper driving bands which they take off the shells which have been fired into the town. They are inscribed 'Siege of Kimberley, 1899–1900.' They are sold at 12s 6d [62½p] each, the odd 12s [60p] being the price of the brooch as a relic. The 6d [2½p] about covers its value. Cecil Rhodes has been well to the fore here in matters of relief and organizing troops, etc. The residents speak well of him, and are getting a 1s [5p] subscription list out to erect a statue to him in Kimberley.[39]

'A Totnes Gunner at Kimberley', *Totnes Times*, 7 April 1900, p. 5

231

Private W. H. Stewart (KOYLI) had other thoughts on his mind when he entered Kimberley amidst 'women and children crying and singing "Soldiers of the Queen" . . . flags and sticks, red shawls and handkerchiefs waving, and men and women . . . cheering as well as they could'. After serving in four costly battles under Lord Methuen, he informed his uncle in Harrogate: 'We have got a very good General now, in Lord Roberts; we are in his command, and I can tell you he is the best General out here. He has done some fine work.'

'War Letters. With the Kimberley Field Force', *Sheffield and Rotherham Independent*, 12 April 1900, p. 6

---

[39] In 1907, Kimberley unveiled a 72-ton bronze statue of Rhodes sitting on a horse, facing north with map in hand. The town also awarded every member of the garrison with a semi-official Mayor's Siege Medal, known as the Kimberley Star, and on 9 July 1902 presented Kekewich with a sword of honour.

British Press Reaction to the Relief of Kimberley

The British public did not react to the relief of Kimberley with the frenzied jubilation that followed the relief of Ladysmith, where the belated release of pent-up emotions reflected anxiety about a much larger British garrison and the costly fighting that preceded the relief.[40] Kimberley's relief still produced widespread satisfaction across the United Kingdom. Although the rift between Rhodes and Kekewich would soon become public knowledge, this was not the case initially. While relatively little had been heard from Kimberley since the previous December, the vast majority of correspondence had come from Methuen's relief force, describing costly victories and one shattering defeat at Magersfontein. As accounts of the cavalry operation only appeared several weeks later,[41] editors had to interpret an unexpected event and the first piece of good news from the front for many months.

Relief was the most pervasive feeling since 'the pall of gloom which has shrouded the war in South Africa' had been lifted,[42] bringing hope of recovery 'from those melancholy disasters to our troops'.[43] The succession of reverses in Natal, following the debacle at Colenso (15 December 1899), and the static front that had ensued along the Modder River following Magersfontein, had caused widespread depression at home, from which the news of Kimberley's relief was such a welcome development. The Southampton-based *Hampshire Advertiser* reported the joy that was felt 'by all classes of the community', and Cardiff's *Western Mail* claimed that the news was 'hailed with general rejoicing in London and the provinces'.[44] The metropolitan *Daily News* confirmed that the 'news created unwonted excitement in the West-end clubs where the utmost satisfaction was expressed at the brilliant achievement of General French'.[45]

The absence of the popular demonstrations that followed the reliefs of Ladysmith and later Mafeking, possibly reflected the somewhat sour observation of the *Bristol Mercury* that 'At last Mr. Rhodes and his diamonds are safe.'[46] The centrality of Rhodes to the siege had long

---

40 E. M. Spiers, *Letters from Ladysmith: Eyewitness Accounts from the South African War* (London: Frontline, 2010), pp. 156–60.
41 'With French to Kimberley', *Daily News*, 19 March 1900, p. 3; 'The March on Kimberley', *The Times*, 6 April 1900, p. 13.
42 'The Outlook. Success at Last', *Daily Mail*, 17 February 1900, p. 4.
43 'The Relief of Kimberley', *Essex County Standard*, 17 February 1900, p. 5.
44 'Good News at Last!' *Hampshire Advertiser*, 17 February 1900, p. 5; and 'Summary of the News', *Western Mail*, 17 February 1900, p. 4.
45 'The Good News from Kimberley', *Daily News*, 17 February 1900, p. 5.
46 'Kimberley Reached', *Bristol Mercury*, 17 February 1900, p. 5.

been recognized, possibly obscuring the broader strategic and economic significance of Kimberley, while underpinning the belief that the Boers simply wanted 'to capture Kimberley because Mr. Cecil Rhodes was within its walls . . .'[47] The *Morning Post* emphasized that the successful defence of 'Diamond City' must have frustrated the Boers and their sense of 'cupidity': 'Mr. Cecil Rhodes', it added,

> whom they feared and hated more than any other man in South Africa, left the comparative safety of Rhodesia in order to inspire the inhabitants, and the recently arrived garrison under Colonel Kekewich, to the utmost resistance . . . The Boers themselves professed with joy . . . that their enemy had been thus delivered into their hands. Fortunately, the result has falsified their most ardent anticipations . . .[48]

Editors were just as impressed by the 'marvellous transformation' in the conduct of the relief operations: 'it was a stroke of genius', declared the *Barnsley Chronicle*, 'conceived by a master mind, and carried out by brilliant commanders and men imbued with high enthusiasm and indomitable pluck'.[49] While the *Belfast News-Letter* commended the 'brilliant operations' of Lord Roberts, hailing his tactics as 'on a par with his strategy – unexpected and vigorous',[50] the *Hampshire Telegraph* was even more blunt, arguing that Roberts had found 'a display of mobility' that had cut 'the Gordian knot which Lord Methuen had so disastrously failed to unravel by delivering frontal assaults'.[51] The *Northampton Mercury* shared the impression that 'brilliant strategic movements' had flowed from the planning of Lord Roberts and the dash and spirit of the cavalry under French, but it also maintained that the war had entered a new phase: 'The Free State is invaded by a British army so far victorious, and it is no longer a case of Boer invasion and British defence, but a case of British advance and Boer defeats.'[52] Even more propitious, argued the

---

47   'Local and General Notes', *Cheshire Observer*, 17 February 1900, p. 5.
48   'The Siege of Kimberley', *Morning Post*, 17 February 1900, p. 5.
49   'The Turn of the Tide', *Barnsley Chronicle*, 24 February 1900, p. 5; see also 'The Morning's News in Brief', *Liverpool Mercury*, 17 February 1900, p. 6.
50   *Belfast News-Letter*, 17 February 1900, p. 4.
51   'Digest of the Week', *Hampshire Telegraph*, 17 February 1900, p. 4.
52   'The War: A New Phase', *Northampton Mercury*, 23 February 1900, p. 5; see also the editorials of the *Glasgow Herald*, 19 February 1900, p. 6; *Birmingham Daily Post*, 17 February 1900, p. 6; *Western Mail*, 17 February 1900, p. 4; and *Inverness Courier*, 20 February 1900, p. 4.

Yorkshire Herald, as Cronjé had been 'hopelessly out-manoeuvred', the Free Staters were likely to be 'disheartened', and, in the opinion of *Lloyd's Weekly Newspaper*, 'completely demoralised'.[53]

The *Sheffield Daily Telegraph* was somewhat more perceptive; while acknowledging that the victory that 'was practically bloodless' (another contrast to the endeavours of Methuen's division), it observed that

> There must have been some urgent reason for the dash to Kimberley. Possibly the condition of the garrison was graver than had been permitted to transpire, for if the relief could have been left for the infantry with a smaller cavalry force, the bulk of the mounted men under General French would have been invaluable in at once following Commandant Cronje . . .
>
> General French may have dined in Kimberley on the night of his relief, and no soldier ever better earned his dinner – a remark which applies to every man with him – but the dashing cavalry officer did not linger for *fêtes* and feasting. He was off again after the fugitive Boers, and the Highland Brigade, under General Macdonald, hurried from Jacobsdal on the same errand. The Highlanders have a heavy score to settle with those Boers of Magersfontein . . .
>
> The one fly in the ointment of the apothecary is the report of the capture by the Boers of a large British convoy.[54]
>
> 'Summary of the News', *Sheffield Daily Telegraph*,
19 February 1900, p. 4

The Battle of Paardeberg

On the evening of 16 February, after an exhausting day chasing the Boers near Dronfield, French received news that Cronjé was on the move towards Bloemfontein. Fortunately he had left Broadwood's brigade in

---

53 'The Relief of Kimberley', *Yorkshire Herald*, 17 February 1900, p. 4; and 'The Relief of Kimberley', *Lloyd's Weekly Newspaper*, 18 February 1900, p. 12.
54 After the reorganization of his transport arrangements, Lord Roberts created a highly vulnerable and slow-moving supply train, without artillery escort. On 15 February 1900 the Boers under Christiaan De Wet intercepted the convoy at Waterval Drift, and captured some 200 heavily laden wagons. Apart from an error in dating the ambush, De Wet provides a good account of the British resistance, and of the booty seized, in *Three Years War*, pp. 47–50. British sources admit the loss of 176 wagons, 2,880 oxen, 500 slaughter cattle and vast quantities of supplies, and accept that the lost grain could have fed the Cavalry Division for a week, Anglesey, *British Cavalry*, vol. 4, pp. 132–3; Maurice, *War in South Africa*, vol. 2, pp. 73–8; Badsey, *Doctrine and Reform*, p. 102.

reserve, and so ordered this brigade and two squadrons of Carabineers (some 1,200 men), with twelve guns,[55] to leave at 3 a.m. for Koodoosrand on the Modder River. The other units were left to recuperate,[56] with some following on once Methuen reached Kimberley.

232

In the diary sent with his letter (**130, 207**), Captain Egerton-Green (12th Lancers) explained that

> 1st Cavalry Brigade left at 3 a. m. for Koodoo's Rand Drift, marching along [the] road to Bloemfontein with the object of preventing Cronje from crossing the Modder on his way to Bloemfontein. We were just in time to prevent his enormous convoy crossing Koodoo's Drift, as our artillery opened fire just as his first waggon reached the Drift. C Squadron in advance of the guns took a small kopje and reported the position of affairs. Cronje's army and laager entrenched themselves on the bank of the river. During the above operations many horses died of want of food and exhaustion, and though they accomplished their object the Cavalry Division is much crippled.[57]
>
> 'March of Cavalry Division to Relief of Kimberley',
> *Essex County Standard*, 31 March 1900, p. 6

233

As Trooper Arthur J. Wardill ('C' Squadron, 6th Dragoon Guards) recalled in (**213**), the cavalry stopped Cronjé's slow-moving convoy

> by coming down on him, higher up the river, on Saturday night. By noon on Sunday our infantry pursuing column came up, and Cronje was nearly surrounded. We attacked him, and had awful fighting all day. I was under shell and rifle fire all the morning. Our troop being advance guard, as usual, were trying to turn the one flank Cronje had open. Our losses were heavy, I am sorry to say. It was a piteous sight to see the wounded crawling about and begging for water. Two

---

55 Goldmann, *With General French*, pp. 101–2.
56 Several cavalry units were in a desperate condition: the 9th Lancers had to leave officers and men in charge of 200 sick and exhausted horses, while another commander had only 28 horses able to 'raise a trot', Colvin and Gordon, *Diary of the 9th (Q.R.) Lancers*, p. 70, and Amery, *Times History*, vol. 3, p. 413.
57 From 11 to 27 February, the Cavalry Division lost 1,581 horses or some 30 per cent over 18 days, Anglesey, *British Cavalry*, vol. 4, p. 144.

days later we took a kopje on Cronje's left flank, thus completely surrounding him.

'War Letters', *Sheffield and Rotherham Independent*, 28 April 1900, p. 7

234

As Gunner Hughes of 'G' Battery, RHA, informed his father in Pontypridd,

The G and P Batteries of Horse Artillery, with the 10th Hussars and Household Cavalry, were the first to come in contact with Cronje's force, but he very quickly let us know that he was there in strong force. He must have had at the time 4,000 men and a good number of guns, but as he had only arrived just before us he had only two guns in position, and those we very soon silenced, but not before he had sent a number of well-directed shells against the battery. This was on Saturday, the 17th of February. We continued to shell their position all day Saturday and again during the night. We had to sleep alongside our guns, taking our turns at them. On Sunday it was one continual heavy fire from the morning until the night, but by the morning of the Sunday we had reinforcements on both sides of the river.

'Local Men at the Front', *Western Mail*, 3 April 1900, p. 6

235

The supporting forces included the 13th and 18th Brigades, which were part of the 6th Division, under Lieutenant-General T. Kelly-Kenny,[58] that had been camped at Klip Drift when Cronjé's convoy passed them by. While they followed and harried Cronjé's rearguard, further units came from the south, notably Major-General H. A. Macdonald's 3rd (Highland) Brigade and Major-General H. L. Smith-Dorrien's 19th Brigade (both part of Colvile's 9th Division). Reinforcements included Lieutenant-General C. Tucker's 7th Division, the Naval Brigade and the 3rd Cavalry Brigade, which helped to deter any Boers from seeking to assist Cronjé from the north.

---

58 Lieutenant-General (later General Sir) Thomas Kelly-Kenny (1840–1914) saw active service in China (1860) and Abyssinia (1867–8) before rising through home-based appointments to assume command of the 6th Division (and later the Orange River Colony) in the South African War. He served finally as adjutant-general to the forces (1901–4), in which post he opposed the introduction of a general staff.

Part of the 13th Brigade, Private R. H. Nicholls (1st Battalion, Oxfordshire and Buckinghamshire Light Infantry) recalled that

> We had to march day and night with very little rest, and not much food, besides getting wet through, and had to lie in it all night without topcoats or blankets. On the morning of the 16th we started an engagement with the Boers, which was our first. It lasted from seven o'clock in the morning until about eight o'clock at night. We drove them from one position in the morning, and they retired back on another, and remained there until dark, and then we drove them out with the bayonet, which they did not stop to have much of. I can tell you we all felt a bit shaky when we heard the bullets whistling around us, and the shells screaming, and I was not sorry when night came and it was over.
>
> 'The Oxfordshires Lost Heavily', *Jackson's Oxford Journal*, 14 April 1900, p. 4

236

Soldiers remembered the privations of the preceding march almost as much as the horrors of the ensuing battle. On 14 February, recalled Sergeant R. A. Cooke (2nd Battalion, Shropshire Light Infantry),

> Reveille sounded at 3.40 a. m., and after a drink of coffee and a biscuit we paraded, moving off about 5 o'clock. Besides our Field Artillery we had two large Naval guns, which we nicknamed 'Little Bobs' and 'Sloper', and were each dragged by 32 oxen. We had a very tiring march. The heat was dreadful, and water was very scarce; in fact none at all. Horses and mules were dropping down dead, and a large number of men in the brigade fell out.
>
> 'Letters from the Front', *Isle of Wight Observer*, 31 March 1900, p. 5

'We covered an average of something like eighteen miles [29 km] a day', in the estimation of Private J. Berry (1st Battalion, Welsh Regiment), and, as soon as the marching halted about noon, 'we dropped off to sleep'. Nevertheless, once the Boer laager was detected 'rolling over the veldt', we put on 'the pace after that, and the Welsh had a very good name for marching. Very few dropped out of our ranks, but some of the other regiments in the division were leaving their men behind like a lot of sheep.'[59]

'A Hero of Paardeberg', *Western Mail*, 20 April 1900, p. 6

237

Once Cronjé's convoy halted on 17 February, it entrenched itself at Paardeberg – an elliptical basin north of the river, with low ridges to the north, trees and thickets providing cover along the riverbank, and several ditches running to the river that formed natural trenches from which to fire at any enemy approaching along the river.[60] In the absence of Roberts, who was recovering from an illness at Jacobsdal, Kelly-Kenny was the senior officer but Kitchener intervened, and set aside Kelly-Kenny's preference for simply investing the Boer position. Uncertain about the number of Boers trapped, or of their chances of breaking out or of receiving external relief, Kitchener advocated an immediate attack on the morning of 18 February. Envisaging a three-pronged assault, he never had sufficient staff officers to co-ordinate operations from the south, east and west of the Boer position.

First into battle were the bulk of the 3rd, 13th and 18th Brigades south of the river. Supported by accurate fire from 38 guns from the south and north of the river, the infantry advanced as Private Hogg (1st Battalion, Princess of Wales's Own Yorkshire Regiment[61]) recollected,

> at 6 a.m. . . . we saw signs of the enemy, and at 6.30 a.m. we were having a cut in at them. They were in force on the other side of the river – four to five thousand of them.[62] Our regiment was the first to enter the firing line, supported by the [6th] division. The fight lasted over fourteen hours, and we were constantly under a murderous fire

---

59 This was the 6th Division, which nominally included the 1st Battalions, Welsh, Yorkshire and Essex Regiments and 2nd Battalion, Royal Warwickshire (18th Brigade) and the 1st Battalions, Oxford and Bucks Light Infantry and West Riding Regiments with the 2nd Battalions, East Kent and Gloucestershire (13th Brigade).
60 For a description of this defensive position, see Pretorius, *A to Z of the Anglo-Boer War*, pp. 310–11.
61 At this time there were five regiments with 'Yorkshire' in their titles, but this regiment was formerly the 19th Foot, then popularly known as the 'Yorkshires', and later renamed the Green Howards. G. Powell and J. Powell, *The History of the Green Howards: Three Hundred Years of Service* (Barnsley: Leo Cooper, 2002), pp. 101 and 107.
62 This is a good estimate. On 27 February, the British accepted the surrender of 4,105 Boers, including 150 wounded. Maurice, *War in South Africa*, vol. 2, p. 484.

from the enemy. We had no shelter whatever. We were on the open veldt, while they were hidden in trees and bushes. Not a thing could we see; we could only hear the deadly sting of bullets, and see our men fall as if by magic.

'A Melsonby Man at the Front', *Northern Echo* (Darlington), 3 April 1900, p. 3

238

Another Yorkshireman, Private Riley, reckoned that when 'our first battalion and the Essex and Welsh charged the laager on the 18th . . . our battalion lost about 80 men missing, killed, and wounded.[63] We couldn't help that, because they had such a good position.'

'A Pudsey Man From The Front', *Leeds Mercury*, 27 April 1900, p. 5

When ordered to join the southern attack the highlanders, as Private Hamilton (Argyll and Sutherland Highlanders) described,

> extended out to about six paces, and slowly made the advance, losing a few men on the way. We got within about 1,500 yards [1,370 m] when the bullets began to get a little too thick for our liking, so the line started a nice steady double till we got within 400 yards [365.3 m],[64] and could just see the enemy on the other side of the river. Then our Major gave the command to halt, and lie down. I had just got my hands on the ground when a bullet struck me in the small of my back.

'Letter from a Wounded Colcestrian', *Essex County Standard*, 31 March 1900, p. 5

239

Meanwhile the rest of 6th Division, the 19th Brigade and two companies of Seaforths pressed the Boers from the west. After an hour's shelling several companies crossed the river, 'joining hands, as it was from 4 ft. to 5 ft. deep'. The other companies, as Sergeant Cooke indicated (**236**), advanced on the south side of the river, 'forming a half-circle from one

---

63 Among the fatalities was Sergeant Alfred Atkinson, who earned a posthumous VC after carrying water from the river to the wounded. For once the estimated number of casualties is low – the Yorkshires in fact suffered 130, Maurice, *War in South Africa*, vol. 2, p. 446.
64 The actual distance was nearer 800 m. Pretorius, *A to Z of the Anglo-Boer War*, p. 311.

side of the river to the other'. Serving with the Shropshire stretcher bearers, he found it 'very hard work', crossing and re-crossing the river, carrying wounded, some of whom were 'big, heavy men' over 'rough' ground, and often under enemy fire. Of the units engaged in this area, he rightly observed that 'The Canadians and Cornwalls suffered most in our brigade, having lost a lot in charging the position and having to retire without accomplishing anything.'

'Letters From The Front', *Isle of Wight Observer*, 31 March 1900, p. 5

240

This brutal appraisal of the afternoon charges on the western flank of the laager was not quite how surviving members of the Duke of Cornwall's Light Infantry chose to recall the events. Writing to his mother in Cowes, Isle of Wight, Private G. Cox simply commented: 'I suppose you saw our regiment was in the thick of it. We charged the position, and lost our colonel, adjutant, and Captain Newbury, besides several wounded. Our casualties are 93 up to the present.'[65]

'Cowes Lads at the Front', *Isle of Wight Observer*, 31 March 1900, p. 5

Lieutenant Hugh Wharton Fife, who would later be killed at Johannesburg (30 May 1900), wrote the fullest account of the 'Cornish Charge' in a letter to the former colonel's daughter.[66] It explained how some companies had already been engaged in reinforcing the Highland Brigade south of the river before the order came to 'lead a rush on the Boers in a donga [large gully] in the river bed'. Lieutenant-Colonel Aldworth then gave a 'splendid address' to officers and men, describing how tales of the 'Cornish charge' would live on 'in all time to come' and gave the men permission to fall out for some food, before crossing the river by rope and forming up in extended order in three lines about 150 yards (137 m) apart. Following the order to charge,

---

65 Of the three companies that charged, these casualties represented 22 per cent, the second highest proportion of losses per unit sustained, Maurice, *War in South Africa*, vol. 2, p. 446. The officers mentioned were Lieutenant-Colonel William Aldworth, DSO (1855–1900), Captain and Adjutant Edgar Penrose Wardlaw (1866–1900) and Captain Bertram Archdale Newbury (1865–1900).

66 In the unpublished part of the letter, Fife reckoned that in both parts of the action, the battalion lost 3 officers and 24 men killed and 74 wounded, a 'very heavy

The men gave a tremendous shout and we rushed pell-mell through the firing lines. We got about 300 yards [274 m] amidst a most terrific hail of bullets, pom-pom shells, and shrapnel, men falling at every yard. At last I saw the colonel discharge his rifle, and then I was struck in the left shoulder and bowled clean over. I believe the colonel was hit simultaneously . . .

Nothing could have been more magnificent than the way he led us, from before we crossed the river to the finish. The time was about 4.45 in the afternoon.

'The Cornish Charge', *Western Morning News*,
3 July 1900, p. 8

241

The MI Brigade, commanded by Colonel O. C. Hannay, led the assault from the east. From early morning, as Trooper Harry Godsmark (Kitchener's Horse) commented,

We were laid down firing for an hour or two, and they were soon all at it. We had advanced a bit too far, so the order was given to retire. We were under a very heavy fire at the time, and I was shot almost directly . . . It was about 10 or 11 a.m. when I was hit . . .

'Letter From The Front', *Yorkshire Herald*,
29 March 1900, p. 2

After the MI received a direct order from Kitchener to launch another attack in the early afternoon, Hannay led some fifty gallopers in an abortive charge and was killed himself. The Welsh and Essex Regiments were then thrown into the attack north of the river: 'About a mile [1.6 km] from the Boer trenches', wrote the Welsh Private J. Berry (**236**),

We formed out in line, and advanced over open ground towards the enemy without having any cover at all. Our men were falling fast, and the only way of getting near the Boers was to lie down flat on the earth for a while, and then make a sudden rush for about twenty yards [18 m], and lie down again. In this fashion we got to within 400 or 500 yards [365.2–457.2 m] of them, and forced them back into closer touch with the main body. We did not cease firing until the light had failed, and it was just then that I was hit . . . The men of the Essex

---

loss', for which he held Lord Kitchener responsible, Cornwall's Regimental Museum, 'Memorials of Colonel Aldworth', Lt H. Fife to Miss Aldworth, 26 March 1900.

were supposed to reinforce us, but they did not turn up until the fighting was nearly over.[67]

'A Hero of Paardeberg', *Western Mail*,
20 April 1900, p. 6

242

The upshot, as Private D. Robinson (Oxford and Bucks Light Infantry) observed, was that 'The day's fighting did not shift them in the least.'

'Letters From The Front: In Pursuit of the Enemy',
Jackson's Oxford Journal, 12 May 1900, p. 3

Even worse was the number of killed and wounded, which as Private W. Meehan (Yorkshire Regiment) correctly calculated, was 'over 1200'.[68]

'The War: Letter from a Spennymoor Man',
(Darlington) *Northern Echo*, 29 March 1900, p. 3

Speculating wildly, Private Hogg (**237**) claimed that 'The enemy lost 1,700 killed and wounded',[69] but more poignantly added that 'It was awful to hear the groans of the dying and the wounded asking for water. The dead and wounded were lying about all night; the men were too weak to carry them in.'

'A Melsonby Man at the Front', *Northern Echo* (Darlington),
3 April 1900, p. 3

243

Undaunted, Private Robert Perry (2nd Battalion, Shropshire Light Infantry) insisted that

> We wanted to charge them out again, but Lord Roberts [who assumed his command on 19 February] would not allow it as he said he was not going to lose any more lives than he could possibly help. On the

---

67 This rankled within the Welsh Regiment and reflected the poor staff work and co-ordination during the day, see 'One of Cronje's Tacklers', *Western Mail*, 4 April 1900, p. 6. Major Brown claimed that four companies of the Essex Regiment pressed along the river's edge until checked. 'Doings of the Essex Regiment', *Essex County Chronicle*, 6 April 1900, p. 8.
68 Officially 1,262 casualties, including 20 officers and 300 men killed or died of their wounds – 8 per cent of the 15,000 men in the field, 'the highest casualties of any one day's fighting in the war', Maurice, *War in South Africa*, vol. 2, p. 445.
69 The British later claimed that Cronjé lost about 100 killed and 250 wounded for the whole period from his flight to his surrender, Maurice, *War in South Africa*, vol. 2, p. 446.

following evening our regiment had orders to crawl as near as possible to the enemy's position and dig shelter trenches, which we did at midnight... We continued this kind of work until 9 a.m. on the 27th February.

'A Bangorian at the Capture of Cronje', *North Wales Chronicle*, 31 March 1900, p. 3

244

Meanwhile Roberts concentrated on bringing up reinforcements, ultimately deploying some 40,000 men and 100 guns in a continual pounding of Cronjé's laager.[70] That laager had caught fire on the 18th, destroying vast quantities of food and ammunition, while killing or stampeding many of the horses and draught animals. Lieutenant G. W. Herbert (Welsh Regiment), who had been taken prisoner and spent the battle in the Boer laager, confirmed that 'Most of the laager containing food was burnt on the first day at Paardeberg, and at the end of the siege they practically had no food left.'

'Welsh Officer in Cronje's Laager', *Western Mail*, 2 June 1900, p. 5

To add to Cronjé's woes, the Naval Brigade with its heavy ordnance arrived on 22 February, and, in the words of a Rochdale Marine, had 'a frightful job' hauling four of their guns with their large teams of oxen across the river:

> Then we saw how things stood. Take a basin, put Cronje and his men at the bottom of it, and Roberts and his guns all round the edge, and there you have it.
>
> We kept them lively all day and night with both artillery and rifle fire, but they stuck to it pluckily. We had three nights of heavy rain, and slept in the trenches in pools of water and wet clothes ... Near the river were dead, stinking cattle, and half-buried Boers in dongas and nullahs gave you a stinking dislike of and longing to get out of the war.

'Naval Brigade on the Modder. A Rochdale Marine's Story of the Pursuit of Cronje', *Manchester Evening News*, 29 March 1900, p. 5

---

70 Pretorius, *The A to Z of the Anglo-Boer War*, p. 313.

245

William Watson Cheyne, FRS, the consulting surgeon with Roberts's force, had already coped with the pervasive bouts of diarrhoea that had afflicted soldiers camped by the Modder River. Now as the river rose,

> there was a constant procession down the stream of dead and putrid horses and other animals from the Boer camp. The stench from these animals was very bad . . . [and] the greatest care had to be exercised in the sanitation of the camp, and it says a great deal for the arrangements adopted that no illness except the ever-present 'Modders' developed.
>
> 'Doctors at the Front', *Daily News*, 7 May 1900, p. 3

246

The only significant distraction occurred in the south-east, where a Boer commando under General Christiaan de Wet, accompanied by General Philip Botha, seized some hills known as the Oskoppies (renamed after the battle as Kitchener's Kopje). Having arrived on 22 February, de Wet saw Cronjé's laager surrounded by 'an encircling multitude', with British guns 'belching forth death and destruction'. By opening up a second front, and holding most, though not all, of these hillsides against counter-attacks over several days, he provided an escape route for Cronjé and his burghers, if they were willing to leave everything behind them: 'But General Cronje would not move . . . it was too much to ask him – intrepid hero that he was – to abandon the laager.'[71]

It was a shock, nonetheless, for Private P. Barrett (2nd Battalion, Lincolnshire Regiment) to find himself 'between two fires. The bullets were striking the ground all around me.'

'War Letters. With the 2nd Lincolnshires', *Sheffield and Rotherham Independent*, 12 April 1900, p. 6

Private Ned Maxwell (Yorkshire Regiment) was equally stunned to find the Boers contesting a hill in the rear: 'After about seven hours we

---

71 De Wet, *Three Years War*, pp. 55, 57 and 63. A Boer prisoner later claimed that 'General Cronje expected all the time to be reinforced, but it was impossible for the relieving and beleaguered forces to join hands', 'Boer Prisoners on Their Defeat', *Daily Telegraph*, 8 March 1900, p. 10.

drove them off, and then got something to eat, for the first and last time that day.'

'Letter from a Stockton Man at the Front',
Northern Echo (Darlington), 30 May 1900, p. 3

Cronjé Surrenders (27 February 1900)

Refused a truce to bury their dead, the Boer council of war[72] resolved to surrender unconditionally on 27 February (Majuba Day, the anniversary of the Boer victory in 1881 that proved the climax of the fighting in the Anglo-Transvaal War). Cronjé's surrender was a major event: of those who surrendered, 18 officers and 2,592 men were Transvaalers, another 18 officers and 1,327 men were Free Staters, and the remainder were women and children. They had only four guns and one pom-pom.[73]

247

British soldiers were stunned by the age, appearance and composition of their enemy: another MI officer had never seen 'a more motley, disreputable-looking crew in his life'.

'Major Manuell at the Front. Interesting Experiences',
Aberdeen (Weekly) *Journal*, 30 April 1900, p. 5

'We had Cronje and his men', wrote Private W. C. Purnell (1st Battalion, Scots Guards),

> and a warm lot they were, ranging from 14 to about 80 years of age . . . Old Cronje looked down on his luck I can assure you . . . Cronje's wife looked worn and weary. She must have gone through something, as did the other women and children who were in the trenches, with the lyddite bursting about them. One little child about two months old had its arm shattered.

'Letters From Swindonians at the Front',
Evening Swindon Advertiser, 1 May 1900, p. 2

---

72 All officers participated in the *krygsraad* (council of war), and, if necessary, they took decisions by a vote in which the views of the junior officers could prevail over those of more experienced seniors, H. C. Hillegas, *With the Boer Forces* (London: Methuen, 1900), pp. 92–4.
73 Maurice, *War in South Africa*, vol. 2, p. 484. The pom-pom was a belt-fed automatic machine gun with a range of 3,000 yards (2,740 m) made by Maxim-Nordenfelt.

Private G. Washington (2nd Battalion, Coldstream Guards), who assisted in cooking the victory dinner, noted that Cronjé would not join Lord Roberts and his staff in the champagne supper

> but had a table laid outside a tent set apart for him. However, Albrecht, who came in to-day with the remainder, showed less contempt, and made the best of matters by having a late breakfast with the staff, and laughing and chatting with them as to the numbers and guns employed at the different engagements.
>
> 'The Umbrella and Waggonette Corps',
> *Wakefield Express*, 31 March 1900, p. 6

248

Soldiers were astonished, too, by the sight of the laager. Captain F. Egerton-Green (12th Lancers) saw

> A sight I shall not forget for some time. Such a scene of wreck and desolation . . . afforded one of the best examples of the horrors of war. Dead horses lay in groups all over the laager, sometimes in batches of ten as they had stood together when a shell killed the lot . . . and the smell of all those dead horses is better imagined than described. There was nothing worth taking as a trophy . . . the whole place being littered with the most filthy old clothes, pillows, and cooking pots . . . The caves they had dug in the river bank were wonderful, a good sized hole to go in led to a fair-sized room, and tunnels branched out of this leading to sleeping places well underground, where no shell could possibly hurt the occupants. The banks of the river are about 25 ft. [8 m] above the surface of the water, and all along these for 1½ miles [1.6 km] or so was a perfect honeycomb of these caves and tunnels.[74]
>
> 'Further Letter from Captain F. Egerton-Green',
> *Essex County Standard*, 31 March 1900, p. 5

---

74 Private A. Thomson (Argyll and Sutherland Highlanders) also regarded the trenches as 'impregnable to infantry', 'Local Men at the Front', *Kilmarnock Standard*, 31 March 1900, p. 3, while Sergeant Cooke (**236**, **239**), possibly arriving in the camp ahead of Egerton-Green, found several Bibles, copies of Walter Scott's works in Dutch, various pieces of music and 'a violin and auto-harp', 'Letters From The Front', *Isle of Wight Observer*, 31 March 1900, p. 5.

249

Further reactions to Cronjé's surrender included some exultation: 'we avenged Majuba', asserted Private W. Robinson (1st Battalion, Oxford and Bucks Light Infantry).[75]

'Letters From The Front: In Pursuit of the Enemy',
Jackson's Oxford Journal, 12 May 1900, p. 3

While Private Houghton (1st Battalion, Yorkshire Regiment) felt sheer relief: 'Old Cronje and four thousand men gave themselves up, and so we have had a day's rest, the first for a month.'

'The Fighting at Paardeberg', *Leicester Chronicle,*
31 March 1900, p. 5

Some like Corporal H. Fallas (10th Royal Hussars), who had been at the relief of Kimberley and Paardeberg, now assumed that the war would soon be over: 'It was a grand sight to see Cronje and his men sitting on the veldt, and our men feeding them on biscuits and tinned meat. I don't think the war will last much longer, and I don't care how soon it is over, as we have had some great hardships and deprivations.'

'Corporal Fallas on Cronje's Surrender',
Ossett Observer, 7 April 1900, p. 8

At least one Free State prisoner of war demurred: 'Cronje', he reckoned, 'is finished for all time. He did well, but I think Delarey [*sic*] or Botha would have done better. This surrender will not end the war, but it brings the termination of our hardships within close range.'

'Homes of the Boers', *Glasgow Herald,*
2 May 1900, p. 8

250

Such prescience only added to the forebodings of L. Harris (Kitchener's Horse):

> It is after the battle that one feels the pangs of war, when one looks through the serried ranks and depleted squads, when one sees small groups of dead soldiers lying in rows on the slopes of small kopjes ready for burial, here Highlanders, there Welsh Regiments. The still bodies – without boots, and but a cloth over their dead faces . . . In another part of the field lie wounded men scattered about.

---

75 See also Driver T. Curzons, in 'Hard Fighting and Short Rations', *Warwick, Leamington and Warwickshire Times,* 28 April 1900, p. 4.

Extemporised hospitals, medical men coatless, their arms reeking with blood, but moving rapidly and skilfully to alleviate the sufferings of the men – and how many lives have been saved by the swift dexterous movements none can tell.

'Soldiers Letters. Nottingham Man with Kitchener's Horse', *Nottinghamshire Guardian*, 14 April 1900, p. 5

Chapter 6

Assessing the Kimberley Siege

Reviewing and ultimately assessing the significance of the Kimberley siege through the eyes of contemporaries poses challenges unlike those of any other Victorian siege. First and foremost, it was a siege conducted primarily by civilians (on both sides ironically). In Kimberley, they constructed and manned the perimeter defences, undertook the bulk of the mounted patrols, and even manufactured their own long-range ordnance. However valuable the advice and services of the 600 regulars, their mobility was strictly limited in range (and direction as they depended largely upon use of the armoured train and the truncated rail network), so ensuring that they eventually became a central reserve. Secondly, the polite and unassuming Kekewich, though able to conduct an aggressive defence of Kimberley over a couple of months, was neither a charismatic nor a commanding figure. Among the pantheon of Victorian siege commanders, he hardly captured the imagination in the way that Henry Havelock did in the first relief of Lucknow or Charles 'Chinese' Gordon at Khartoum, or Baden-Powell at Mafeking. He was, too, dwarfed by the towering personality of the siege, Cecil Rhodes, being likened in one commentary to a 'Lilliputian obliged to sit on the head of a pinioned Gulliver'.[1] Thirdly, the Boers conducted this siege in a remarkably passive manner that was relatively ineffective until their introduction of the 'Long Tom' gun. Their failure to exploit the shock of investment at the outset has fuelled speculation about what might have happened had they done so,[2] but their tactical performance in facing the relief forces revealed many of their strengths and weaknesses in fighting from

---

1 R. Kruger, *Goodbye Dolly Gray: A History of the Boer War* (London: Nel Mentor edition, 1967), p. 104.
2 Pretorius, *A to Z of the Anglo-Boer War*, p. 213.

prepared positions. Those weaknesses exposed towards the end of the battle of Modder River, and then more noticeably at the battle of Paardeberg, underpinned the widespread but premature confidence in Britain that the tide had turned in the war. For soldiers and civilians alike, this would prompt speculation about how Britain, its army, and empire would benefit from the outcome.

Sources: Searches, Selection and Significance

This account of the siege of Kimberley and its relief, including new material in this chapter, has employed some 261 letters, with 49 from civilians and a handful from Boer prisoners, selected from 99 metropolitan and provincial newspapers. It has required a more extensive search technique than that required to find correspondence from Victorian soldiers on active service, namely the search for letters in newspapers published within the recruiting districts of the regiments engaged, or near their depots and bases used prior to embarkation. Those methods were used to detect correspondence from soldiers in the relevant infantry-of-the-line battalions sent to family and friends at home, and then passed on to the local press, usually about four weeks or more after despatch from South Africa. These uncensored letters attracted editorial attention by virtue of their local interest, particularly for the provincial newspapers; their often blunt and graphic phraseology; and their readiness to make points about commanders, battles, the enemy, and campaign generally that would never be found in official despatches.[3] Moreover, in a war that attracted huge press attention, with the leading metropolitan and provincial newspapers, as well as news agencies like Reuters, retaining at least 70 special correspondents in the field by early 1900 – newspapers sought to cover the war extensively, readily filling columns with 'Letters from the Front' among other material.[4]

This search process uncovered numerous letters from soldiers of the principal infantry units involved, including correspondence from soldiers in the Highland Brigade not used in previous accounts of Magersfontein,[5]

---

3 E. M. Spiers, 'Military correspondence in the late nineteenth-century press', *Archives*, vol. 32, no. 116 (2007), pp. 28–40.
4 S. Badsey, 'The Boer War as a Media War', in P. Dennis and J. Grey (eds), *The Boer War: Army, Nation and Empire, The 1999 Chief of Army/Australian War Memorial Military History Conference* (Canberra: Army History Unit, 2000), pp. 70–83, at p. 81.
5 In seeking letters other than those used in Spiers, *Scottish Soldier and Empire*, ch. 8, the author profited from the need of so many Scottish regiments to recruit from south of the border.

and from soldiers of the Loyal North Lancashire Regiment, with a rich array of material on the latter coming from the newspapers of Preston, Bolton, Burnley and Blackburn.[6] While these searches found some correspondence from soldiers in the Guards, cavalry, artillery and the support arms – all of which recruited nationally – as well as from civilians in the siege, a national sample had to be undertaken to find a more representative range of writings. The sample had to reflect the primary sources of recruitment, namely the cities and towns from which the cavalry found some 75 per cent of its troopers by the mid-nineteenth century, and from which the artillery and infantry found over 80 per cent of its men by 1891.[7] Although this sampling also revealed correspondence from civilians sent after the relief of Kimberley, further letters were found by searching newspapers from the Highlands. As a Presbyterian church had been founded in Kimberley as early as 1878, and had catered for many of the Scottish migrants who sought their fortunes in the diamond diggings,[8] the search through newspapers such as the *Aberdeen Journal, Inverness Courier, Northern Scot and Moray and Nairn Express, Elgin Courant* and the *Caithness Courier* proved extremely productive.

Of the letters found, which greatly exceeded the number used, it was possible to select an array of letters from all the major regiments and support arms engaged, both in the relief forces and inside Kimberley. So many accounts had to be consulted because, as Samuel Hynes once remarked, 'The stories that soldiers tell are small-scale, detailed, and confined',[9] and as historical evidence they require amplification, corroboration where possible, correction in some respects, and additional insights from differing perspectives. It was also possible to find a range of commentary, often in the form of siege diaries that spread over several columns of newsprint, from the English-speaking community in Kimberley. They included letters from the mayor (**6**) and a councillor (**183**); a range of military personnel in the Kimberley Rifle Volunteers, Kimberley Light Horse, the Town Guard, Cape Mounted Police and

---

6 With seven letters from the besieged and another twelve from the relief force, this sample exceeds the nine used in the regimental history, see Downham, *Red Roses on the Veldt*.
7 A. R. Skelley, *The Victorian Army at Home: The Recruitment and Terms and Conditions of the British Regular, 1859–1899* (London: Croom Helm, 1977), p. 294.
8 J. M. MacKenzie with N. R. Dalziel, *The Scots in South Africa: Ethnicity, identity, gender and race, 1772–1914* (Manchester: Manchester University Press, 2007), pp. 179, 219, 225.
9 S. Hynes, *The Soldiers' Tale: Bearing Witness to Modern War* (London: Allen Lane, 1997), p. 12.

those engaged in the communications systems; another thirteen from women, including the letter from the irrepressible Manx lady (**1**), which is almost as long and detailed as the well-known diary of Mrs Rochfort Maguire (**173**), and includes a first-hand account of living in the mines; and correspondence from the Kimberley suburbs, Beaconsfield (**179**) and the more exposed and vulnerable, Kenilworth (**17** and **171**).

The significance of such writing merits further comment. As personal narratives they are inherently fallible, often shaped by prior assumptions, restricted in scope, biased in perspective (especially among regiments competing for battlefield glory), coloured by emotion, and prone to error.[10] Such errors may reflect either an attempt to account for (and explain) the heavy casualties after each battle or the infusion of rumour from camp or hospital gossip. 'Memories', wrote Dan Todman, 'are shaped socially', and 'the more frequently a story is told, the more likely it is to be remembered': later if the story is retold, individuals can repeat it with as much conviction as if it were their own.[11] However Todman, like many commentators on military memoirs, focused upon the accounts of Great War veterans, often retold many years after the event when the narratives could be affected by 'rehearsal', that is, the social act in which memories are described to others. Such effects in South Africa, though evident in some of the exaggerations, were offset by the fact that most of these letters were sent relatively soon after the event. The immediacy with which these letters were composed, despatched, and later printed, enhances their evidentiary significance, even if the odd soldier, like Private John William Smith (Loyal North Lancashire MI), doubted that he had stories worth retelling: as he informed his wife, 'The papers can tell you more than anyone else even on the battlefield, because we can't see all over the field and it takes us all our time to look after ourselves.'[12]

Smith's diffidence was rare. Sergeant Alf Linley (Northumberland Fusiliers) was not alone in recognizing that the special correspondents, unlike the soldiers, were writing under the constraints of censorship hence

---

10   After Modder River, Lance-Corporal Green (**95**) wildly exaggerated in claiming that 'There were about 15,000 Boers on the other side of the river', and while he was correct in describing how the Boers fled once the British forces crossed the river (**91**), he exaggerated again in claiming that the 'Boers have lost 2,000 of their men, and our loss is 500' ('Letters From Soldiers: A Gainsbronian at Modder River', *Sheffield Daily Telegraph*, 3 January 1900, p. 7).

11   D. Todman, 'The Ninetieth Anniversary of the Battle of the Somme' in M. Keren and H. H. Herweg (eds), *War Memory and Popular Culture: Essays on Modes of Remembrance and Commemoration* (London: McFarland & Co., 2008), pp. 23–40, at p. 25.

12   'Two Horses Shot from Under Him', *Blackburn Times*, 24 February 1900, p. 3.

'The papers' account [*sic*] out here are a long way from the mark, and I daresay it is the same at home, so I will try and give you my experience of what occurred.'[13] Able to write without censorship, many soldiers were desperate to share their experiences with their readers, whether they were veterans comparing this war with previous campaigns[14] or soldiers reflecting upon the strangeness and intensity of their first battles – the confusion, sights, smells and sounds of men wounded and dying. They also wanted to bear witness: as a Lismore Lancer informed his aunt, 'You must know what it is to have shot and shell coming around you like hail stone.'[15] Some, like Private William Almond (1st Battalion, Coldstream Guards), dwelt on the horrors of war and the loss of comrades: with emotions raw after fighting three battles in six days, he protested that 'War is awful. It is cruel. It is murder. Actually being shot down side by side!' After Magersfontein, he described how, 'We cannot see them in the hills and trenches until we get very close to them, and they open fire upon us. The last time we tried to rush their positions we lost over a thousand men, and that is a great loss. This war is worse than the Crimea.'[16]

Others were keen to describe how they had survived the rigours of campaigning over the veld. Of the Kimberley relief column, wrote Trooper Pegler (Scots Greys), 'It was a forced march, and a very hard one, and beat the record march.'[17] They could explain, too, in a way that official despatches would not, that recourse to looting (**86, 95**) enabled exhausted men to overcome their pangs of hunger after the ferocious battle along the banks of the Modder River. Self-censorship probably held such accounts in check; there are only passing references to drink (**167**) and fraternization with ladies in Kimberley (**170**) but these writers held the attention of British readers by graphic descriptions of the African environment. Lieutenant J. Brander Dunbar of the Town Guard was fascinated with the local insect life, describing the 'thousands of locusts' that afflicted Kimberley, the 'damnable' mosquitoes that feasted on his men during a night at Otto's Kopje, and the 'innumerable' flies in the

---

13 'War Correspondence', *Yorkshire Herald*, 9 January 1900, p. 2.
14 'Wounded men', wrote a Gordon Highlander, 'can lie, as was the case in the retirement at Magersfontein, in the knowledge that they will receive the best of treatment at the hands of their enemies, and not the "coup de grace" as from the Afridis', 'A Gordon Highlander on Indian v. African Warfare', *Edinburgh Evening News*, 15 March 1900, p. 6; see also 'The Battle of Magersfontein', *Derby Daily Telegraph*, 19 January 1900, p. 3.
15 'At the Modder River', *Cork Constitution*, 13 January 1900, p. 6.
16 'A Narrow Shave', *Blackburn Times*, 24 February 1900, p. 3.
17 'One of the Scots Greys', *Cheltenham Chronicle*, 14 April 1900, p. 4; see also 'Kimberley Relief. An Auckland Man's Letter', *Northern Echo*, 21 March 1900, p. 4.

tents, food, and, on one memorable occasion, in his breeches: 'Those which I did not squeeze on the saddle "came to" with the warmth of my person, and began a promenade, not conducive to steadiness on parade.'[18] Finally, there were soldiers only too ready to express pride in their achievements and those of their regiments; as Trooper Edward Dunner (Royal Horse Guards) informed his sister and brother-in-law in Pultneytown, Caithness, 'I am proud to say that I was at the relief of Kimberley and at Koodooransdrift, where we captured Cronje and his army of 4,000.'[19]

The Siege: Sufferings, Passivity and Civil–Military Strife

The many correspondents from Kimberley were delighted by the outcome of the 124-day siege. 'Kimberley men', wrote Frank Elkington, who had fled from Johannesburg and served in the Town Guard, 'feel very proud at having held the town, as the defence was worthy of the residents and about 1,000 from Johannesburg.'[20] The victory, though, had been bought at a significant price. The shelling may have caused relatively few deaths and physical injuries but, as Reverend George W. T. Laverack recalled, it had frayed the nerves of many inhabitants and caused 'considerable damage to property'. The siege, too, had brought all mining to a standstill and, as a consequence, had produced a 'good deal of destitution . . . in the town'. As Laverack observed, this had only worsened after the ending of the siege and the disbanding of the town guard: the mines could not reopen until the railway brought coal and dynamite to Kimberley.[21]

More significantly, as stocks of food dwindled over the four months of the siege, infant mortality had surged. From 133 deaths in the first month, the numbers of infant deaths grew to 302, 585 and 609 in the successive months, or a total of '1,679' (*sic*: 1,629), which almost equalled the usual number of deaths in a complete year. Among European infants the death rate rose to 500 per thousand while among the black infants it was 935 per thousand. The blacks also proved peculiarly susceptible to the most serious disease that erupted during the siege, namely scurvy.[22] The Manx lady explained how conditions had become increasingly severe for young mothers:

---

18 'A Diary of the Siege of Kimberley', *Northern Scot and Moray & Nairn Express*, 24 March 1900, p. 6.
19 'A Letter from Bloemfontein', *John O'Groats Journal*, 20 April 1900, p. 4.
20 'In Kimberley during the Siege', *North Wales Chronicle*, 31 March 1900, p. 3.
21 'The Siege of Kimberley', *Leeds Mercury*, 11 April 1900, p. 6.
22 Kekewich (Q. 21,853), Evidence before the Elgin Commission, vol. 2, p. 560.

There was a great deal of sickness throughout Kimberley and Beaconsfield during the siege. The death rate was very high, amongst children in particular – poor little mites dying for want of milk. Those who had young children were allowed one tin of condensed milk every five days, but could any mother . . . manage to feed and keep a baby well on that quantity? And so the poor little babies faded and died, and my opinion is that the Boers were accountable for the deaths of these children, and also of scores of delicate people, who simply died simply for want of nourishing food. Most people call it the fortunes of war. I call it wholesale murder.[23]

The townsfolk were at least spared any direct assault upon Kimberley, as the Boers never showed any inclination to storm the defences. George Lunt (**169**) ascribed this good fortune to the natural defences provided by the heaps of 'tailings'[24] from the mines, similar to the cinder heaps of his native Black Country; the fortifications erected by the engineers and artillery; the 'incessant patrolling' by bodies like the Kimberley Light Horse; and the several miles of open ground between the town and the kopjes which surrounded it.[25] Yet the passivity of the Boers may have reflected other factors, too. While the Boers would happily have accepted the surrender of Kimberley, their armed forces, despite invading Cape Colony and Natal, were not bent upon conquest and the seizure of territory. They were hoping to repeat the triumphs of the Anglo-Transvaal War (1880–1) by defeating the British armies before the latter could invade their territory, and so persuading the British to seek a negotiated settlement.

As in the previous war, this was essentially a defensive strategy and it involved concentrating the bulk of their forces in Natal, where the British were strongest. In the western theatre they proved reluctant to probe deep into Cape Colony despite the possibility of arousing a rebellion among the large number of Boers who lived in the colony, and preferred to mount sieges as they had done in the previous war,[26] fighting from defensive positions. This defensive approach was undoubtedly fortified by deep religious convictions. The Boers did not want to strike first, and assume a full-scale offensive because they believed that it would be unbiblical and

---

23 'Horrors of the Siege', *Isle of Man Weekly Times*, 16 June 1900, p. 5.
24 These are by-products from the diamond extraction process.
25 'Birmingham Men in Kimberley', *Birmingham Post*, 26 May 1900, p. 5.
26 Of the seven British garrisons besieged during 1880–1, only Potchefstroom surrendered, I. Bennett, *A Rain of Lead: The Siege and Surrender of the British at Potchefstroom* (London: Greenhill Books, 2001).

could jeopardize the support of foreign countries.[27] Nevertheless, by this instinctive caution, they allowed British commanders to mount offensives from the Cape.

Compounding these weaknesses was the fact that the Boers fought in a citizen army in which the men elected their own officers. In wartime the burghers (citizens) were not disciplined and trained soldiers in prime physical condition but merely white men from either republic, aged between sixteen and sixty years of age. If British soldiers were surprised by the age and appearance of those captured at Paardeberg (**247**), Howard C. Hillegas, an American reporter with the Boer forces, explained that virtually 'the entire population of the two Republics' had journeyed to the front, and that many were unfit for military duty, either too young, too old, sick or maimed. Moreover although the burgher was compelled to join the army, he was not obliged to fight unless he volunteered to do so (hence the limited numbers who joined the firing lines at Belmont and Graspan). Nevertheless, if they had a respected and firm general like Cronjé, the men willingly entered battle because they realized that they had to fight.[28] When armed with rifle and horse, the Boer proved a fiercely independent and mobile adversary but he was also extremely conscious of his own safety whenever danger seemed near. The unedifying retreat from the Modder River (**91**) reflected the jibe of Hillegas that 'The Boer was quick in noting when the proper time arrived for retreat, and he was not slothful in acting upon his observations.'[29]

Such characteristics ensured that the Boers who invested Kimberley were instinctively risk-averse and reluctant to suffer casualties. Consequently, they missed the opportunity to storm the town at the outset, when it was most vulnerable to 'a determined assault by disciplined men'.[30] But these Boers were neither a disciplined force like their British adversaries nor part of an army that could absorb and replace casualties; they relied instead upon a desultory bombardment in the hope of inducing surrender. They proved just as feckless when de Villebois-Mareuil arrived with the 'Long Tom' gun. As he wrote in his diary of 9 February 1900, 'The gun fires continuously on the town and produces great effects. Still the Boer generals refuse to march. It is an opportunity lost through their heedlessness.'[31] Councillor W. T. Anderson (**183**) attributed this passivity

---

27 A. Wessels, 'Afrikaners at War' in J. Gooch (ed.), *The Boer War: Direction, Experience and Image* (London: Frank Cass, 2000), pp. 73–106, at pp. 82–5.
28 Hillegas, *With the Boer Forces*, pp. 69–74, 90–1, 104.
29 Ibid. p. 130.
30 Maurice, *War in South Africa*, vol. 2, p. 69.
31 De Villebois-Mareuil, *War Notes*, p. 221.

to 'a strong belief that Kimberley was mined with dynamite for 15 miles [24.1 km] around'. He had learned from Captain Brown, whom the Boers had taken prisoner, and then released after a trial in Bloemfontein, that his captors had pressed him for information on the placement of mines, exhibiting 'a great dread of dynamite'. Increasing this fear, argued Anderson, was the inability of the Boers to move without being observed: at night the searchlights proved 'a wholesome deterrent', while during the day the observation posts, particularly the conning tower, provided a 'splendid view of the country for miles around'.[32]

Yet the source of greatest controversy during the siege was the rift between Kekewich and Rhodes. As the pre-eminent figure of the siege, Rhodes was the main target of Boer enmity. Likened subsequently by Field Marshal Jan C. Smuts to a 'caged lion' in Kimberley,[33] he was depicted quite wrongly by Kruger as the instigator of the war through his desire for a South African empire.[34] The controversy over his conduct both during and after the siege inspired debate and recriminations, with many of the incidents becoming public knowledge within a month of the town's relief. As indicated in the Introduction, copies of O'Meara's diary, which were fiercely critical of Rhodes, circulated within Kimberley and, in one of the first histories of the war, Conan Doyle criticized the role of Rhodes in a manner that many commentators would follow. While the official historian described Rhodes as 'almost impossible to work with', if 'a tower of strength' for the citizens of Kimberley,[35] one of the principal histories of these events denounced Rhodes for his 'megalomaniac quest for power during the siege'.[36]

If the citizens of Kimberley could hardly comment upon all of the private meetings and disputes between Kekewich and Rhodes, many had read the blistering editorials of the *Diamond Fields Advertiser* pressing for an early relief of the town, and had heard of the public spat at the Sanatorium when Rhodes ordered the colonel out of his house. They briefed reporters on this friction,[37] and Mrs Rochfort Maguire, a personal friend of Rhodes, when interviewed on her return to London, tried vainly to downplay accounts of the rift and instead offered assessments of the relative contributions of the two men in the defence of Kimberley.

---

32 'An Aberdeen Gentleman on The Siege of Kimberley', *Aberdeen* (Weekly) *Journal*, 8 May 1900, p. 4.
33 Field Marshal J. C. Smuts, 'Introduction', in Green, *An Editor Looks Back*.
34 Hillegas, *With the Boer Forces*, p. 242.
35 Maurice, *War in South Africa*, vol. 2, p. 70.
36 Gardner, *Lion's Cage*, p. 173.
37 'Our South African Letter', *Lancashire Daily Post*, 27 March 1900, p. 5.

Kekewich, she praised, for his 'admirable tact' and 'indefatigable' endeavours and then eulogized the contribution of Rhodes: 'It was very largely due to Mr. Rhodes' generosity and untiring labours that Kimberley held out so long.'[38] She later expanded on this comparison in her published diary, devoting over a column in *The Times Weekly Edition* to the many services of Rhodes (**173**) before concluding that Kimberley owed 'much to the foresight, tact, and resolution of Colonel Kekewich' and 'to the genius, breadth of mind, and unwearying and unfailing resourcefulness of Mr. Rhodes'.[39] Many citizens, who were not part of Rhodes's intimate circle, praised his contributions in a similar manner (**172, 187, 188**).

Kekewich never fully grasped the limitations upon his 'supreme command' of a town of 50,000 people, many of whom depended upon the De Beers Company for their livelihoods. He blamed Rhodes as the sole source of the 'very serious trouble' he encountered, and dismissed any actions by other members of the town council as merely following in his wake.[40] Doubtless from his own point of view the command would have passed much more smoothly without the interference of Rhodes, and without his increasing irritability as Methuen's relief operation stalled and the Boers mounted more effective bombardments. Kekewich, though, completely absolved Rhodes of ever threatening to surrender the town, an imputation that had exercised Lord Roberts and had been seized upon by the many critics of Rhodes.[41] Unlike his biographer, O'Meara, Kekewich also vouchsafed that Rhodes had contributed significantly to the defence of Kimberley.

Quite apart from all the material support that Rhodes supplied from the De Beers Company and the various mines, he had realized on arriving in Kimberley that the town desperately required a mobile force if it was to mount an effective defence.[42] Only Rhodes could raise, pay, and support such a body, which helped to keep the enemy at bay, not least by utilizing artillery that was otherwise hopelessly inadequate in range. Until the engineering plant of De Beers manufactured the 'Long Cecil'

---

38 'Under Siege', *Courier and Argus* (Dundee), 19 March 1900, p. 5.
39 'Life in Kimberley during the Siege', *The Times Weekly Edition*, 23 March 1900, p. 184.
40 Kekewich (Qs. 22028–9), Evidence before the Elgin Commission, vol. 2, p. 566; on his command assumptions, see the transcript of his meeting with French, RH, Rhodes Mss., Afr. S228/C28, f. 189, transcript for Rhodes, 2 March 1900.
41 Ibid; Roberts was reassured that surrender was not being considered, NAM, Roberts Mss., Acc. 1971-01-23, 110/1, f. 117, Roberts to Lord Lansdowne, 12 February 1900.
42 Smuts, 'Introduction', in Green, *An Editor Looks Back*.

gun, the only artillery pieces available for the defence of Kimberley were the 7-pounder guns. As they had an effective range of only 2,500 yards (2.3 km), and were inaccurate at their maximum range of 4,500 yards (4.1 km), these guns had to be brought fairly close to the enemy positions and protected by the mounted units. At the end of the siege Rhodes was absolutely right to complain about the woeful state of British artillery[43] and to commend the services of the volunteer soldiers – services that were deprecated by regular soldiers (**11**) and not even officially acknowledged by Kekewich when volunteers paid the ultimate sacrifice in defence of their town.[44]

Undoubtedly Kekewich understood the mechanics of siege warfare. He moved with alacrity to control and later ration foodstuffs (**8**), monitored the movements of the enemy on a daily basis, engaged them as and when he could, and tried to maintain discipline and control of communications. Rhodes, having clamoured for an early relief, was much more concerned with the mood and morale of those besieged.[45] He earned plaudits for his mounted tours of the fixed defences, posing for photographs with the men and boosting morale (**172**, **188**), especially in the more exposed positions at Kenilworth. As Mrs Griffiths, a resident of Kenilworth, observed, Rhodes was a regular visitor:

> He was generally on horseback, but sometimes he walked. He was dressed in an ordinary way. It was good for us that he was there. He did everything he could for us. He spared neither money nor pains to make our lot during the siege easier. A splendid man is Mr. Rhodes.[46]

Many of his initiatives during the siege, whether in relieving internal pressures by expelling black workers or in supplying soup kitchens, and ultimately in providing shelter within the mines, were as much to do with boosting morale (**191**) as with conserving food or saving lives.[47] Moorie

---

43 'Grateful Kimberley', *Daily Mail*, 3 March 1900, p. 5; on the range of the guns, see Kekewich (Q.21919), Evidence before the Elgin Commission, vol. 2, p. 563.
44 'The Siege of Kimberley. A Talk with Mr. Cecil Rhodes', *Daily Mail*, 17 March 1900, p. 4.
45 RH, Rhodes Mss., Afr. S227, f. 1304, Rhodes to the governor, Cape Colony, 5 November 1899.
46 'Kimberley during the Siege', *Western Mail*, 28 April 1900, p. 4. For further confirmation that 'Mr. Rhodes has acted well during the siege', see the third Kimberley resident quoted in 'Letter from the Front', *Southern Guardian*, 31 March 1900, p. 2.
47 'He did a great deal to inspire the people and to cheer them up.' Jourdan, *Cecil Rhodes*, p. 112.

MacBean was probably not the only town guardsman, who feared lest the 10,000 blacks in the compounds 'would become wild' with the idleness and shelling, break loose, and run amok. As his brother commented, 'You see they would have had a free run of the town, as everyone with arms was on duty somewhere. I was very glad when they were nearly all sent away in January, through the Boer lines'.[48]

In essence the rift between Kekewich and Rhodes became a matter of control, especially about the flow of information and how that information should be used both internally and externally. From the outset Kekewich tried to control that flow and was appalled to learn that Rhodes had flouted the censorship in his early communications with the Cape, and had revealed confidences. He not only became more circumspect in his dealings with Rhodes but also more cautious in the public dissemination of news (whether of Boer offers of free passage for women and children or of the scale of British losses at Magersfontein, including the decimation of elite units such as the Black Watch). Yet this caution merely fed rumour, alarm and dismay, and Rhodes was by no means the only person incensed. Luard of Reuters protested that townsfolk had been kept in ignorance of the 'results' of the 'heavy fighting on which our fate depended'. The 'military authorities', he added, 'often failed to grasp that even a mere civilian may possess an understanding mind, and, consequently, does not care to be treated like a machine'.[49] Another journalist, H. O. Oliver, who was on the staff of the *Diamond Fields Advertiser*, deplored 'the red tape which makes the strain heavier than it would otherwise be',[50] while MacBean, a town guardsman, who regarded the censorship as among the worst features of the siege (**163**), remained furious about another incident:

> Personally, I would blame Colonel Kekewich for not letting us all know, by proclamation or notice, that the Boers were mounting such a large gun, and so close in. Much terror might have been avoided and some life saved. He must, of course, have known about it but he left it to ourselves to make 'dug-outs'.[51]

Maintaining morale may have been only one of many tasks confronting Kekewich, and in a sprawling, overcrowded town it may have had a some-

---

48 'A Highland Family in Kimberley', *Inverness Courier*, 13 April 1900, p. 6.
49 G. M. C. Luard, 'The Siege of Kimberley', in *Graphic History of the South African War* (London: Graphic Office, 1900), pp. 52–4, at p. 54.
50 'The Rival Armaments', *Norwich Mercury*, 24 March 1900, p. 2.
51 'A Highland Family in Kimberley', *Inverness Courier*, 13 April 1900, p. 6.

what intangible quality compared with the routines of manning the defences, monitoring the enemy and distributing dwindling supplies. Yet as conditions worsened with the much heavier bombardments from 'Long Tom', and the disrupted distribution of supplies that it caused (with people cowering in dug-outs or down the mines), morale became increasingly fragile. In these foetid and overheated conditions, Rhodes behaved petulantly and unforgivably towards Kekewich but the latter merely responded by trying to shoot the gunners: in doing so, he neither stopped the shelling nor reassured the citizens. The ladies down the mine thanked Rhodes (**189**) and not Kekewich; as one observed, 'we were put down the mine, through the kindness of Mr. Cecil Rhodes, who did all in his power to make us comfortable under the circumstances'.[52] Lance-Corporal Arthur Ernest Togwell, one of the section of 7th Field Company, Royal Engineers, who served in Kimberley throughout the siege, was just as complimentary. Although he approved of Kekewich's censorship on the grounds that 'ill news is best unheard',[53] Togwell commended the efforts of Rhodes in organizing road building, and the soup kitchens, and in providing 'every comfort' for the women and children down the mines. Rhodes, he claimed, 'deserves great praise, for his great encouragement to all, his name is quite a household name in Kimberley'.[54]

Kimberley might not have been on the brink of surrender (or even near it) when the relief forces arrived, but civil–military relations had reached their nadir. French, on arriving in Kimberley, may have sided too quickly with the man who owned the town and was 'a power not only in the Empire but in Europe', but he was probably correct in some of his criticisms of Kekewich's mode of command. While it was unfair to complain that Kekewich had not always exercised command 'with discretion'[55] since Kekewich had impressed most civilians with his calm and courteous manner, Kekewich was neither an inspirational nor particularly imaginative commander, and so left a gap in his handling of the siege that Rhodes could exploit.

---

52 'Four Days Down a Mine', *Lloyd's Weekly Newspaper*, 1 April 1900, p. 4; see also RH, Rhodes Mss., Afr. 228/C28, f. 171, 'From the Ladies at present in the Kimberley Mine to The Right Hon. C. J. Rhodes', n.d, and Jourdan, *Cecil Rhodes*, p. 113.
53   REMLA, Togwell diary, 2 January 1900.
54   REMLA, Togwell diary, 11 February 1900.
55   RH, Rhodes Mss., Afr. 228/C28, f. 189, transcript for Rhodes, 2 March 1900.

Relief and its Aftermath

In mounting the relief operation, Methuen's soldiers found themselves thrown into action within weeks of landing at Cape Town. Moved relatively rapidly by rail to the Orange River, they had scant opportunity to acclimatize before engaging the Boers in three battles in six days. For these soldiers (and sailors), many of who were fighting for the first time, the first week of the relief mission proved a shocking, unexpected, and challenging ordeal. Only some of them fought in all three battles but many fought in at least two of the engagements, crossing fire-swept zones in broad daylight, with comrades falling all around (**47, 50, 52, 74**).[56] They protested repeatedly that they barely had a sight of a Boer other than when they were withdrawing from battle (**49, 78, 80, 223**). At Belmont, wrote one guardsman, 'What made it the more terrible was that you could not see the enemy, for they were three-quarters of a mile away among the rocks, while we were on the sky line.'[57] Many speculated wildly about the numbers faced (**114** and p. 168 n. 10 of this chapter) and the casualties inflicted. In so doing, they were desperately seeking ways of coming to terms with the traumatic aftermaths of battle, with so many of their comrades dead or wounded, as well as the cries of the injured and the sights and smell of corpses, both human and animal.

With remarkable stoicism, doubtless derived from years of discipline and a determination to avenge fallen comrades, they proffered scant criticism of their commanding officer (**75**) and his tactics. Lord Methuen had secured three victories, however costly, and had secured the crossing of the Modder River, even if he had not reached Kimberley as forecast. Moreover, he had done so despite a chronic weakness in reconnaissance, and in a mounted arm that proved unable to pursue the retreating Boers. Few questioned his strategy of moving along the railway[58] or his tactical preference for advancing at night prior to dawn assaults, at least until disaster ensued at Magersfontein. Even then the crescendo of criticism came largely but not exclusively[59] from the decimated Highland Brigade

---

56 'War as Seen by a Cumbrian', *Lancashire Daily Post*, 2 January 1900, p. 2.
57 'Belmont, Graspan, and Modder River Fights Described', *Coventry Times and Warwickshire Journal*, 3 January 1900, p. 7.
58 There were some critics, notably Lt Hugh Crispin in his diary, 29 November 1899, FMN, where he argues that the three victories 'were dearly bought at the price, and a dearly bought victory is sometimes called a moral defeat. One can stand losing 1000 men if you have 1000 or more of the enemy stretched out as a set off, but I believe the Boer losses in these fights were very small compared with ours.'
59 Private William Stott (1st Battalion, Coldstream Guards), who was shot in the throat in the battle, reckoned that 'it was simply throwing men's lives away to attack

(**147, 150, 151**); in an extreme example, a soldier from the Highland Light Infantry described how

> Somebody shouted 'Retire!' and we did – well not a retire but a stampede, 4000 men like a flock of sheep running for dear life . . . Twelve hours' fighting and no result! Had we been handled properly the result would have been different. Every man, and officer too, is heart sick of the whole affair, all through the stupid blundering and bad generalship of Lord Methuen.[60]

Many guardsmen and other soldiers still defended Methuen (**152**). 'I am in Lord Methuen's column', wrote Private J. Bolton after Magersfontein, 'and I think we couldn't have a better commander over us.'[61] Such support was not destined to last. Several weeks spent in the trenches at the Modder River hardly improved morale (just as it caused similar problems within the Boer ranks), and, when Lord Roberts arrived with massive reinforcements and a more ambitious (and successful) strategy, confidence in Methuen began to wane (**231**).

Soldiers sought to explain how the relief mission had stalled and even suffered a calamitous defeat. They tried to disabuse the impression at home that this was going to prove a relatively easy, and rapidly triumphant, campaign. After the battle of Modder River, Private W. Billson (1st Battalion, Coldstream Guards) asserted that 'Most English people thought we should have as easy a time as we had when the British were fighting savages, but I can tell you that is wrong, for the Boers are a civilised nation with the latest weapons, and know how to use them'.[62] After Magersfontein, a driver in the Royal Field Artillery feared that the war 'is not the picnic that everyone thought it was going to be. I am sure there will be thousands lost on both sides yet before it is ended.'[63]

The more perceptive were also keen to convey some impression of the inhospitable climate, and the vast open terrain that afforded scant cover for advancing soldiers, as well as the determination of a well-armed enemy. Accordingly, they wrote not only about the effects of magazine rifles firing smokeless, flat-trajectory ammunition across open fire zones,

---

them as we did', 'A Bolton Man Wounded at Magersfontein', *Bolton Chronicle*, 13 January 1900, p. 7.
60 'Soldiers' Accounts of Magersfontein', *Glasgow Herald*, 10 January 1900, p. 9.
61 'Letters from Local Men', *Wakefield Express*, 10 February 1900, p. 6.
62 'Will be "Glad When Peace is Proclaimed"', *Sheffield Daily Telegraph*, 3 January 1900, p. 7.
63 'Local Men at the Front', *Alnwick and County Gazette*, 10 February 1900, p. 2.

but also about the resolve of the Boers and the tactical leadership of their generals. By withdrawing men from the sieges at Mafeking and Kimberley to concentrate upon blocking the relief mission, the Boer commanders had sought to inflict another major defeat on the British, as they had done at Majuba in February 1881, and thereby precipitate peace negotiations. Three retreats in six days had not helped but even after the hasty withdrawal from the Modder River, the British were not convinced that the enemy had become demoralized. Sergeant T. Kirby (Loyal North Lancashires) discounted reports that the Boers 'were starving' as 'very few give themselves up'. On the contrary he had heard that 'They seem to be making a determined stand against Buller's advance to Ladysmith and in my opinion they will strongly oppose Lord Methuen's advance to Kimberley.' Writing on the eve of Magersfontein, Kirby added that 'The Boer is not the ignorant farmer some people take him for. They have some very clever men amongst them, as no one could select better positions than they do.'[64]

More fundamentally some had already noticed that the nature of war had changed. Modern weaponry, if fired from concealed positions at ground level, maximized the effects of smokeless, flat-trajectory ammunition, and enhanced the fire-power of soldiers fighting on the defensive. Hence when Sergeant Richard Wilkinson (2nd Battalion, Coldstream Guards) praised the generalship of Cronjé, and the resolve of Boers 'as fighting men', holding firm in spite of shelling from British artillery, he observed: 'Of course, they are all on the defensive, they never attack us, but always wait for us to go for them . . . They are playing a waiting game and playing it well.'[65] Being faced with such tactics, and a barely visible enemy, had caused immense frustration in British ranks. Writing after Magersfontein, an officer in Methuen's force complained that the Boer 'is the invisible enemy . . . We want brains here, and rough riders and bold riders. The old system of war is played out. England wants to turn over a new leaf in this woefully-managed war.'[66] Even in the wake of Paardeberg, a signaller in the King's Shropshires felt that Britain had to cope with the near-term requirements as well as considering army reforms for the longer term. 'The generals who have made mistakes are the best, or supposed to be, that we have,' he wrote, 'so we must perforce abide by both system and generals.'[67] However, he maintained that if Britain

---

64 'With the North Lancashires', *Lancashire Daily Post*, 12 March 1900, p. 5.
65 'A Nelson Soldier at Modder River', *Nelson Chronicle*, 12 January 1900, p. 6.
66 '"This Woefully-Managed War"', *Birmingham Daily Post*, 10 January 1900, p. 9.
67 This was quite prescient as Methuen was one commander who would serve throughout the war.

wanted 'an army to be ready and efficiently equipped for the field, and have the latest improvements in armament, we must be prepared to pay for it . . . A nation must either keep forging ahead with the rest, or go to swell the list of decayed powers. We cannot remain stationary.' What he feared was that, once peace returned, 'the whole matter will pass away from the minds of men . . . and "Tommy" himself will again become an isolated being'.[68]

Cavalrymen were less beset by self-doubt and introspection. They had participated in one of the epic events of the war (**207, 210**), the first charge for many of them (**208**), and a demonstration of what a cavalry division could accomplish under a 'brilliant' general (**218, 219**). Both at the time, and subsequently, the charge was hailed as a stunning example of what the mounted arm could achieve on the battlefield against an enemy armed with magazine rifles. As the interception of Cronjé's forces at Paardeberg followed the relief of Kimberley, and led to the first major surrender of Boer forces in the war, it bolstered the reputations of French and of his chief staff officer, Haig,[69] enhancing their ability to champion the cavalry arm in the subsequent debates over army reform.

Haig was quite prepared to seize the initiative in such matters. In a letter dated 2 March 1900, he revealed that he knew that army reform was once again under scrutiny at home and he wanted to publicize that 'the Cavalry – the despised Cavalry I should say – has saved the "Empire" to quote Lord Kitchener's word'. The army, he argued, could not rely upon mounted infantry because they could not charge with lance or sword. Conversely French had decided, 'without a second's hesitation', to launch the charge at Klip Drift despite passing 'within 1,000 yards [914 m] of the Boer position' and encountering a 'very hot rifle fire'. The division had incurred very few casualties in relieving Kimberley, without the garrison making the 'slightest attempt to assist us', and then sent units ahead to pin the Boers at Paardeberg, so demonstrating that the cavalry 'can charge in the open as well as act dismounted'.[70]

While some commentators assert that these events vindicate their description of Haig as a reformer intent on preserving a properly trained 'hybrid' cavalry that could act effectively in different ways on the modern battlefield,[71] two crucial features of the Klip Drift charge were the four-day

---

68 'The Cronje Surrender', *Burnley Express and Advertiser*, 14 April 1900, p. 8.
69 On Haig's role as French's deputy, see Badsey, *Doctrine and Reform*, pp. 100–1 and n. 100.
70 NLS, Haig Mss., Acc. 3155/334(e), Haig to unidentified colonel, 2 March 1900.
71 Badsey, 'The Boer War (1899–1902) and British Cavalry Doctrine', pp. 85 and 90; G. Sheffield, *The Chief: Douglas Haig and the British Army* (London: Aurum

preparatory manoeuvre and the open-order formation. By moving south and thence east away from the railway line and into the Orange Free State, French exploited mounted resources in cavalry, MI and horse artillery that Methuen had never possessed. More significantly, he was able to move his forces to confront the Boers where they were relatively weak. By launching the charge in open order to minimize British casualties, he did not know that he faced only about 900 men spread thinly over the hills and nek. While nothing should detract from the boldness of his decision and the spectacular nature of the event,[72] it was surprising that Haig, as a purported reformer, should choose to criticize the open-order formation. In the cavalry war diary, he regretted that the leading 3rd Brigade 'was unable to retain a squadron in close order in hand', claiming that the enemy would have lost more heavily 'had this been done'.[73]

Understandably, the British citizens of Kimberley had scant interest in such debates or in the details of army reform. They had survived an unexpected ordeal and had built up a strong animus against the Boers (**21, 22**). They were 'not men, they are fiends', wrote one lady, a resident of Kimberley for the past twenty-five years; while C. P. J. Coghlan, a captain in the Town Guard, disparaged the Boers as 'awful scoundrels' for 'deliberately' shelling 'the town, with a result that mostly women and children have been killed and maimed'.[74] Nevertheless Willie Campbell, like many others, was proud that they had remained resolute after Magersfontein and had kept 'the Dutch out of Kimberley' (**226**). Whether the citizens were simply pleased to have survived the experience or were just relieved that the siege was over, they had a common desire for security. In the short term they welcomed the arrival of a larger garrison of British soldiers, the restoration of the railroad and with it the resumption of supplies from the Cape, and the confirmation that all the diamonds and mining plans, which had been buried during the siege, had survived.[75] Economically, the town could recover relatively quickly and many of those trapped in their flight from the Rand could travel on to Cape Town.

Press, 2011), p. 45.
72 G. J. de Groot, *Douglas Haig, 1861–1928* (London: Unwin Hyman, 1988), p. 80; J. P. Harris, *Douglas Haig and the First World War* (Cambridge: Cambridge University Press, 2008), p. 35.
73 NLS, Haig Mss., Acc. 3155/34, Cavalry Diary and Orders, 15 February 1900, p. 170.
74 'The Siege of Kimberley from Within', *Birmingham Daily Post*, 22 March 1900, p. 5; 'Another Letter from Kimberley', *Essex County Chronicle*, 30 March 1900, p. 3.
75 'The Kimberley Diamonds How They Were Saved', *Western Mail*, 18 April 1900, p. 6.

Returning home, though, could prove a daunting experience. When Sergeant Harvey C. Merry of the Cape Mounted Police and his wife got back to their house in Barkly West, they found that they had lost 'everything belonging to our home . . . The Boers looted or smashed up everything they could not take away.'[76] Understandably, such revelations appalled English-speaking survivors of the siege and they deprecated the behaviour of the Boers and expressed uncertainty about the future. All too aware of the settlement that followed the Anglo-Transvaal War, which restored the sovereignty of the South African Republic (Transvaal), they feared a similar outcome. 'If autonomy is to be given back to these rascals as it was in 1881', wrote the Kimberley lady, 'we may expect another serious war in five years . . . The Dutch have proved themselves utterly incapable of governing themselves or anybody else.' For her, the future depended 'on the English Parliament. But there lies the real danger – far worse than the Boers – that when all is over they will return the country to the Boers, and we shall be worse off in the colony than ever.'[77] Just as this lady saw the only solution as 'a united South Africa, and Federal Parliament under the English flag', the Campbells saw salvation in an expanded empire from the Cape to Cairo.[78] Indeed, Willie Campbell embraced fully the vision of Cecil Rhodes:

A few days before we were in the valley of the shadow of death; but now we believe we may live to see the day when the British Empire shall extend from the Cape to Cairo, when there will no more Free State and South African Republic, but a united South Africa, happy and prosperous, under the Sceptre of British Sovereignty.[79]

Ironically the citizens of Kimberley, like the soldiers who relieved their siege, were not simply revelling in the moment of triumph. The 124-day siege had left lasting scars that found reflection in many of the letters chronicling their recent experience. Dislike of the invading enemy was more than matched by a loss of confidence in the conduct of the war, even if the arrival of Lords Roberts and Kitchener and their additional forces had bolstered morale and revived confidence about the military outcome. For Kimberley's civilians, success on the battlefield represented

---

76 'Letter from a Derby Man Serving in the Cape Mounted Police', *Derby Daily Telegraph*, 20 March 1900, p. 3; see also 97.
77 'The Siege of Kimberley from Within', *Birmingham Daily Post*, 22 March 1900, p. 5.
78 Ibid.; 'Letters from Kimberley', *Caithness Courier*, 23 March 1900, p. 3.
79 'Part II of the Siege of Kimberley', *Caithness Courier*, 20 April 1900, p. 3.

only the first stage on the path towards political security and economic prosperity; the nature of the subsequent political settlement would remain an imponderable and, if the full vision of Rhodes would not be realized in its entirety, the unification of South Africa was a critical requirement.

Select Bibliography

Primary Sources

Black Watch Regimental Archive (BWRA)
    Cameron Mss.
Cornwall's Regimental Museum
    Aldworth Memorials
Fusiliers Museum of Northumberland (FMN)
    Crispin diary
    Porteous diary
    Smith diary
Lancashire Infantry Museum (LIM)
    Gregson letter
    Kekewich diary
    O'Meara diary
    Webster reminiscences
National Army Museum (NAM)
    Bly Mss.
    Haddock letter
    Roberts Mss.
National Library of Scotland (NLS)
    Haig Mss.
Rhodes House (RH)
    Rhodes Mss.
Royal Engineers Museum, Library and Archive (REMLA)
    Togwell diary
Wiltshire and Swindon Historical Centre (WSHC)
    Methuen Mss.

Newspapers

Aberdeen (Weekly) *Journal*
Alnwick and County Gazette
Argyllshire Herald
Auckland Times and Herald
Ayr Advertiser or West Country and Galloway Journal
Bath Daily Argus
Belfast News-Letter
Birmingham Daily Post
Blackburn Times
Bolton Chronicle
Bradford Observer
Bridge of Allan Reporter
Bristol Mercury and Daily Post
Burnley Express and Advertiser
Bury and Norwich Post, and Suffolk Standard
Caithness Courier
Cheltenham Chronicle
Cheshire Observer
Chronicle (Doncaster)
Cork Constitution
Courier and Argus (Dundee)
Coventry Times and Warwickshire Journal
Crewe Guardian
Daily Free Press (Aberdeen)
Daily Mail
Daily News (London)
Daily Telegraph
Derby Daily Telegraph
Derby Mercury
Devon Weekly Times
Doncaster Gazette
Dover Express
Dundee Advertiser
Dundee Weekly News
Edinburgh Evening News
Elgin Courant and Courier
Essex County Chronicle
Essex County Standard, West Suffolk Gazette and Eastern Counties Advertiser
Evening News (London)
Evening Swindon Advertiser
Glasgow Herald
Gloucestershire Chronicle
Gloucestershire Echo
Graphic
Hamilton Advertiser
Inverness Courier
Isle of Man Weekly Times and General Advertiser
Isle of Wight Observer
John O'Groats Journal
Kentish Mercury
Kilmarnock Standard
Lancashire Daily Post
Leeds Mercury
Leicester Chronicle and Leicestershire Mercury
Lennox Herald
Lichfield Mercury
Liverpool Mercury
Lloyd's Weekly Newspaper
Manchester Evening News
Manchester Weekly Times
Morning Post
Motherwell Times
Nairnshire Telegraph
Nelson Chronicle
Newcastle Daily Chronicle
North-Eastern Daily Gazette
North Wales Chronicle
Northern Echo (Darlington)
Northern Scot and Moray & Nairn Express
Norwich Mercury
Oban Times
Ossett Observer
Paisley and Renfrewshire Gazette
Perthshire Advertiser
Perthshire Constitutional and Journal
Pontefract Telegram
Preston Herald

Select Bibliography

Rotherham Advertiser
Sheffield and Rotherham
  Independent
Sheffield Daily Telegraph
Somerset County Gazette
Somerset Standard
Southern Guardian
Stirling Observer
Strathearn Herald
The Star (Saint Peter Port)
The Times
The Times Weekly Edition

Totnes Times
Wakefield Express
Warrington Guardian
Warwick, Leamington and
  Warwickshire Times
Weekly Standard and Express
  (Blackburn)
Wells Journal
Western Mail
Yorkshire Evening Press
Yorkshire Herald and The York
  Herald

Secondary Sources

Amery, L. S. (ed.), *The Times History of The War in South Africa 1899–1902*, 7 vols (London: Sampson Low, Marston and Co., 1900–9)

Anglesey, Marquess of, *A History of the British Cavalry 1816–1919*, vol. 4: *1899–1913* (London: Leo Cooper, 1986)

Ashe, E. Oliver, *Besieged by the Boers A Diary of Life and Events in Kimberley during the Siege* (London: Hutchinson, 1900)

Badsey, S., *Doctrine and Reform in the British Cavalry 1880–1918* (Aldershot: Ashgate, 2008)

Beet, A. J., and Harris, C. B., *Kimberley Under Siege* (Kimberley: Diamond Fields Advertiser, n.d.)

Bennett, E. N., *With Methuen's Column on an Ambulance Train* (London: Swan Sonnenschein, 1900)

Bennett, I., *A Rain of Lead: The Siege and Surrender of the British at Potchefstroom* (London: Greenhill Books, 2001)

Bredin, Brigadier A. E. C., *A History of the Irish Soldier* (Belfast: Century Books, 1987)

Brooks, R., *The Long Arm of Empire: Naval Brigades from the Crimea to the Boxer Rebellion* (London: Constable, 1999)

Cammack, D., *The Rand at War 1899–1902: The Witwatersrand and the Anglo-Boer War* (London: James Currey, 1990)

Carver, Field Marshal Lord, *The National Army Museum Book of The Boer War* (London: Pan Books, 2000)

Changuion, L., *Silence of the Guns: The History of the Long Toms of the Anglo-Boer War* (Pretoria: Protea Book House, 2001)

Childs, L., *Kimberley: Belmont/Graspan/Modder River/Magersfontein* (Barnsley: Leo Cooper, 2001)

Colvin, Brevet Lieutenant-Colonel F. F., and Gordon, Captain E. R., *Diary of the 9th (Q.R.) Lancers during the South African Campaign, 1899 to 1902* (London: Cecil Roy, 1904)

Creswicke, L., *South Africa and the Transvaal War*, 6 vols (Edinburgh; T. C. & E. C. Jack, 1900)
De Groot, G. J., *Douglas Haig, 1861–1928* (London: Unwin Hyman, 1988)
De Villebois-Mareuil, G., *War Notes The Diary of Colonel Villebois-Mareuil from November 24, 1899 to April 4, 1900* (London: Adam & Charles Black, 1902)
De Wet, C. R., *Three Years War (October 1899–June 1902)* (London: Archibald Constable and Co., 1903)
Downham, Lieutenant-Colonel J., *Red Roses on the Veldt: Lancashire Regiments in the Boer War, 1899–1902* (Lancaster: Carnegie Publishing, 2000)
Doyle, A. Conan, *The Great Boer War* (London: Smith, Elder & Co., 1900)
Evans, M. Marix, *Encyclopedia of the Boer War* (Santa Barbara, Cal.: ABC-CLIO, 2000)
Gardner, B., *The Lion's Cage* (London: Arthur Barker, 1969)
Garvin, J. L., *Life of Joseph Chamberlain*, 6 vols (London: Macmillan, 1932–69)
Goldmann, C. S., *With General French and the Cavalry in South Africa* (London: Macmillan & Co., 1902)
Gooch, J. (ed.), *The Boer War: Direction, Experience and Image* (London: Frank Cass, 2000)
Gordon-Duff, Lieutenant-Colonel L., *With the Gordon Highlanders to the Boer War and Beyond: The story of Captain Lachlan Gordon-Duff* (Staplehurst, Kent: Spellmount, 2000)
Green, G. A, L., *An Editor Looks Back: South African and other Memories, 1883–1946* (Cape Town: Juta & Co.,1947)
Harris, Colonel Sir D., *Pioneer, Soldier and Politician: Summarised Memoirs* (London: Sampson, Low, Marston & Co., 1930)
Harris, J. P., *Douglas Haig and the First World War* (Cambridge: Cambridge University Press, 2008)
Headlam, C. (ed.), *The Milner Papers*, 2 vols (London: Cassell, 1933)
Henderson, R. H., *An Ulsterman in Africa* (Cape Town: Unie-Volkspers Beperk, 1944)
Hensman, *Cecil Rhodes: A Study of a Career* (Cape Town, C. Struik, 1974)
Hillegas, H. C., *With the Boers* (London: Methuen, 1900)
Holmes, R., *The Little Field Marshal: A Life of Sir John French* (London: Jonathan Cape, 1981)
Jeans, Surgeon T. T. (ed.), *Naval Brigades in the South African War 1899–1900* (London: Sampson Low, Marston & Co., 1902)
Jourdan, P., *Cecil Rhodes: His Private Life by His Private Secretary* (London: John Lane, The Bodley Head, 1911)
Kruger, R., *Goodbye Dolly Gray: A History of the Boer War* (London: Nel Mentor edition, 1967)
Lloyd, Captain E., *Boer War. Diary of Captain Eyre Lloyd 2nd Coldstream Guards* (London: Army and Navy Co-operative Society, 1905)

Select Bibliography

Lockhart, J. G., and Woodhouse, the Hon. C. M., *Rhodes* (London: Hodder & Stoughton, 1963)

Longford, E., *Jameson's Raid* (London: Weidenfeld & Nicolson, 1982, 2nd edition)

Lunderstedt, S., *From Belmont to Bloemfontein: The Western Campaign of the Anglo-Boer War, February 1899–April 1900* (Kimberley: Diamond Fields Advertiser, 2000)

MacKenzie, J. M., with Dalziel, N. R., *The Scots in South Africa: Ethnicity, identity, gender and race, 1772–1914* (Manchester: Manchester University Press, 2007)

Macnab, R., *The French Colonel: Villebois-Mareuil and the Boers, 1899–1900* (Oxford: Oxford University Press, 1975)

Maurice, Major-General Sir F. B., and. Grant, M. H, *History of the War in South Africa 1899–1902*, 4 vols (London: Hurst & Blackett, 1906–10)

Meintjes, J., *De la Rey – Lion of the West: A Biography* (Johannesburg, Hugh Keartland Publishers, 1966)

Meyer, C., *Days of Honour during The Siege of Kimberley 1899/1900*, trans. by V. Matter (Kimberley: Kimberley Africana Library under the auspices of the Friends of the Library, 1999)

Mileham, P. J. R., *Fighting Highlanders! The History of the Argyll & Sutherland Highlanders* (London: Arms and Armour Press, 1993)

Miller, S. M., *Lord Methuen and the British Army: Failure and Redemption in South Africa* (London: Frank Cass, 1999)

Nasson, B., *The South African War 1899–1902* (London: Arnold, 1999)

O'Meara, Lieutenant-Colonel W. A. J., *Kekewich in Kimberley: Being an Account of the Defence of the Diamond Fields October 14th, 1899–February 15th, 1900* (London: Medici Society, 1926)

Pakenham, T., *The Boer War* (London: Weidenfeld & Nicolson, 1979)

Pemberton, W. Baring, *Battles of the Boer War* (London: Pan Books, 1969)

Phillipps, L. March *With Rimington* (London: Edward Arnold, 1902)

Powell, G., *Buller: A Scapegoat?* (London: Leo Cooper, 1994)

_____, and J. Powell, *The History of the Green Howards: Three Hundred Years of Service* (Barnsley: Leo Cooper, 2002)

Pretorius, F., *The A to Z of the Anglo-Boer War* (Lanham, Maryland, and Plymouth, UK: Scarecrow Press, 2009)

_____, *Life on Commando during the Anglo-Boer War 1899–1902* (Cape Town: Human & Rousseau, 1999)

Ralph, J., *Towards Pretoria: A Record of the War between Briton and Boer to the Hoisting of the British Flag at Bloemfontein* (London: C. Arthur Pearson, 1900)

Roberts, B., *Kimberley: Turbulent City* (Cape Town: David Philip, 1976)

Rotberg, R. I., *The Founder: Cecil Rhodes and the Pursuit of Power* (New York: Oxford University Press, 1988)

Sheffield, G., *The Chief: Douglas Haig and the British Army* (London: Aurum Press, 2011)

Skelley, A. R., *The Victorian Army at Home: The Recruitment and Terms and Conditions of the British Regular, 1859–1899* (London: Croom Helm, 1977)

Spiers, E. M., *Letters from Ladysmith: Eyewitness Accounts from the South African War* (London: Frontline, 2010)

———, *The Scottish Soldier and Empire, 1854–1902* (Edinburgh: Edinburgh University Press, 2006)

Thomas, A., *Rhodes: The Race for Africa* (London: Penguin Books, 1997)

Trollope, A., *South Africa*, reprint of the 1878 edition with an introduction and notes by J. H. Davidson (Cape Town: A. A. Balkema, 1973)

Villebois-Mareuil, Georges de, *War Notes. The Diary of Colonel de Villebois-Mareuil* (London: Adam and Charles Black, 1902)

Wallace, R. L., *The Australians at the Boer War* (Canberra: The Australian War Memorial and the Australian Government Publishing Service, 1976)

Warwick, P. (ed.), *The South African War: The Anglo-Boer War 1899–1902* (London: Longman, 1980)

Wessels, A. (ed.), *Lord Roberts and the War in South Africa 1899–1902* (Stroud, Glos.: Sutton Publishing for the Army Records Society, 2000)

Williams, A. F., *Some Dreams Come True: Being a Sheaf of Stories Leading up to the Discovery of Copper, Diamonds and Gold in Southern Africa, and of the Pioneers who took part in the Excitement of those Early Days* (Cape Town: Howard B. Timmins, 1948)

Wilson, H. W., *With the Flag to Pretoria: A History of the Boer War of 1899–1900*, 2 vols (London: Harmsworth Brothers, 1900–1)

Articles and Chapters

Badsey, S., 'The Boer War (1899–1902) and British Cavalry Doctrine: A Re-Evaluation', *Journal of Military History*, vol. 71 (2006), pp. 75–97

Beaumont, J., 'The British Press during the South African War: The Sieges of Mafeking, Kimberley and Ladysmith', in M. Connelly & D. Welch (eds), *War and the Media: Reportage and Propaganda, 1900–2003* (London: I. B. Tauris, 2005), pp. 1–18

Miller, S. M., 'Lord Methuen and the British Advance to the Modder River', *Military History Journal*, vol. 10 (1964), pp. 121–36

Peddle, Col. D. E., 'LONG CECIL: The Gun made in Kimberley during the Siege"', *Military History Journal*, vol. 4, no. 1 (1977) http://samilitaryhistory.org/vol041dp.html (accessed 31 May 2011)

'Reminiscences of the Siege of Kimberley', *Lancashire Lad*, no. 2 (1908), pp. 15–16

Spiers, E. M., 'Military correspondence in the late nineteenth-century press', *Archives*, vol. 32, no. 116 (2007), pp. 28–40

Index

Aberdeen Journal, 167
Ackroyd, Lt Charles H., 57n31
Adlam, Leon, 32
Akenhead, A. G., 19
Albrecht, Maj Richard F. W., 75, 162
Aldworth, Lt-Col William, 156n65, 157
Alexandersfontein, 16, 117, 126, 143; Boer positions at, 125–6, 136
Allason, Maj R. Bannatine, 132n16
Almond, Pte William, 169
ambulance, 70, 98, 143; fired on, 50, 57, 69, 97
Amery, Leo, 38n3, 115n8
Anderson, Pte Harry, 95
Anderson, W. T., 119–20, 146, 172–3
Anglo-Transvaal War (1880–1), 8n30, 47–8, 161, 171, 183
Anthony, Pte W. J., 74–5
armoured train, 20, 23, 28–9, 31–2, 38, 61, 78n2, 165; ambush of, 8n30, 16; reconnaissance duties of, 51, 63
army corps, 37–8
army reform, 46n18, 180–2
artillery, Boer, 78, 103, 132–3; at Belmont, 42, 46, 75; at Graspan, 51–2, 54; at Kimberley, 4, 15–16, 22, 24–9, 31, 33, 114, 118–22, 124–5, 136, 141–2, 144, 174, 182; at Klip Drift, 134–5; at Magersfontein, 81, 91; at Modder River, 61, 63–4, 66–8, 70, 72; at Paardeberg, 152, 161; Creusot, 116n11, *see also* 'Long Tom' gun
artillery, British, 1, 41, 79, 103, 131–2, 167; at Belmont, 46, 48, 60; at Graspan, 52, 54, 56, 58, 60; at Kimberley, 14, 17, 22, 28, 32, 35, 175; at Klip Drift, 134–5, 140; at Magersfontein, 83n10, 84–5, 89–91, 96, 107–8; at Modder River, 66–7, 69; at Paardeberg, 152–4, 159–60, 180; naval, 46, 52, 63, 77, 103, 153, 159; *see also* 'Long Cecil' gun
Ashe, Dr E. Oliver, 35, 123n22
Atkinson, Sgt Alfred, 155n63
Atkinson, L/Cpl W. H., 63–4

Austin, Pte J., 100
Australian forces, 75, 77; for specific Australian units, *see* regiments, Volunteer
Ayres, Sgt-Maj, 142

Baden-Powell, Col Robert S. S., 1, 165
balloon, observation, 74, 95–6, 107–8
Barnard, Pte Thomas Walter, 68
Barnsley Chronicle, 149
Barrett, Pte P., 160
Beaconsfield, 12, 119, 125, 168, 171; ambulance corps of, 118; town guard, 32, 125
Bechuanaland expedition (1884–5), 3, 21n12
Belfast News-Letter, 149
Belmont, 37, 40, 42, 44, 51, 79, 128, 130; battle of (1899), 41n7, 42–51, 54, 60, 63, 75, 77, 81, 83n9, 130, 143, 172, 178
Bennet, Thomas, 17, 21, 27, 121–2
Bennett, QMS, 67–8
Bergandel, battle of (1900), 3n6
Berry, Pte J., 153–4, 157
Billson, Pte W., 179

192   Index

Blackburn, Pte F., 37
Blackburn Times, 9
black people, 1, 8n30, 51, 117; drivers, 69; labourers, 73, 122; runners, 7; *see also* Kimberley
'Black Week', 103
Bloemfontein, 41, 75, 113, 127–8, 150–1, 173; Boer from, 69, 75, 84–5. 96; commando, 75; conference (1899), 3n6, 16n6
Boers, 2, 8, 78, 80, 132, 146, 179, 183; and Rhodes, 2–4, 148–9; at Belmont, 42, 44–8, 50; at Graspan, 51–2, 54–60, 69; at Kimberley, 5, 15–18, 21–5, 28–36, 58, 69, 111–12, 116–17, 120, 125–6, 128, 142–4, 165, 171–2, 176; at Klip Drift, 133–4, 140–1, 182; at Magersfontein, 74–5, 81, 83–6, 88–94, 108; at Modder River, 60–71, 74, 168; at Paardeberg, 151–61; concealment of, 8, 57, 63–4, 72, 75, 81, 84–6, 100, 178, 180; ill-discipline of, 58, 69–70, 168, 172; mobility of, 8, 55n28, 67, 73, 172, 178; shooting of, 38, 64–5, 78, 85–6, 91, 126, 131, 140; ultimatum of, 1, 3n6, 16–17; *see also* artillery, Boer
Bolton, Pte J., 179
Boshof, 116n12; commando, 16
Botha, Gen Philip, 160, 163
Bourne, L/Cpl, 890
Bristol Mercury, 148
Broadwood, Maj-Gen Robert G., 129

Brooke, Lt Edward, 67
Brooks, Pte S., 125
Brown, Maj Frederick J., 158n67
Bryson, Sgt John, 44–5
Buckley, Tpr Robert, 49
Buller, Gen Sir Redvers, 38, 41, 103, 127, 180
Bultfontein Mine, 11
Bunbury, Lt William, 142n35
Butler, Sgt Harry, 140–1
Butler, Lt-Gen Sir William F., 4
Byrne, J. F., 15–16

Caithness Courier, 167
Callendar, Cpl, 135, 137
Campbell, William J., 107–12, 114, 122, 125, 141, 183
Canadian contingents, 75, 77, 156
Cape Colony, 1–4, 7, 15, 20, 39, 109, 113–4, 116, 128–9, 171–2; Boers in, 41, 109, 171; British forces in, 1, 37
Cape Medical Volunteer Corps, 85
Cape Mounted Police, 12, 17, 21–2, 29, 137, 167, 183
Cape Town, 2, 15, 37–41, 73–4, 109n3, 127, 129, 178, 182; Cape to Cairo, 183
Cardwell, Edward T., 46n18
Carter's Ridge, 16, 27; action at (1899), 31–4
cavalry, brigades, 54n26, 128–9, 133, 150–2, 154, 182; division, 130, 134, 140–1, 146, 150n54, 151, 181
censorship, 5, 107n1, 109–10n4, 168–9, 176–7
Chalmers, Sapper W. C., 69

Chamberlain, Joseph, 7
Chamier, Maj George D., 31–2, 35
Cheyne, William Watson, 160
Clarke, Pte J. H., 90
Clements, Maj-Gen Ralph A. P., 127
Clucas, Albert, 26–7, 33, 35–6, 115, 123
Cockcroft, Pte J., 99
Coghlan, C. P. J., 182
Coldstream Guards, 64; *see* regiments for 1st and 2nd Battalions
Colenso, battle of (1899), 103, 148
Colesberg, cavalry operations (1899–1900), 128–9, 135
Colvile, Maj-Gen Sir Henry Edward, 83, 152
communications, 19, 175–6; alarms, 17–18, 119; despatch riders, 7; heliograph, 7, 23, 31, 116; telegraph, 17–18, 38, 73, 138; telephone, 12, 18, 115n7
conning tower, 12, 107, 115n7, 119, 173
Consolidated Gold Fields of South Africa, 3
Cooke, Sgt R. A., 153, 155–6, 162n74
Cookson, Sapper, 74n54
Cox, Pte G., 156
Crimean War (1854–6), 169
Crispin, Lt Hugh T., 58–9, 178n58
Cronjé, Gen Piet A., 61, 70, 81, 116–17, 141, 150–1, 160, 162, 172, 180; forces of, 61, 71n50, 127–8, 151–2, 154, 158–61, 168n10; surrender of, 161, 163, 170, 181
Crossley, Pte A. E., 58

Index

Daily Mail, 7
Daily News, 148
Dargai, storming of (1897), 94n17
De Aar, 40, 59, 72, 98, 109n3, 128; *see also* hospital
De Beers Consolidated Mines, 2–4, 6, 12, 14, 112, 146; and 'Long Cecil' gun, 111, 115n7, 116, 174; employees of, 11, 20, 27n18, 113, 115n7, 123, 145, 174; shell production of, 28, 115n7
De Beers Mine, 12, 18, 123, 143
De La Rey, Gen Jacobus H. (Koos), 8, 16, 21n12, 51, 71n50, 128, 163; tactics of, 60–1, 69, 81
De Villebois-Mareuil, Col Georges H. A.-M. V., 116–17, 172
De Wet, Gen Christiaan, 128–9, 131n13, 150n54, 160
De Wet, Gen Pieter (Piet) D., 131n13
Diamond Fields Advertiser, 6–7, 124, 173, 176
Diamond Fields Artillery, 12, 17, 23, 32
Diamond Fields Horse, 12, 17, 21, 23, 138
diamonds, 1–3, 11, 113, 124, 148–9, 167, 182
Downman, Lt-Col George T. F., 94
Doyle, Arthur Conan, 4–5, 173
Doyle, Pte P., 44–6, 52, 65, 69
Dronfield Ridge, 16, 27; action at (1899), 23; action at (1900), 138, 142–3, 150
Drummond, 2nd Lt The Hon Maurice C. A., 86

Duffield, Tpr, 135
Dunbar, Lt James Brander, 24, 31n31, 169–70
Dundee (Talana Hill), battle of (1899), 38
Dunner, Tpr Edward, 170
Du Toit, Gen Sarel Petrus, 117, 141
Dutoitspan Mine, 11
Dutton, Pte Harold, 89

Eadie, Pte W., 74
Eagar, Capt Edward B., 47, 50
Edwards, Pte A. G., 55
Edwards, Sgt, 95–6
Egerton-Green, Capt Francis, 92, 134, 151, 162
Egypt, campaign (1882), 21n12, 39, 83n9, 98n22
Elandslaagte, battle of (1899), 140
Elgin Courant, 167
Elkington, Frank, 170
entrenchments, at Kimberley, 12, 14, 16, 18, 21, 115, 126, 144; Boer, 31, 33, 61, 66, 69, 75, 81, 84–7, 89–91, 96–8, 102n28, 125, 128, 135, 151, 154, 157, 161–2n74, 169, 179; British, 103–4, 159, 179
Ewart, Col J. Spencer, 98

Fallas, Cpl H., 163
Feilden, Capt Cecil W. M., 130, 133, 136–7
Fernyhough, Lt Hugh C., 57n31
Ferreira, Gen Ignatius, 17, 116
Fife, Lt Hugh Wharton, 156–7
First World (Great) War (1914–18), 168
Fitches, Tpr G., 136
Fordyce, Lt Robert D., 142n35

Fort Rhodes, 113
Foster, Gnr A., 56
Freeland, Capt Lewis G., 47
French, Sgt James T., 87
French, Maj-Gen John D. P., 5, 118, 132, 135, 181; and Kekewich, 137n20, 174n40, 177; and relief operation, 122, 127, 134–5, 140–2, 144, 148–9, 181; and Rhodes, 5, 137, 150, 177; at Klip Drift, 134–5, 140–1; relief force of, 127–9, 132n14, n15, 142, 144, 149–50, 182
Frontier Mounted Rifles, 39
Furness, Sgt Walter, 97

Gatacre, Maj-Gen Sir William F., 41, 127
gold, 2–3
Gordon, Maj-Gen Charles 'Chinese', 165
Gordon, Drummer F., 85–6
Gordon, Brig-Gen James R. P., 129
Gosling, Arthur, 59
Gough, Lt-Col Bloomfield, 51, 58n32
Graham, Lt Richard B., 88
Grant, Lt W. Gordon, 27n18m 113, 116, 142
Graspan (Enslin), battle of (1899), 51, 53–60, 69, 77, 79, 83n9, 143, 172; action at (1899), 78
Gray, Clr Sgt A. J., 100–1
Gray, Pte J., 38–9
Gray, Pte W., 47
Green, L/Cpl C., 146–7
Green, George, A. L., 6–7n22, 137n20
Green, L/Cpl James A., 72, 168n10
Gregory, Pte G., 73

Gregson, Pte Robert, 15
Griffiths, Mrs, 27, 175
Griqualand West, 2, 4
Groundwater, Pte Alexander, 143
Guards Brigade, 41, 47, 49, 61, 65, 83, 89, 92; *see* regiments for specific Guards battalions
Guild, Jessie R., 26, 34, 121

Haddock, Mrs William, 35n31
Haig, Lt-Col Douglas, 119n18, 128n6, 132n16, 137, 181–2
Hamilton, Pte 155
Hamilton, Sgt William, 79–80, 104
Hampshire Advertiser, 148
Hampshire Telegraph, 149
Hannay, Col Ormelie C., 129, 157
Harris, Sir David, 6
Harris, L, 163
Harrison, Tpr Claude, 77–8
Havelock, Maj-Gen Henry, 165
Hawley, Pte H., 72
Hayes, Pte J., 69
Haygarth, Sgt Harry, 144
Hayworth, Pte J., 102
Heberden, Dr G. E., 30
Henderson, Robert H., 6
Henry, Adam, 138
Herbert, Lt Louis. W., 159
Hewitt, Pte George, 56, 59–60, 92–3
Hex River Valley Pass, 109
Hicklin, Pte Ted, 90
Highland Brigade, 41, 77, 81, 87, 90, 93, 95, 100–2, 104–5, 150, 152, 156, 166, 178
Hill, Gnr E., 130–1, 133–4
Hill, Pte, 40–1
Hillegas, Howard C., 172

Hilliard, R., 27, 125
Hirst, Pte J. T., 50
Hitchcock, Sgt, 104
Hodgson, L/Cpl W. H., 94
Hogg, Pte 154, 158
Hope, Bandmaster Harry, 84
hospital: De Aar, 98, 100; Cape Town, 74, 98; field, 97, 164; Kimberley, 11, 24, 34, 114, 119–20; Orange River, 79; Wynberg, 74, 100
Houghton, Pte, 163
Hubbard, Gnr H., 132, 135, 138
Hughes, Gnr, 152

India, 103n29; reinforcements from, 1n2; tactics developed in, 94; wars, 8, 103n29
Ingham, Pte John M., 85n12, 87–8
Ingram, Tpr Harold C., 129–30

Jackson, Pte Edgar, 91
Jackson, Pte L., 52, 54
Jackson, Maj Spenser, 67, 71
Jacobsdal, 136, 150, 154; commando, 16
James, Pte Frank, 139
James, Pte W., 47–8
Jameson, Dr Leander Starr, 3, 81n5
Jameson Raid (1895–6), 3, 14, 16n6, 81n5
Jenner, Tpr, 139
Joel, Sgt H., 85
Johannesburg, 2, 156, 170
Jones, Cpl U. W. J., 238
Joubert, Comdt-Gen, Piet, 116n12
Jourdan, Philip, 5n15

Kamfersdam, 27, 117, 125, 141

Keate, Robert William, 2
Kekewich, Lt-Col Robert G., 12, 24, 35–6, 137n20, 149; and Kimberley's defences, 12, 14; and Kimberley's food supplies, 14, 19, 139n23, 175, 177; censorship of, 107n1, 109, 176–7; command of, 4, 14, 145, 174, 177; diary of, 5, 36; feud with Rhodes, 4–7, 124, 127, 148, 173–7; politeness of, 6, 145, 165, 174, 177; post-war honours of, 5, 147n39; siege tactics of, 20, 32, 124, 141, 165, 175, 177; staff officers of, 5–6, 146n37
Kelly-Kenny, Lt-Gen Thomas, 152, 154
Kenilworth, 11, 27, 29, 113, 168, 175; Defence Force, 27n18, 113, 142
Kersley, Pte John, 51
Khartoum, 165
Kimberley, 2–4, 7, 11–12, 14, 23, 32–3, 38–42, 51, 59, 63, 74, 80–1, 122, 124, 126, 133–4, 141–2, 150–1, 168; besieged, 1, 6, 16–20, 24, 27, 31n21, 34, 36n33, 41, 61, 107–8, 110–14, 121, 137–8, 144–6, 148, 150, 165–7, 170–1, 173, 175–7; blacks in, 6, 11, 14, 27, 110–12n6, 117, 122, 145, 170, 176; Boers in, 24, 111, 120; casualties in, 24, 27, 30–6; defences of, 11–12, 14, 17–18, 21–2, 25–6, 30, 36, 115–16, 119, 125, 139n23, 145, 171, 174–7; infant mortality, 170–1; memorials, 36n33, 114, 147; Presbyterian Church, 17,

167; rationing, 108–12, 117, 138–9n23, 175–7; refugees, 1, 15, 17, 38, 170, 182; relief of, 9, 81n5, 107, 113, 117–18n18, 127–30, 135–7, 139–40, 144, 147–50, 163, 166–7, 170, 173, 175, 177–8, 181; relief works, 110, 114, 145, 147, 177; shelling effects, 24–8, 114–15, 117–19, 122, 137–9, 144, 147, 170, 172, 176, 182; vulnerability of, 1, 4, 7, 15–16, 75n56, 117, 124, 139, 177; water supplies of, 12, 14, 18, 111, 115n7, 143, 145
Kimberley Club, 12, 125
Kimberley Light Horse, 14–15, 20–2, 26, 29–30, 33, 36, 112, 167, 171
Kimberley Mine, 12, 123
Kimberley Rifle Volunteers, 12, 15, 17–18, 20, 22, 36, 144, 167
Kimberley Town Guard, 12, 14, 16–22, 24, 27, 32, 107, 110n4, 144–5, 167, 169–70, 176, 182
Kirby, Sgt T., 180
Kitchener, Maj-Gen H. Herbert, Lord, 104, 128, 181, 183; at Paardeberg, 154, 157, 160
Kitchener's Horse, 128n6, 157, 163
Klerksdorp commando, 61
Klip Drift, 131, 133, 152; casualties, 133–5, 140–1, 181–2; charge (1900), 134, 139–40, 181–2
Knight, Edward F., 47n19
Kraaipan, ambush (1899), 8n30, 16
Kroonstad, commando, 16; surrender (1900), 131n13

Kruger, President Paul, 3, 6n30, 16n6, 40, 173

Labram, George, 115, 119–20
Ladysmith, 116, 180; relief of, 148; siege of, 1, 37, 41, 109, 116
Lambton, Maj The Hon. William, 90
land mines, 12, 173
Laverack, Rev George W. T., 118, 170
Lawry, Rev E. P., 83
Lawson, Lt Algernon, 142
Lazenby, Pte J., 48–9
Lees, Pte, 49
Léon, Sam, 116–17, 125
Levi, Pte J., 43
Lindley, battle of (1900), 83n9, 131n13
Linley, Sgt A., 168
Linworth, L/Sgt B., 88–9
Lloyd's Weekly Newspaper, 150
Lombard's Kop, battle of (1899), 41
'Long Cecil' gun, 111n5, 115–16, 119, 125, 174
Longthorn, Cpl W., 49–50
'Long Tom' gun, 4, 115n7, 116–19, 121, 125, 139n23, 141, 144, 165, 172, 177
looting, 72, 128n6, 131–2, 162, 169, 183
Luard, G. M. C., 7, 176
Lunson, W. O., 18, 107–8, 115, 118
Lunt, George, 112, 171
Lunt, Mrs L. E., 113–14
lyddite, 72, 79, 83–4, 96, 161

MacBean family, 22–3, 109; Moorie, 175–6
Macdonald, Mrs, 138–9, 143–4
Macdonald, Sgt, 138–9

Macdonald, Brig-Gen Hector A., 105, 150, 152
McDougall, Sgt, 93
Macfarlane, L/Cpl W., 99
machine guns, 14, 51, 107; Maxim, 18n18n, 20n11, 23, 30n30, 32, 65
MacInnes, Lt Duncan Sayre, 146
MacKay, Pipe Maj James, 87n14
MacKenzie, John, 136
Mafeking (Mafikeng), 147; relief of, 148; siege of, 1, 15–16, 37, 61, 165, 180
Magersfontein, 75, 93, 128; battle of (1899), 17, 21n12, 72n52, 74, 81–103, 107–9, 114, 127, 144, 148, 150, 166, 169, 176, 178–80, 182; casualties at, 85n12, 86–98, 179; post-battle stalemate, 103–4, 116, 128–9, 148, 179
Maguire, James Rochfort, 124
Maguire, Mrs Rochfort, 6n16, 36, 112n6, 114, 120, 122–3, 168, 173–4
Main, James, 22
Majuba, battle of (1881), 105n31, 161, 163, 180
Mannion, Pte Reg, 95, 99
Manx lady, 14–15, 25, 28, 34–5, 109, 117–18, 121n20, 145, 168, 170–1
Marchant, Capt A. E., 56n30
Matabeleland expeditions (1893–4, 1896), 31n22
Maxwell, Pte Ned, 160–1
Meehan, Pte W., 158
Mercer, Pte R., 45
Merry, Sgt Harvey C., 183
Methuen, Gen Lord Paul S., 21, 47–8, 50n23, 57–8, 64–6, 70, 74, 79,

98n22, 101–3, 105, 151; command of, 4, 60, 101, 108, 113, 127, 147, 179; line of communications, 77, 128; mounted forces of, 41, 58, 61, 63, 91–2, 182; relief force (division) of, 4, 7–8, 32, 41–2, 51, 60, 73, 77, 99, 108, 113, 148, 150, 174, 178–80; tactics of, 45, 48, 51, 55n27, 61, 65, 81, 93, 100, 149, 178; wounded, 65–6, 75, 83n9
Middleton, Pte A., 78
Middleton, Maj William C., 134
Millard, Sgt J., 73–4
Milner, Sir Alfred, 4, 7, 16n6
Milton, Maj Percy W. A. A., 51–2
mines, *see* Bultfontein, De Beers, Dutiotspan, Kimberley, Premier and Rhodes
Modder River, 7, 61, 63, 70, 108, 116, 128, 131–2, 148, 151, 178–9; battle of (1899), 59n34, 60–74, 79, 81, 83n9, 166, 168n10, 169, 172, 179–80; bridge, 73–5n56; camp, 71–2, 77, 79–80, 103–4, 113, 127, 130–1, 143n36, 160; casualties at, 64–8, 71–5n56, 79; station, 14, 16
Moore, Pte P. H., 38
Morning Post, 47n19, 149
Morris, Sgt T. G., 102
mounted infantry (MI), 37, 40, 51, 58–9, 77, 128–9, 168, 181–2; at Klip Drift, 134; at Paardeberg, 157, 161; *see also* French, Kitchener's Horse, Roberts's Horse

Natal, 1n2, 2, 38n3, 41, 116, 129, 148, 171; British forces in, 1, 37–8n2, 116n11, 127
Naval Brigade, 41, 52, 55–6n30, 57, 59, 152, 159
Nazareth Home, 27
Newbury, Capt Bertram A., 156
New Rush, 2
Newsham, A. W., 19, 29, 119
newspapers, 8–9, 38n3, 102, 113, 168–9; Highland, 167; metropolitan, 7, 148, 166; provincial, 7, 96, 166–7
New Zealand contingents, 142
Nicholls, Pte R. H., 153
Nicholson's Nek, battle of (1899), 41
Nightingale, Drummer Ben, 22, 118–19
Nightingale, John, 39
Nixon, Pte David, 32–3
Nobron, Tpr William, 54
Northampton Mercury, 149
Northern Scot and Moray and Nairn Express, 167

Oliver, Mayor H. A., 17–18, 23–4, 26, 33, 110, 124–5, 142
Oliver, H. O., 176
Omdurman, battle of (1898), 83n8, 98n22, 104n30, 105n31
O'Meara, Maj Walter A. J., 5–6, 36, 122, 174; diary of, 5, 173; faulty map of, 61
Orange Free State, 1–3n6, 15–17, 54, 59, 84, 117, 128, 131n13, 132, 149, 182–3; forces of, 16–17, 42, 51, 69, 75n57, 123, 150, 161

Orange River, 2, 39, 79, 178; camp at, 37–9, 42, 130; Colony, 152n58; station, 128, 178
Otto's Kopje, 31–2, 169; field fort at, 117
Owens, Pte J. H., 45

Paardeberg, battle of (1900), 81n5, 96n20, 119n18, 150, 154–64, 166, 172, 180–1; casualties at, 155–8, 163–4
Pakenham, Thomas, 124n24, 139
Palmer, George, 24–5
Parsons, Edward, 119
Pattrick, Horace, 20–1, 29, 31
Pegler, Tpr, 169
Perry, Pte Robert, 158–9
Pipes, Driver J., 66
Porter, Brig-Gen Thomas C., 129
Potchefstroom, commando, 61; surrender of (1881), 81n5, 171n26
Premier Mine, 12
Pretoria, 38, 41, 116
Price, Pte W., 143
Priest, Pte Charles V., 78–9
Prinsloo, Gen Jacobus, 42, 51, 69
prisoners of war: Boer, 30–1, 48, 60, 74, 81n5, 131, 140, 142, 160, 163, 166, 172; British, 159, 173; in Kimberley, 33, 122, 145
Pugsley, Gnr W. F. C., 147
Purnell, Pte W. C., 161
Purnett, Pte O., 102

railway, 1, 14, 61, 68, 71, 74, 77, 81, 97–8, 127, 141n33, 182; and Kimberley, 2, 11, 15–17, 19, 38, 109n3, 146, 170;

bridges, 39, 61, 73–5n6; British advance along, 39–42, 48, 51–2, 61, 67, 178; *see also* armoured train, De Aar, Orange River
Ramdam, 128, 130, 132n15
Rea, L/Cpl Robert, 42, 44, 63
reconnaissance, 20, 28, 40, 45, 51, 61, 63, 74, 80, 178
Redgrave, Pte W. S., 141
regiments (in alphabetical order in each category)
Footguards: 1/Coldstream, 41, 50, 85n12, 90, 92, 95, 99, 169, 179; 2/Coldstream, 41, 48–9, 51, 63, 65, 71n51, 103, 162, 180; 3/Grenadier, 41–2, 44–7, 49, 52, 63, 65, 69, 90; 1/Scots, 38–9n4, 42n12, 44–6, 58, 65, 94, 102, 161
Cavalry: Carabineers (6th Dragoon Guards), 136, 141, 151; 10th Hussars, 152, 163; 14th Hussars, 141; Inniskilling Dragoons, 133–4n17, 138–9; King's Dragoon Guards, 133; 9th Lancers, 38, 40–1, 46, 49, 51, 54, 58, 61, 63, 83, 133–4, 140, 143, 151n56; 12th Lancers, 41, 77–8, 80, 84, 91–2, 102, 133–5, 138, 140, 151, 162; 16th Lancers, 135, 140; Royal Horse Guards, 170; Royal Scots Greys, 130, 134, 142–3, 145, 169
Infantry: 1/Argyll and Sutherland Highlanders, 41, 61, 65, 67–9, 71, 74, 77, 80, 85, 87–8, 101, 155, 162n74; 2/Black Watch, 6, 31n22, 41, 77, 85–9, 95n19, 97, 176; 2/Duke of Cornwall's Light Infantry, 156–7; 1/Essex, 154n59, 155, 157–8; 2/Gloucestershire, 154n59; 1/Gordon Highlanders, 41, 77–8, 81, 93–5; 1/Highland Light Infantry, 41, 77, 79, 85, 87–9, 104, 179; 2/King's Own Yorkshire Light Infantry, 41, 46, 52, 56–7, 67, 72, 85, 92; 2/King's Shropshire Light Infantry, 79, 153, 156, 158–9, 180; 2/Lincolnshire, 160; 1/Loyal North Lancashire, 7, 12, 14–15, 17, 22–3, 32, 37–8, 40–1, 52, 56–7, 67, 71, 102, 104, 112, 118, 125–6, 136, 139, 167–8, 180; 2/Northamptonshire, 41, 45–8, 51, 60, 78–9; 1/Northumberland Fusiliers, 38, 41–2n12, 46n15, 47, 50, 58, 70, 74, 85, 93, 168; 1/Oxfordshire and Buckinghamshire Light Infantry, 153–4n59, 158; 1/Princess of Wales's Own Yorkshire, 154–5n63, 158, 160, 163; 2/Royal East Kent (The Buffs), 154n59; 1/Royal Munster Fusiliers, 38, 41; 2/Royal Warwickshire, 154n59; 2/Seaforth Highlanders, 41, 77–9, 84–5, 87–9, 96, 99–101, 155; 1/Welsh, 153–5, 157–9, 163; 1/West Riding (Duke of Wellington's), 154n59

Volunteer: New South Wales Lancers, 41, 74–5; Queensland Mounted Infantry, 142; Rimington Guides (Scouts), 41, 52, 61, 80, 137
Reuters, 7, 166, 176
Rhodes, Cecil John, 2–5, 36, 112, 114–5, 137, 139–40, 148–50; and expulsion of blacks, 6, 112n6, 175; and Kimberley's defences, 4–5, 14, 121, 145–7, 174–5, 177; and mine refuge, 114, 121–4, 175, 177; critics of, 4–5, 121–2, 124n24, 139, 141, 173–4; feud with Kekewich, 4–7, 14n5, 124, 127, 148, 165, 173–7; generosity of, 20, 113–14, 121–2, 143, 145, 174–5, 177; imperialism of, 3, 173, 183–4; relief works of, 114, 145, 147, 177
Rhodesia, 3, 6, 149
Ridley, Col. Charles P., 129
Riet River, 60–1, 128, 130, 132
rifles, 8, 14, 17, 30–2, 35, 49n22, 78, 90, 134, 172, 179, 181
Riley, Pte, 155
Rimington, Maj Michael, 54–5; Guides, *see* regiments
Ripley, Capt George E., 47
Roberts, Brian, 6
Roberts, Field Marshal Frederick S., Baron (later 1st Earl) of Kandahar, 103–4, 124, 127, 141, 147, 150n54, 154, 174, 183; at Paardeberg, 158–9; forces of,

159–60; strategy of, 127, 139, 149, 179
Roberts's Horse, 128–9
Robertson, Rev J., 98
Robinson, Pte Albert, 71
Robinson, Pte D., 158
Robinson, Pte W., 163
Royal Army Medical Corps, 72
Royal Artillery, 12, 17, 22, 31–2, 35, 85; Field, 41, 52, 66–7, 77–9, 83, 90, 147, 153, 179; Garrison, 28, 31n21; Horse, 41, 77, 79, 91, 128, 130, 142, 152, 182
Royal Engineers, 52, 69, 73–4, 77, 85, 95, 97; in Kimberley, 12, 17, 22, 31–2, 146, 171, 177
Royal Marines, 55–6, 59, 159
Rudd, Charles, 3
Rushton, Pte Clifford, 102

Sampson, Sgt W. Herbert, 79
Sannaspost, battle of (1900), 83n9
Scandinavian corps, 81, 89
searchlights, 7, 12, 21, 74, 80, 115n7, 145, 173
Sharples, Pte J., 64
Sheffield Daily Telegraph, 150
Simpson, Tpr T., 133, 138
Sinclair, Hugh, 15
Sivell, Cpl V., 141–2
Smith, Cpl H., 57
Smith, Pte John W., 168
Smith, Pte T., 103
Smith-Dorrien, Maj-Gen Horace L., 152
Smuts, Field Marshal Jan C., 173
Snape, Pte J., 57
South African Republic, *see* Transvaal
South African War (1899–1902), 1, 37,
54n26, 105n31, 118n18, 152n58
special correspondents, *see* war correspondents
Stewart, Pte W. H., 147
Steyn, President Marthinus T., 3n6, 16, 81
Stockwin, Pte, 51
Stopford, Lt-Col Horace P., 64n42
Stormberg, 41; battle of (1899), 103, 127
Sutcliffe, Pte Walter, 126

Taylor, Pte, 71
Thomson, Pte A., 162
The Times, 38n3; *Weekly Edition*, 174
Times History of the South African War, 140
Tirah campaign (1897–8), 77, 94n17
Todman Dan, 168
Togwell, L/Cpl Arthur E., 177
Transvaal, 2–3, 8n30, 14–16n6, 38, 183; forces of, 16–17, 51, 69, 161
Trollope, Anthony, 11
Tucker, Lt-Gen Charles, 152
Turnbull, Pte, 47
Turner, Lt-Col H. Scott, 6, 23, 31–6
Tweebosch, battle of (1902), 8n30, 21n12
Tyson, Capt 'Tim', 110

Uitlanders, 2–3
Upstone, Pte J., 138

Van der Merwe, J. A. P., 42
Vereeniging, Peace of (1902), 8n30
Vooruitzigt farm, 2
Vryburg station, 14

Wallace, Sgt John, 96–7
Waller, Pte George, 89
Walsh, Sgt, 46
Walton, L/Cpl. J., 50
war correspondents, 4, 7, 166, 168
Wardill, Tpr Arthur J., 136, 151–2
Wardlaw, Capt Edgar P., 156n65
War Office, 108
Warren, Maj-Gen Sir Charles, 21n12
Washington, Pte, 65–6
Washington, Pte G., 162
Waterboer, Nikolaas, 2
Waterval Drift, convoy captured at (1900), 150n54
Wauchope, Maj-Gen Andrew G., 83, 86, 95, 100–2; staff officers of, 98
Webster, Maj A. MacCullum, 20n10, 23
Wessels, Gen Christiaan J., 16, 24
Wesselton Mine, 145
Western Mail, 148
White, Lt-Gen Sir George, 41
White, Pte Sidney, 129
white flag, abuse of, 31, 47–8, 50, 56
Whitehead, Pte S., 57
Wilkie, Cpl, 93–4
Wilkinson, Sgt Richard, 180
Williams, Alpheus F., 122
Williams, Gardner, 123
Witwatersrand, 2–3
Wolseley, Field Marshal Garnet J., Viscount, 21n12, 103n29
Wood, Lt Charles C., 40
Woodhead, Sgt, 92

Yate, Capt Charles A. L., 57n31
Yorkshire Herald, 150